UNIVERSITY LIBRARY
UW-STEVENS POINT

W9-AOV-827

European Monographs in Social Psychology
The political system matters
Social psychology and voting behavior in Sweden and the United States

European Monographs in Social Psychology

Executive Editors:
J. RICHARD EISER and KLAUS R. SCHERER
Sponsored by the European Association of Experimental Social Psychology

This series, first published by Academic Press (who continue to distribute the numbered volumes), appeared under the joint imprint of Cambridge University Press and the Maison des Sciences de l'Homme in 1985 as an amalgamation of the Academic Press series and the European Studies in Social Psychology, published by Cambridge and the Maison in collaboration with the Laboratoire Européen de Psychologie Sociale of the Maison.

The original aims of the two series still very much apply today: to provide a forum for the best European research in different fields of social psychology and to foster the interchange of ideas between different developments and different traditions. The Executive Editors also expect that it will have an important role to play as a European forum for international work.

Other titles in this series:

Unemployment by Peter Kelvin and Joanna E. Jarrett
National characteristics by Dean Peabody
Experiencing emotion by Klaus R. Scherer, Harald G. Wallbott and Angela B. Summerfield
Levels of explanation in social psychology by Willem Doise
Understanding attitudes to the European Community: a social-psychological study in four member states by Miles Hewstone
Arguing and thinking: a rhetorical approach to social psychology by Michael Billig
The child's construction of economics by Anna Emilia Berti and Anna Silvia Bombi

The political system matters

Social psychology and voting behavior in
Sweden and the United States

Donald Granberg
Center for Research in Social Behavior, University of Missouri-Columbia

and

Sören Holmberg
Department of Political Science, University of Göteborg

The right of the
University of Cambridge
to print and sell
all manner of books
was granted by
Henry VIII in 1534.
The University has printed
and published continuously
since 1584.

Cambridge University Press
Cambridge
New York   New Rochelle   Melbourne   Sydney

Editions de la Maison des Sciences de l'Homme
Paris

Published by the Press Syndicate of the University of Cambridge
The Pitt Building, Trumpington Street, Cambridge CB2 1RP
32 East 57th Street, New York, NY 10022, USA
10 Stamford Road, Oakleigh, Melbourne 3166, Australia
and Editions de la Maison des Sciences de l'Homme
54 Boulevard Raspail, 75270 Paris Cedex 06

© Maison des Sciences de l'Homme and Cambridge University Press 1988

First published 1988

Printed in Great Britain by the
University Press, Cambridge

British Library cataloguing in publication data
Granberg, Donald
The political system matters: social psychology and voting behavior in Sweden and
the United States.–(European monographs in social psychology).
1. Sweden. Electorate. Voting behavior
2. United States. Electorate. Voting behavior
I. Title II. Series
324.9485

Library of Congress cataloguing in publication data
Granberg, Donald.
The political system matters.
(European monographs in social psychology)
Bibliography.
Includes index.
1. Political participation–Sweden.   2. Political participation–United States.
3. Voting–Sweden.   4. Voting–United States.   5. Political psychology.
I. Holmberg, Sören, 1943–   . II. Title. III. Series.
JN7945.G73 1988   323′.042′09485   88-9525

ISBN 0 521 36031 5
ISBN 2 7351 0242 4 (France only)

Contents

JN
7945
.G73
1988

vi   *Contents*

Contents

Acknowledgements

This book is the result of interdisciplinary collaboration between an American social psychologist and a Swedish political scientist. The bulk of the analyses and writing occurred during two years when we worked together in Sweden. During the first (1982–83), Donald Granberg was on a sabbatical leave from the University of Missouri and also the recipient of a fellowship from the Svenska Institutet. During the second (1986–87), Donald Granberg was on a research leave granted by the Research Council and the Provost's office of the University of Missouri. It is not easy to see how this book could have been done without such support, so we feel very grateful for the opportunity afforded us.

Overall, our work can best be seen as an effort to understand the operation of social psychological processes within two democratic – yet very different – political systems. Among the goals of democracy are to give citizens a sense of control and efficacy, to resolve conflicts in a nonviolent manner, to create justice, and to facilitate the solution of ever-changing and emerging problems faced by societies. Understanding how democracies work and comprehending the potential of voters and how individual citizens function within democracies is a big order. Our hope is that our analyses make at least a small contribution toward that objective.

For the many analyses to be reported, we depended heavily on the advice and assistance of Mikael Gilljam, Peter Esaiasson, Maria Oskarson, Hans Nordlöf, and Iris Alfredsson of the Department of Political Science at the University of Göteborg. So great was our dependence in that regard that it is doubtful that we will ever be able to reciprocate adequately. So to these helpful and light-hearted souls, we offer our sincere and deeply felt thanks.

When things go smoothly in academia, it is sometimes easy to take effective administration for granted. We want to avoid that, and, therefore, it is fitting to acknowledge, with gratitude, efforts on our behalf by Bo Särlvik, Dean of the Social Sciences and Professor of Political Science at the University of Göteborg and Bruce Biddle, Director of the Center for Research in Social Behavior at the University of Missouri. Barbara Bank, James McCartney, and Kenneth Benson, who have rotated chairing the Sociology

Department of the University of Missouri during these years, have also facilitated our work administratively when necessary.

The typing and processing of several drafts, including the many graphs and tables, several of which ultimately were excluded, were handled effectively and with great patience and good cheer in Columbia, Missouri by Patricia Shanks with the able assistance of Cathy Luebbering, Diane Chappell, Teresa Hjellming, and Mark Henry under the supervision of Billye Adams. In Göteborg, Anna-Gun Andersson was very helpful. Many colleagues have provided constructive comments and suggestions on drafts of chapters in various stages of development. Richard Niemi, Samuel Barnes, Richard Braungart, and David Sears were especially helpful in that regard. We also wish to thank J. Richard Eiser, coeditor of this monograph series, who responded positively with encouragement when we initally approached him with the idea of the book. The editing was done by Penny Carter and Trudi Tate at Cambridge University Press with great care.

Finally, we wish to salute and pay homage to the pioneers who were responsible for initiating the national election studies, Angus Campbell and Warren Miller in the United States, Jörgen Westerståhl and Bo Särlvik in Sweden, and the many others who have worked in one way or another in maintaining, continuing, and extending these series over the years. The data from these election studies were obtained through the Inter-University Consortium for Political and Social Research at the University of Michigan and through the Svensk Samhällsvetenskaplig Datatjänst at the University of Göteborg. Whatever the merit of our particular analyses, we were fortunate to be working with such high-quality data sets.

In spite of all the help we were fortunate to have received and have gratefully acknowledged, the customary caveat is in order. We are solely responsible for the analyses and interpretations appearing in this book.

Donald Granberg   Sören Holmberg
Columbia, Missouri   Washington, D.C.
February, 1988

1 Social psychological processes in political context

In the parlance of contemporary social science, the thesis of our book, that "the political system matters," must be considered as a valence issue rather than a position issue (Butler and Stokes, 1974; McLean, 1981). That is, we do not see ourselves arrayed against some unnamed competitors who are somehow asserting that the political system does not matter. It is rather a matter of emphasis. For it is often the case that social psychologists and political scientists take the political system for granted. Sometimes they act and write *as if* the political system did *not* matter. Yet, if you asked them, most would concede that of course it matters. There are times, however, when analysts become so engrossed in the details of a particular system or type of system that they lose sight of the fact that there are alternatives. In making a series of comparisons between Sweden and the United States, our purpose is to provide a gentle but well-documented reminder. In analyzing political behavior and political psychology, it is essential to bear in mind the nature of the political system in which people are thinking and acting, and which they may be seeking to alter or maintain.

If the political system matters, the obvious question is how it matters. A truly general social psychological analysis of politics would state principles abstractly enough to be applicable to a wide range of political systems and the ways in which people function psychologically within those systems. Truth be told, we may not yet even be close to being able to do that. What we can do, and indeed, what we do in this book, is examine principles, effects, and relationships in a series of comparative empirical analyses. If the political system matters, then at the very least the strength of various effects and relationships might be expected to vary. At most, it is possible that a relationship observed in one system might be absent or conceivably even be reversed in a different system.

It should also be stated at the outset that we take for granted and shall not argue the advantages and benefits of an interdisciplinary approach (Sherif and Sherif, 1969a). In the case of this work, the subject matter is a meeting ground for social psychology and political science. Over the years it has been common to assume that psychology matters in politics, e.g., that the personality of leaders may make an impact on policy, that perception or how people define a situation psychologically can affect the outcome. Our focus generally is on the flow in the other direction – namely, the impact of living in a particular political system on how people appear to function psychologically.

Systemic effects on psychological processes

In further delineating our approach, we shall describe briefly what our study is not and then point to what can be regarded as the closest analogue in prior research. First, we do not focus on the differences in the policy making process nor on the policy differences between Sweden and the U.S. (Heclo and Madsen, 1986). Such differences are both real and significant. We also do not focus on a specific issue and how it is treated in the two countries, e.g., air pollution (Lundqvist, 1980), health and occupational safety (Kelman, 1981), or unemployment (Ginsburg, 1983). Nor is our focus on the consequences of political policies on how people live in the two nations, a question of obvious relevance.

While our approach is somewhat broader and more basic in orientation, we do not seek to be exhaustive as to the differences between Sweden and the U.S. We have, for the most part, avoided questions pertaining to stratification and demography. It would, for example, be a relatively simple matter to show that social class has been a far more important determinant of voting in Sweden than in the United States (Korpi, 1981; Lipset, 1981), although within Sweden in recent years ideology may have been increasing in importance and class may have become relatively less important (Holmberg and Gilljam, 1987). Without denying in any way the importance of such abiding issues in political sociology, we have decided to limit the scope of our present inquiry and not to take up such matters.

The comparative analysis of politically relevant survey data is a rich tradition going back to Gabriel Almond and Sidney Verba's (1963) study of the "civic culture" in Britain, the United States, Germany, Italy, and Mexico. Strangely enough, however, the closest analogue to what we are trying to do in this monograph may be a study that had practically nothing to do with politics but focused on a matter of basic research in psychology. In 1966, an interdisciplinary team of Northwestern University professors Marshall Segall, Donald Campbell, and Melville Herskovits published a book entitled *The influence of culture on visual perception*. They reported a comparative study of the degree to which people in very different cultures are susceptible to optical illusions. Briefly, they found that people in western, technologically advanced, urbanized, and industrialized societies were more susceptible to some visual illusions (e.g., Müller–Lyer) but less susceptible to others than people in the technologically less advanced non-western cultures. Their results were theoretically equivocal. In support of Gestalt or nativist theories of perception, they did not find any culture in which these illusions did not occur at least to some degree. On the other hand, behavioristic or empiricist theories of perception were supported by the fact that the degree of susceptibility to basic optical illusions was affected by the cultural context in which the person had been living (Segall, Campbell, and Herskovits, 1966). For example, people in western cultures who had lived in a "well-carpentered" environment with many straight lines and right angles were more susceptible to the Müller–Lyer illusion but less susceptible to some other illusions.[1] The findings could have been cast as evidence that "the cultural system matters."

Our approach is similar to that of Segall *et al.* in a couple of important respects. First, we are comparing systems that are very different. While Segall *et al.* studied a large number (23) of cultural systems, their most relevant comparisons were between people from systems that were very different. Among the western democracies, Sweden and the United States are about as different as any two political systems. Thus, in the logic of comparative analyses, we are using the "most different systems" design rather than the "most similar systems" design (Przeworski and Teune, 1970).

The design of Segall *et al.*, though using materials that had been studied extensively in the laboratory, was nonexperimental. That is, their independent variable was not manipulated by the experimenter, and their subjects were, of course, not randomly assigned to the experience of being born and socialized into one of several cultures. Similarly, the data in our analyses are derived from nonexperimental surveys in which people who are citizens of Sweden or the U.S. are asked a series of questions. Closer to home, our approach is similar in design to that of Niemi and Westholm (1984), who compared the attitude stability of people in Sweden and the U.S. Our approach, necessitating a book rather than an article, expands this method by making a series of systematic comparisons between Sweden and the U.S. rather than concentrating on only one.

Building blocks from social psychology

The basic concepts in our analyses are drawn from standard conceptual distinctions in contemporary social psychology (e.g., Eiser, 1986; Myers, 1987; Sears, Freedman, and Peplau, 1985). For years, *attitude* has been a central concept in social psychology. We use attitude to refer to a relatively specific evaluative (i.e., affectively charged) judgment people make which reveals a preference that they hold. Stating that abortion should be legal, that nuclear power should be phased out within ten years, that one likes the

Liberal Party more than the Center Party, or that one likes the Republican Party more than George Bush reflects attitudinally instigated judgments (Eiser, 1984).

We are also interested in how parties, candidates, and leaders appear to individual citizens. We are using the concept of *perception* to refer to beliefs or cognitions people have about political phenomena. If people think that the Communist Party is against nuclear power, that President Jimmy Carter is opposed to a tax cut, that the Conservative Party is further to the right than the Liberal Party, or that Walter Mondale is more liberal than Ronald Reagan, these would be examples of what we treat as political perceptions. We recognize that our usage is somewhat broader than the classical definition of perception which referred to the more or less immediate organization by the individual of sensory stimulation occurring at a given time (Granberg and Seidel, 1976). However, such relatively broad usage has become more or less standard in political psychology (Conover, 1981; Granberg and Brent, 1980).

Thirdly, we deal with a special kind of belief that pertains to a person's *expectation* about what will happen in the future. Believing that there will be a change in the government after the election, that nuclear power will continue to be used as a source of electricity in the twenty-first century, or that George Wallace will carry one's state are examples of the sort of expectations we have in mind. Since they are usually asked and stated as unqualified and unconditional statements about what will occur in the future, technically these expectations should be regarded as prophecies rather than as predictions (Popper, 1959).

The fourth analytical concept we distinguish and use is *behavioral intention*. This is measured simply by asking people what they plan on doing or think they will do at some designated point in the future. The obvious intention questions in election studies concern whether the person intends to vote in an upcoming election and, if so, for which party or candidate.

Finally, we are interested in the *behavior* of people, what they actually do. In the main, we are limited to self-report as to whether people voted and for what party or candidate. In the Swedish data, there has been a sustained and effective program, using official records, to validate people's reports as to whether they voted. For the U.S. data, such validation is more sporadic but has been improving in recent years. There is no way of directly validating party or candidate selection behavior in either country, although comparing the overall distribution in the sample with the electoral outcome provides indirect hints of validity in that regard (Holmberg, 1981). We also consider how people report voting with a longer interval between behavior and measurement. This can, with panel data, be used to assess the reliability of self-report, and it can also be used as an indicator of *recalled behavior*.

These concepts – attitude, perception, expectation, intention, and behavior – are the focus of our analyses. They each have been measured in similar ways in several surveys in both Sweden and the United States. How they are interrelated and implicated in social psychological processes is the central problem of this book. Among other problems, we shall examine the degree to which attitudes are interrelated to form an ideology and the link between ideology and voting in the two countries. Perceptions of the parties and candidates are studied to determine the degree of perceptual consensus and the extent to which perceptual distortion occurs in placing liked and disliked political actors. We also examine the linkages among preference, expectation, and behavior in order to test various models. The intention–behavior relationship is analyzed to see how strong it is, whether variables can be identified that intervene to determine this strength, and to identify the characteristics of the intention–behavior changers. Finally, we examine accuracy in recalling one's prior behavior and whether prior behavior or recalled behavior can be used more effectively to predict subsequent behavior.

Why Sweden and the United States?

There are several reasons why comparisons between Sweden and the United States hold considerable potential for fruitful analyses. Not the least of these is the quality of the data sets that will be described shortly. Hopefully, however, we have even better reasons for proceeding than solely because high quality data are available.

Suppose, by way of analogy, that we do a mental experiment involving random assignment of people who initially know nothing about art to two conditions. In condition A, people are shown works of art that differ from each other on several dimensions but on balance are not very different from each other. The slides of works of art shown to people in condition A are poorly focused, and there are several other things that distract people's attention from the slides that are being shown. In condition B, the works of art are shown with a clear sharp focus and few distractions. Moreover, in B, the pieces of art differ mainly on one salient dimension and are substantially different from one another.

After being shown the slides people in both conditions A and B are asked a series of questions about their attitudes and perceptions pertaining to art. If a scientist studied only condition A, it would be easy to conclude that the average person does not know much or care much about art, has a hard time articulating any organized view of art, and demonstrates little coherence or stability in artistic preferences. Admittedly, this analogy is a bit overdrawn, but clearly a comparative analysis between conditions A and B will tell us more about human inclinations and capacities than concentrating exclusively on either A or B. In Sweden, the strong and stable party system may provide cues used to facilitate the opinion-formation process, leading to coherent ideological views among the citizenry. In the United States, by comparison, such strong cues are by and large lacking.

In concentrating on the differences, it is well to remember that there are several ways in which Sweden and the United States are similar. Both are highly industrialized and urbanized societies in which there is a substantial commitment to civil liberties and a democratic tradition. In recent decades, both nations have enjoyed a high standard of living.

There is, however, more inequality in the United States, and that means the rich people in the United States and the poor people in Sweden are probably better off in material terms than their counterparts in the other country (Hochschild, 1981). Verba and Orren (1985a, 1985b) have shown that the difference between Sweden and the United States on actual degree of economic equality has a parallel finding at the social psychological level of analysis. At both the elite and mass levels, people in the United States express a preference for much more inequality than do people in Sweden.

When people in the two countries are compared as to how they rank the terminal values identified by Milton Rokeach (1973), the rank correlation is +.54 (Reimer and Rosengren 1986; Inglehart, 1985). This indicates that the values are more similar than different but also implies some substantial differences. This seems about right, given the across-time (1968–1981) stability correlation for the United States alone of +.94 (Inglehart, 1985). The largest differences between the two nations by this measure occurred when people in Sweden tended to rank "true friendship" and "mature love" higher, and people in the United States ranked "salvation," "self-respect," and "a sense of accomplishment" higher. The latter differences are readily interpretable as reflecting the greater importance of religion and the emphasis on individualism within the United States. Another comparison found local leaders in Sweden to attach greater value to economic equality than do their counterparts in the United States (Strömberg, 1986). Similarly, Swedish youth expressed a consistent preference for the principle of equality over need or equity as a basis for allocating scarce resources. In contrast, U.S. youth gave more mixed responses, but preferred the equity or contribution principle when it came to dividing money (Törnblom, Jonsson, and Foa, 1985).

These value differences are very substantial and obviously are a consequence of socialization into different systems. Our focus, however, is on the political system, and here the differences are quite pronounced. Sweden has a disciplined multi-party system with a unicameral parliament in which seating is based on proportional representation. Most votes within the

Swedish Parliament take place strictly along party lines, whereas this is generally not true in the U.S. Congress. The U.S. has a relatively weak and undisciplined two-party system with a bicameral legislature and an independent executive branch headed by a president, and elections based on the principle of winner-take-all. Perhaps related to these differences, participation is much higher in Sweden, roughly 90 percent in Swedish parliamentary elections, compared to about 55 percent in recent U.S. presidential elections.[2]

With these very substantial differences between Sweden and the U.S., the objection may be raised that comparisons between them are as futile as that proverbial comparison between apples and oranges. In fact, apples and oranges can be meaningfully compared on a variety of dimensions such as nutritional value and costs of production.

The United States and Swedish election studies

The rich sources of data that we use in our analyses are available thanks directly and indirectly to the contributions of many innovators and leaders of research in this area. George Gallup is often granted primary credit for seeing in the 1930s the potential of systematic sample surveys to describe the state of public opinion. By now, his innovations have diffused to many, perhaps most, countries in one form or other (Lipset, 1984). Gallup's contribution was largely methodological rather than theoretical. But his impact on our ·work and that of many others is very great nonetheless. Theoretically oriented political scientists, such as V. O. Key (1961; 1966), found immense possibilities for secondary analyses in the data being accumulated by Gallup and others (Natchez, 1985).

The advantages of tracing the same specific individuals over time in a panel design were carefully developed and exploited by Paul Lazarsfeld and his colleagues in the community panel studies of the 1940 election in Erie County, Ohio by Lazarsfeld, Bernard Berelson, and Hazel Gaudet (1944) and of the 1948 election in Elmira, New York by Berelson, Lazarsfeld, and William McPhee (1954). They sought to analyze the process of opinion formation in an election campaign. The methodology, modes of analysis, and conceptual distinctions we use are heavily influenced, and, in some instances, directly derived from these two landmark studies, *The people's choice* and *Voting*, emanating from the research program at Columbia University.

A short time later, what has become the dominant or focal election studies project was initiated at the University of Michigan under the direction of Angus Campbell and Warren Miller. These studies, though similar in some respects to the Columbia studies, differed in orientation, placing more emphasis on social psychological and political concepts and less emphasis on sociological concepts and multi-wave panel analyses. In the Michigan studies, the analysis also shifted from a single community to representative samples of the entire nation. It would be a gross understatement to say that the major works coming out of this research program – *The voter decides* by Campbell, Gerald Gurin, and Miller (1954), *Elections and the political order*, by Campbell, Philip Converse, Miller, and Donald Stokes (1966), and especially *The American voter*, also by Campbell, Converse, Miller, and Stokes (1960) – had a major impact on political science and the study of voting behavior. Much of what has been done since has been in response or reaction to their theses (e.g., Niemi and Weisberg, 1976; Nie, Verba, and Petrocik, 1976; Himmelweit *et al.*, 1981; Särlvik and Crewe, 1983). Moreover, the data archive they gradually accumulated has been subjected to secondary analysis and resulted in numerous books and articles by literally scores of social scientists and thousands of students.

The U.S. data used in our analyses are drawn from the Michigan election studies. Because these data are so well known and widely used, they will be described here only briefly. In each of the nine most recent U.S. presidential elections (1952 to 1984), a large representative sample of U.S. adults was interviewed at length prior to the election and then again after the election. These preelection interviews for the panel took place during the eight-week period just before the election, and the postelection interview as soon as possible after the election. In this series, there are also two across-election panels (1956–1960 and 1972–1976) which we use in our analyses. These people were interviewed five times, before and after two presidential elections and after the intervening congressional election.[3]

Because they are less well known and have been less extensively analyzed, we shall take care to describe the Swedish election studies in somewhat greater detail. The Swedish election studies project was initiated by Jörgen Westerståhl and Bo Särlvik in the mid 1950s, shortly after the Michigan election studies project began. It was begun in conjunction with the local elections in 1954 and expanded in the parliamentary election of 1956. In the parliamentary elections since then, a large representative sample of adults in Sweden has been interviewed. The basic design is a rolling panel in which a random sample of Swedish adults is interviewed at length before or after the election. Half of the sample will have been interviewed in connection with the previous election, and the other half will be interviewed in connection with the succeeding election. In recent years, the response rate in these surveys (percentage of people in the sample who are successfully interviewed) has been about 75 to 80 percent. Those who are interviewed before the election are sent a brief questionnaire to complete after the election. Swedish voters cast their ballots for slates of candidates who have been nominated by a party to be Members of Parliament. Although citizens may delete or add names from the lists provided by the party, practically no one does. So, in effect, nearly everyone votes a straight party ticket. Hence, the questions on the surveys pertaining to voting intention and voting behavior ask only what party people intend to vote for or voted for in the election. In addition to the leadership of Westerståhl and Särlvik, Olof Petersson shared the responsibility for directing the 1973 study and was the principal investigator in the 1976 study. Sören Holmberg has directed the Swedish election studies project since 1979, including the parliamentary elections of 1979, 1982, and 1985, and the nuclear power referendum of 1980. Also, in conjunction with the 1985 parliamentary election study of citizens, a survey was conducted shortly after the September elections of the newly elected Members of Parliament. These data, based on an unusually high response rate of 97 percent, will be used to a limited extent in chapters 4 and 6.

In addition to the parliamentary election studies, we also use data from the 1980 panel surveyed in connection with the national referendum on nuclear power. In that referendum, voters chose from among three alternatives or "lines" (Granberg & Holmberg, 1986c; Holmberg & Asp, 1984). Data from the referendum study are used in chapters 3, 7, 8, and 9. It is important to understand that in the referendum, people voted for one of three alternatives endorsed by the five main parties. By comparison, in regular parliamentary elections, people vote directly for one of the five main parties by casting as their vote the slate of candidates nominated by the parties to be Members of Parliament. Most of our analyses of Swedish data focus on recent parliamentary elections and the associated across-election panels.[4]

2   Subjective ideology: left–right and liberal–conservative

The left–right dimension in Sweden and the liberal–conservative dimension in the United States form a more or less clear foundation for understanding the politics within these two nations. By and large, these ideological dimensions have focused in recent decades upon domestic policies, questions of a market versus a planned economy, inequality, and the role of government in assuring the welfare of citizens. The relevance of such dimensions and the utility of scales designed to measure them are widely assumed in contemporary political analysis (Sani and Sartori, 1983; Mair, 1986). This is not to say that everything that goes on within these countries is linked to the ideological dimensions. But many things are, and it is a good place to start – provided one keeps in mind the complexity of political realities that ultimately must be incorporated into the analysis.

In both Sweden and the United States, there have been sustained attempts to measure ideology by having people place themselves and the parties and candidates on a scale. At the individual level, it is reasonable to expect a high degree of subjective ideological agreement between a citizen's own political ideology and that of the political party favored by that citizen. Subjective ideological agreement involves the apparent congruence between the ideological position taken by the individual and the position of a preferred political stimulus, whether that be a party or a particular candidate.

Subjective ideological agreement is, however, complex. Several underlying processes may exert a force toward congruence. Three rather distinct processes promote ideological congruence between the self and a preferred political party (Holmberg, 1981; Judd, Kenny, and Krosnick, 1983; Markus, 1982; Page and Brody, 1972; Shaffer, 1981). The first is a tendency for citizens to prefer and choose political parties and candidates that represent an ideological position close to their own views. Second is the tendency for parties and candidates to try to persuade citizens toward their position. And third is the tendency for individuals, in the organization of their cognitive structure, to distort or exaggerate the similarities and differences in political stimuli in relation to their personal ideological views.

We assume at the outset that the actual level of ideological agreement that can be observed within a given system at a given time is problematic. One of our goals in this chapter is to compare the extent to which Swedish and American citizens differ in their ideological consistency and whether ideological agreement varies much from election to election within each country. As implied previously, we are interested in the underlying processes that promote subjective ideological agreement and whether these processes operate differently in different contexts. The three processes that have been alluded to can now be spelled out in more detail. First there is the process of *rational selection* where voters choose the alternative that is in the closest proximity to themselves. To the extent that this process occurs, there would be people with ideological positions selecting parties and candidates on the basis of proximity and thereby forming distinct ideological voting groups. If the variation among the alternatives in an election corresponds to variation among voters, the process of rational selection *could* by itself, conceivably, produce complete agreement between citizens and their respective preferred party or candidate. Secondly, insofar as the party's position is known, there will be an inclination to try to place oneself in close proximity to the position of one's preferred party. In this process, there are people with a party or candidate preference who then form or alter their own position on an issue or on an ideological dimension to correspond with the position of the preferred party or candidate. This is often referred to as a persuasion effect but can also encompass the party's influence in the opinion-formation process. Given that most citizens will not have the time, energy, or resources to master the entire political agenda, it is often appropriate and more manageable for them to take cues from a party which has been acting ideologically in their interests (Downs, 1957). This process is referred to as the *influence of a preferred party on self-placement*. While analytically distinct from rational selection, it *can* also be regarded as essentially rational and democratic in nature. Although opinion formation is an essential and central part of any democracy, analysts often imply approval when citizens form opinions in response to information and ideas from the mass media, friends, or relatives, but somehow view it as irrational when opinions are formed in relation to a preferred party's position. We *reject* that distinction, stemming as it does from a negative view of political parties. When these first two processes are operating, one should observe real differences between how people in various voting groups place themselves on ideology.

Thirdly, when the party's position is not altogether fixed or certain, citizens may be motivated to distort their perceptions of a party's position. That is, in order to foster a state of cognitive balance (Heider, 1958), individuals may exaggerate the similarity between their own position and that of a preferred party or candidate. This tendency was tacitly recognized

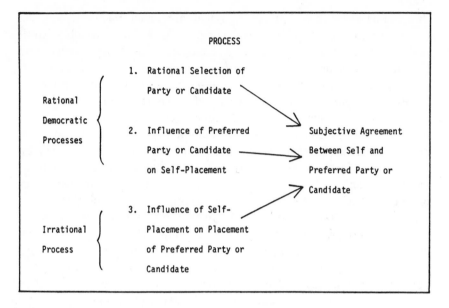

Figure 2.1 Model of three processes producing subjective agreement.

in the 1950s (Berelson, Lazarsfeld, and McPhee, 1954, pp. 215–233) and has been pursued subsequently by several investigators (e.g., Conover and Feldman, 1982; Granberg and Brent, 1974; Holmberg, 1981; Kinder, 1978; King, 1978; Sherrod, 1972). This process has been referred to variously as "projection," "assimilation," "autism," or the tendency toward "wishful thinking." More generally, it may be related to an egocentric bias, in which humans are prone to make an assumption of similarity to self (Granberg, 1972; Ross, 1977). In the present context, the process refers to the *influence of self-placement on placement of a preferred party*. Distinct from the first two processes, this tendency essentially is irrational in nature inasmuch as it involves the influence of affect on cognition. The model implied thus far is shown in figure 2.1. The three processes in the figure are not mutually exhaustive. For instance, a fourth possibility is that a responsive preferred party or candidate could move closer to the person's position. Finally, the positions of the citizen and the preferred party could also converge over time toward greater similarity. To observe these processes occurring would require elite–mass comparisons across time. Although we shall not pursue these possibilities, we would regard these processes as also essentially democratic in nature. Moreover, the extent to which these democratic processes have occurred should be reflected jointly in objective differences that can be observed when comparing party or candidate preference groups on the ideology dimension.

Our primary focus here is on the relationship between a person's own position and that ascribed to a preferred party or candidate. It is normatively important for a democracy that this relationship be strong and based in the main on the more rational processes. The same three processes that produce subjective agreement between a person and a preferred party also ought to produce subjective disagreement between a person and a nonpreferred party. That is, if people choose rationally from among alternatives on the basis of proximity, if they form or alter their own positions so as to depart from the positions of a nonpreferred party, and if they distort their estimates so as to exaggerate the difference between self and a nonpreferred party, the result will be subjective disagreement between oneself and a nonpreferred party.

When the difference between self and a nonpreferred party is exaggerated, this can be referred to as "negative projection" (Conover and Feldman, 1982). Projection and, presumably, negative projection are defense mechanisms in psychoanalytic theory. Instead of this rather awkward usage, however, we shall use terms derived from basic studies of human judgment processes, namely, *assimilation* and *contrast*, drawn from social judgment theory (Eiser and Stroebe, 1972; Granberg, 1982; Sherif and Hovland, 1961). Assimilation refers to the tendency to exaggerate the similarity between oneself and a preferred party or candidate, while contrast refers to the tendency to exaggerate the difference between oneself and a nonpreferred party or candidate. Several studies of specific issues have reported assimilation to be stronger than contrast in the context of presidential politics in the U.S. (Berelson *et al.*, 1954; Granberg and Brent, 1974; Kinder, 1978; Sherrod, 1972), although the validity of that asymmetrical finding has been questioned (Judd *et al.*, 1983; Shaffer, 1981).

It should be emphasized that subjective agreement is more encompassing than assimilation, in that the former could be the result of the effects of all three processes in figure 2.1, while assimilation refers only to the third. Similarly, subjective disagreement encompasses all three processes, while contrast refers only to the third. Figure 2.2 presents a pure subjective placement model that shows abstractly how things would look if the three processes operated as described previously, and if there were no other factors or reality checks exerting an effect. The positions of a person and that of a preferred party or candidate would coincide, while the distance between a person and that of a nonpreferred party or candidate would be maximized.

The problem with the subjective placement model, and with several prior research reports, is that there has often been little attempt to disentangle or unravel the three processes that produce subjective agreement. As pointed out before, the same level of subjective agreement could be produced by different underlying processes of radically different strengths. For instance, a

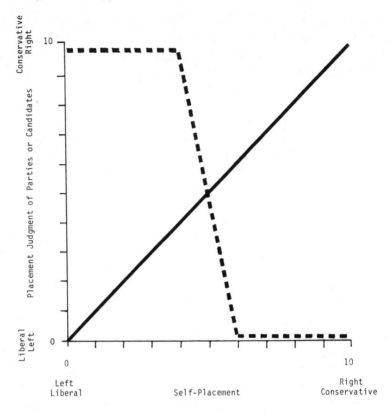

Figure 2.2. A "pure" subjective placement model, depicting relationship between self-placement on a scale and placement of a preferred party or candidate (solid line) and a nonpreferred party or candidate (broken line) on the same scale.

certain level of subjective agreement could be observed but be due entirely to the operation of the first *or* the third process. Therefore, one of our goals is to try to separate the effect of the first two more democratic processes from the third more irrational process.

In the analyses that follow, we first give an overall description of how U.S. and Swedish citizens place themselves, their political parties, and candidates on the left–right or liberal–conservative ideology dimension. The extent of consensus in the perceptions is also analyzed. Correlations between ideological self-placement and attitudinal positions on various political and social issues are considered as indicators of the relevance of the left–right and liberal–conservative dimensions in the two countries. Autocorrelations of self-placements on the ideology dimensions are calculated as measures of stability. Subjective agreement is assessed by evaluating the degree of association between self-placement on the ideology dimension and placement of the preferred party or candidate (resulting from all three processes in figure 2.1). This estimate is compared to the degree of association between self-placement on the ideology dimension and party or candidate preference (resulting from the first two processes in figure 2.1). Assimilation and contrast effects in perception of parties and candidates are also considered *within* party or candidate preference groups in order to get relatively more "pure" measures.

A brief detour

Before turning to the main part of our analyses, let us take a brief detour by examining in a preliminary way some data from the Swedish national election study of 1968. This was the first such survey in which Swedish citizens were asked to place their preferred party and themselves on an 11-point left–right scale. Note that in this survey people were asked to make only two ideological judgments in short succession, first where they would place the party they liked best and then where they would put themselves on the same scale. In subsequent Swedish surveys, which become the focus of our attention later, people were asked to make several placement judgments of parties and then where they put themselves. However, the results from 1968 are presented here briefly because they proved to be instructive as to how analyses of subsequent surveys should proceed.

The upper portion of figure 2.3 shows a very strong linear relationship between where the Swedish people placed themselves on the left–right scale and where they placed their respective preferred party on the same scale (eta = .90). Of the 2546 people represented in figure 2.3, 62 percent put their most preferred party and themselves at exactly the same point on the 11-point scale. The overall subjective agreement coefficient of .90 is even slightly stronger among people who consider themselves as strong sup-porters of the party (.94) and only slightly weaker among people who are not so strong supporters of the party (.89) and among people who only prefer the party and do not identify themselves as supporters of it (.85). This certainly provides strong support for one part of the subjective placement model in figure 2.2. Thus, a very strong empirical relationship has been observed between where people in Sweden place themselves and where they place their preferred party on the left–right ideology scale. Of course, one could argue that when the two questions are asked in such quick suc-cession, there will be a natural tendency to place oneself where one has just placed one's most-liked party. That this is *not* just a fantasy world in which a party can mean all things to all people becomes apparent in a second analysis in which party preference is the independent variable and self-placement on the ideology scale the dependent variable. The resulting eta

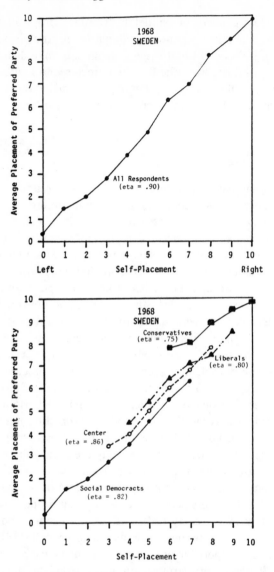

Figure 2.3. Overall relation between self-placement on a 0–10 left–right scale and placement of one's preferred party on the same scale in Sweden in 1968 (upper graph) and within party preference groups (lower graph).

(.71) indicates that there are *large* and very real differences among people in the five main party preference groups as to where they place themselves on the ideology dimension.

Our third stop in this brief detour involves repeating the initial analysis, looking at the effect of self-placement on placement of the preferred party, but this time *within* each party preference group. The results for four of the party preference groups are shown in the lower portion of figure 2.3. The obtained eta values (.79, .82, .86, .80, and .75 for the Communist, Social Democratic, Center, Liberal, and Conservative party preference groups, respectively) show that *within* each party preference group there is a very strong relationship between where people place themselves and where they place their preferred party on the left–right ideology dimension. In these analyses, party, and thus the party's position (if we can assume each party has *a* position), are in effect being held constant. Thus, it seems reasonable to infer from the lower portion of figure 2.3 that considerable assimilation is also occurring in these placement judgments.[1]

Of course, we cannot say for certain whether people alter their perception of the preferred party's position to coincide with their own position or change their own position to coincide with their *perception* of their preferred party's position. What we do know beyond a reasonable doubt is that there is a very strong link between self-placement and placement of a preferred party – both overall and within a given party.

Ideological placements in Sweden and the United States

For all of the remaining analyses in this chapter, the Swedish data are from national election studies done in relation to Sweden's parliamentary elections of 1979, 1982, and 1985. The U.S. data are from the American election studies done by the Center for Political Studies (CPS) of the University of Michigan for the presidential elections of 1976, 1980, and 1984. In Sweden, respondents were asked to place the largest political parties and then themselves on an 11-point *vänster–höger* (left–right) scale. In the United States, people were asked to place themselves, the presidential nominees of the two largest parties, and then the parties on a 7-point liberal–conservative scale.[2] For the U.S., our primary focus is on the placements of the candidates for president, the most prominent actor in the American political system. In Sweden, citizens in effect vote for the party rather than for individual candidates, and thus political parties are the principal actors.[3]

For the U.S. surveys, the preelection question asking for whom the person intended to vote in the coming election is taken as a measure of candidate preference. For Sweden, direct questions regarding party preference are used.

There is not very much difference between the two countries in how respondents place themselves on the respective ideology scale, although a much higher percentage in Sweden placed themselves somewhere on the scale than in the United States (e.g., 94% in Sweden in 1979, 62%

Table 2.1 *Average self-placement and average placement of the parties on the left–right ideology scale (0–10) by party preference groups in Sweden in 1979, 1982, and 1985*

Placement of:	Year		Party preference group in Sweden					Eta
			vpk	s	c	fp	m	
	1985	5.2	2.3	3.6	6.3	6.3	7.8	.76
Self	1982	5.0	1.9	3.4	6.2	6.0	7.7	.79
	1979	4.9	1.9	3.4	5.8	6.0	7.5	.77
	1985	1.0	1.6	1.2	0.8	0.6	0.7	.22
Communist party (vpk)	1982	0.9	1.3	1.1	0.6	0.6	0.5	.22
	1979	1.0	1.2	1.2	0.8	0.6	0.6	.20
	1985	2.8	3.4	3.0	2.4	2.6	2.3	.20
Social Democratic party (s)	1982	2.8	3.2	3.0	2.3	2.6	2.4	.20
	1979	2.9	3.6	3.1	2.5	2.8	2.4	.22
	1985	6.2	6.5	6.2	6.4	6.0	6.1	.10
Center party (c)	1982	6.3	6.7	6.3	6.6	6.1	6.2	.10
	1979	6.2	6.6	6.3	6.7	5.8	6.1	.14
	1985	6.5	6.9	6.4	6.3	6.5	6.7	.20
Liberal party (fp)	1982	6.0	6.9	6.1	5.8	6.1	5.6	.20
	1979	6.0	6.6	6.1	5.8	6.1	5.9	.10
	1985	9.0	9.6	9.1	8.7	8.9	8.9	.22
Conservative party (m)	1982	8.9	9.5	9.1	8.9	9.0	8.8	.10
	1979	8.8	9.6	9.1	8.6	8.8	8.7	.17

Note: The initials for party preference groups here are as they are used in Sweden: vpk = Communist Party; s = Social Democratic Party; c = Center Party; fp = Liberal Party; and m = Conservative Party. The eta values in the right-hand column measure the degree of association between the independent variable, party preference, and the dependent variables, self-placement and placement of the parties. Eta, which has a possible range of .00 to 1.00, is similar to the standard Pearson product moment correlation coefficient, but whereas the latter is sensitive only to linear effects, eta can detect any systematic relationship between two variables.

in the U.S. in 1980).[4] In each case, the distribution of responses approximated a bell-shaped distribution with the average close to the center of the scale.[5] Citizens in the United States have been quite stable, leaning slightly to the right (average = 4.1, 4.2, 4.3, and 4.2 in 1972, 1976, 1980, and 1984, respectively, on the 1–7 scale). The averages for Sweden (4.9, 5.0, and 5.2 in 1979, 1982, and 1985, respectively) were very near the center of the 0–10 scale and may have shifted slightly to the right in recent years. Thus, whatever differences are observed in this study are *not* likely due to differences in the distribution of self-designated ideology between Swedish and American citizens (cf. Granberg, 1987). This does not, of course, mean that ideological positions reflect exactly the same content in the two countries.

The average placement judgments concerning the position of self, parties,

Table 2.2 *Average self-placement and average placement of the candidates and parties on the liberal–conservative ideology scale (1–7) by candidate preference groups in the United States in 1976, 1980, and 1984*

Placement of:	Year	Overall	Placement by people preferring		Eta
			Democratic candidate	Republican candidate	
	1984	4.2	3.5	4.7	.43
Self	1980	4.3	3.9	4.9	.37
	1976	4.2	3.6	4.8	.45
	1984	3.4	3.8	3.1	.22
Democratic Candidate	1980	3.7	4.1	3.3	.26
	1976	3.2	3.4	2.9	.22
	1984	5.0	5.0	5.1	.00
Republican Candidate	1980	5.2	5.0	5.3	.10
	1976	4.9	5.0	4.9	.00
	1984	3.4	3.7	3.0	.20
Democratic Party	1980	3.3	3.7	2.9	.24
	1976	3.0	3.2	2.6	.24
	1984	4.9	5.0	5.0	.00
Republican Party	1980	5.1	5.1	5.1	.00
	1976	5.0	5.1	4.9	.00

Note: The Democratic Presidential candidate in 1976 and 1980 was Jimmy Carter and in 1984 was Walter Mondale. The Republican Presidential candidate was Gerald Ford in 1976 and Ronald Reagan in 1980 and 1984.

and candidates on the ideology scale are given in table 2.1 (Sweden) and table 2.2 (United States). Except for the Liberal and Center parties, political parties in Sweden were seen as distinct from each other on the left–right dimension, with the five parties covering nearly the entire political spectrum. In the United States, parties and candidates were seen as closer to the center and closer to each other. These distributions are about as expected based on Downs' (1957) economic theory of democracy as it pertains to two-party and multi-party systems. It is evident that not only the number but also the *range* of viable alternatives is seen as much greater in Sweden than in the U.S. In both countries, the perceived distinctness among the parties or candidates appears to be somewhat larger than the own position differences among supporters of the parties or candidates (cf. Holmberg, 1981).

A strong consensus in these placement judgments is one indicator of shared meaning on the ideological dimension within the two countries. If all the people were to place a party at the same point on a scale, this does not, of course, *guarantee* that there is complete shared meaning as to what ideology means and what this party's ideology is. But it is at least a strong hint that there is some shared meaning among the people making the placement

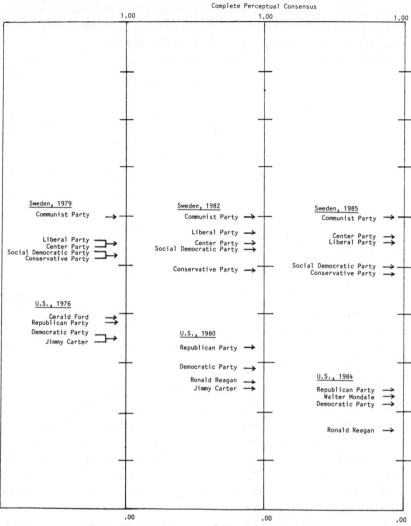

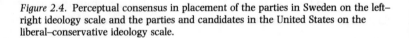

Figure 2.4. Perceptual consensus in placement of the parties in Sweden on the left–right ideology scale and the parties and candidates in the United States on the liberal–conservative ideology scale.

judgments. Consensus here refers then to perceptual agreement about the position of a political stimulus (party or candidate) on the ideology scale.[6] For each set of placement judgments, we calculated a *perceptual consensus coefficient* by dividing the empirically derived standard deviation by the standard deviation that would result if the placement judgments were random (given the number of categories used and the number of people making the placement judgments), and then subtracting the resulting fraction from one.[7] As indicated in figure 2.4, the level of perceptual consensus was considerably and consistently higher in Sweden than in the United States, despite the much *higher percentage of missing data* in the U.S. than in Sweden. Over 90 percent of the Swedish samples made the requested placement judgments on the prescribed scale, compared to about 60 percent of the U.S. samples.

For the United States, the consensus coefficients averaged .36 in 1976, .28 in 1980, and only .21 for 1984 for placements of the two candidates and the two parties. This may indicate that the concept of ideology was relatively more salient in the U.S. in 1976. Other considerations (e.g., Iran, inflation, retrospective evaluations of the incumbent) may have been more salient in 1980 and 1984. It was also true that the response rate was higher in 1984 than in the previous studies. A decrease in missing data may thus be associated with a decrease in the perceptual consensus coefficients.

For Sweden, the consensus coefficients averaged .54 for placement judgments of the five political parties on the left–right scale in each year, 1979, 1982, and 1985.[8] Thus, there can be little doubt that Swedish citizens showed substantially more perceptual consensus than U.S. citizens. This is, in all probability, because political parties in Sweden are more distinct and have much clearer profiles on the left–right ideology dimension than the parties or candidates in the U.S. have on the liberal–conservative dimension. The consensus coefficients for the U.S. indicate more perceptual consensus than would occur by chance – but not much more.

An alternative approach to assessing consensus focuses on the extent to which people in different political groups agree or disagree in their average placement judgments – that is, whether the placement judgments are "stimulus" or "perceiver" determined (Nimmo and Savage, 1976; Sigel, 1964). If opposing groups agree in their placements, the placements are said in this respect to be stimulus determined. To the extent that opposing groups differ in their placement judgments, the judgments are perceiver determined.

In nations where ideology is distributed more or less normally with the bulk of the people at or near the center, such as Sweden and the U.S., one way in which politicians and political parties can enhance potential effectiveness is to emphasize how extreme the opposition parties are, how their opponents radically depart from the center, and how moderate their own party is. To the extent that voters supporting opposing parties showed such tendencies, the result would be a set of placement judgments in which the intergroup differences would be substantial and indicative of a perceiver determined process. Table 2.1 compares supporters of the five parties in

Sweden as to how they placed the five parties in 1979, 1982, and 1985.

In Sweden party preference exerted an effect on the placement of the five parties, but in no instance was the effect especially strong, explaining only about 3 percent of the variance, on the average. For example, differences occurred in placing the Social Democratic Party. The Communists were most likely to place the Social Democratic Party toward the center, and the supporters of the three bourgeois parties (Center, Liberal, and Conservative) tended to place the Social Democratic Party toward the left, thus "pushing" it away from their own party's position. The Communists also tended to place the three bourgeois parties toward the right extreme. Social Democratic supporters showed a similar but weaker tendency. The Social Democrats tended to displace the Conservative Party toward the extreme right, although to a lesser extent than did the Communist supporters. However, contrary to expectation, supporters of a given party generally did not shift their preferred party toward the center.

The scale seemed to be somewhat different, or to be used somewhat differently by the Communists from how it was used by people preferring one of the other four parties. This seems to be a reasonable inference given that the Communists shifted all five parties, including their own, to the right, in comparison with the average placement judgments made by supporters of the other four parties. While some significant differences were observed in these comparisons, we do not want to exaggerate the magnitude of the effects. Overall, the placement judgments may not have been completely stimulus determined in these comparisons, but they were nearly so.

The results for the United States were quite similar to those of Sweden in that they tended to be stimulus determined. In two of three instances, supporters of the Republican candidate actually placed the Republican candidate farther from the center than did supporters of the Democratic candidate. Perhaps the most intriguing finding in table 2.2 was that in each year the candidate preference groups differed much more in placing the Democratic Party and its nominee than in placing the Republican Party and its nominee. The candidate preference groups, in fact, did not differ much at all in their placements of the Republican Party and its nominee. But supporters of the Republican candidate tended to see the Democratic Party and its nominee as farther to the left than did supporters of the Democratic candidate. Another way of viewing these differences is to say that supporters of the Republican candidates tend to see a larger difference between the two major candidates than do supporters of the Democratic candidates. Overall, candidate preference did exert an effect on placement of the parties and candidates in the United States, although this effect was not dramatic and should not be overstated.

Coherence and stability of self-designated ideology

If our assumptions and general understanding of the two political systems are correct, we would expect ideological positions to be more closely related to attitudinal positions on specific issues in Sweden than in the U.S. In each survey, a large number of attitudinal items was correlated with self-placement on the ideology scale. The five issues in each survey that correlated most strongly with left–right or liberal–conservative ideology are given in table 2.3. Attitudes on the five issues were also combined in each year to form an index which was then correlated with the ideology scale. Although the issues were not the same across years, the results are very consistent. Self-designated ideology was clearly more strongly related to position on contemporary issues in Sweden than it was in the U.S., with the correlation between ideology and the attitude index being .70 (1979), .71 (1982), and .72 (1985) in Sweden, compared to .54 (both 1976 and 1980) and .43 (1984) in the United States.

If left–right ideology is more coherent, meaningful, and salient in Sweden than the liberal–conservative dimension in the U.S., self-designated ideology would be expected to be more stable across time in Sweden. In the 1979–1982 Swedish panel, the correlation for self-placement on left–right ideology was .75 (N = 985). The same autocorrelation for the 1982–1985 Swedish panel was .76 (N = 990). The closest comparison we could make to U.S. data involved the CPS 1972–1976 panel. For this panel, the autocorrelation for self-designated liberal–conservative ideology from one presidential election year to another was .56 (N = 821).[9]

Based on evidence presented thus far, including the data on perceptual consensus, it appears clear that left–right ideology is relatively more meaningful, stable, and coherent in Sweden than liberal–conservative ideology is in the United States. However, ideology in the U.S. is by no means meaningless or incoherent. Correlations as high as .54 (between the issue index and ideology) and .56 (autocorrelation for self-designated ideology across time) could not be obtained if ideology were devoid of meaning in the United States.

Subjective agreement

We now return to the central problem in this chapter: subjective agreement between a person and the person's preferred party or candidate. Our approach will be to present a picture of the results pertaining to the subjective placement model and then to break down subjective agreement into its principal components.

To examine the overall relationship between a person's self-placement

Table 2.3 Correlations between self-designated left–right or liberal–conservative ideological positions and attitudes toward current issues in Sweden and the United States

Sweden

Issue	1979	Issue	1982	Issue	1985
1 Wage-earner funds	.60	1 Wage-earner funds	.60	1 Wage-earner funds	.65
2 Socialize large companies	.60	2 Socialize large companies	.54	2 Privatize medical care	.51
3 Government influence on private enterprise	.43	3 Sick-leave policy	.49	3 Socialize large companies	.50
4 Taxes on large incomes	.39	4 Size of public sector	.43	4 Size of public sector	.48
5 Defense spending	.35	5 Social welfare programs	.41	5 Social welfare programs	.44
Average for five issues	.47	Average for five issues	.50	Average for five issues	.52
Five-item index	.70	Five-item index	.71	Five-item index	.72

United States

Issue	1976	Issue	1980	Issue	1984
1 Government health insurance	.36	1 Equal Rights Amendment	.39	1 Guarantee job and living standard	.28
2 Marijuana	.36	2 Guarantee job and living standard	.32	2 Military spending	.28
3 Aid to minority groups	.32	3 Government social services	.30	3 Status women	.28
4 Guarantee job and living standard	.32	4 Aid to minority groups	.30	4 Aid to minority groups	.26
5 Urban unrest	.32	5 Military spending	.28	5 Government social services	.26
Average for five issues	.34	Average for five issues	.32	Average for five issues	.27
Five-item index	.54	Five-item index	.54	Five-item index	.43

and placement of that person's preferred party or candidate, new composite variables were created. The independent variable in this case is the person's self-placement on the ideology scale, while the key dependent variable is the person's placement of the preferred party or candidate. We also constructed a variable for placement of a nonpreferred party or candidate, which was somewhat easier for the U.S. data where there were only two major candidates, compared to Sweden with its five parties. Swedish respondents were asked to rate the five parties on a -5 to $+5$ like–dislike scale (see chapter 5). We used the party rated lowest on this like–dislike scale as a measure of the person's least-liked party. Where respondents placed the least-liked party on the left–right scale was taken as the placement of the most nonpreferred party in each year.[10]

Figure 2.5 presents the results for the subjective placement model in Sweden and the United States. There was a remarkably close resemblance between the empirical results for Sweden in figure 2.5 and the pure subjective placement model in figure 2.2. The correlation between self-placement and placement of the *preferred* party, which may be called the *subjective agreement coefficient*, was robust ($+.87$ in 1979, $+.89$ in 1982, $+.86$ in 1985). The average for each of the 11 categories of self-placement was significantly different from all of the other categories, and there was essentially no nonlinear variance in placing the preferred party. As with the results for 1968 reported previously, the robustness of subjective agreement with preferred party was higher for those who identified strongly with their preferred party, slightly lower among those who identified weakly with their preferred party, and somewhat less for those people who preferred the party but did not identify with it.

When it came to placing the *least-liked* party in Sweden, a step function occurred (figure 2.5), giving strong support to the pure subjective placement model. Swedish respondents whose self-placements were at positions 0, 1, 2, and 3 did not differ significantly from each other in their placement of the least-liked party, as was also the case for those at positions 7, 8, 9, and 10.[11] This step function is also indicated by the statistical departure from linearity. The correlation between self-placement and placement of the least-liked party was $-.70$, $-.72$, and $-.73$ for 1979, 1982, and 1985, respectively, and the eta was .75, .77, and .79 for 1979, 1982, and 1985. Thus, about 8 percent of the variance in the relationship between self-placement and placement of the least-liked party was nonlinear.

The results for the United States (also in figure 2.5) showed considerably weaker effects and less resemblance to the subjective placement model. This is undoubtedly due in part to the wider range of alternatives available to Swedish voters as they select their most preferred and most disliked party. In placing the preferred candidate in 1980, U.S. citizens whose self-placements

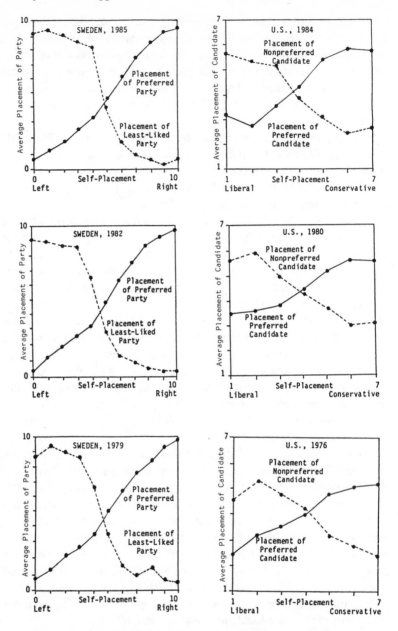

Figure 2.5. Relationship between self-placement and placement of one's preferred party and one's least-liked party in Sweden on a 0–10 left–right dimension and between self-placement and placements of one's preferred candidate and one's nonpreferred candidate in the United States on a 1–7 liberal–conservative dimension.

were at positions 1, 2, and 3 did not differ significantly, nor did those at positions 5, 6, and 7. This is obviously a departure from the subjective placement model (figure 2.2). The correlations between self-placement and placement of a preferred candidate were moderate, +.50 for 1976, +.47 for 1980, and +.58 for 1984. The correlations between self-placement and placement of the nonpreferred candidate were −.50, −.47, and −.55 for 1976, 1980, and 1984, respectively. These correlations were in the expected direction, but noticeably weaker than the corresponding coefficients for Sweden. The correlations for the U.S., as might be expected, increased somewhat if only strong partisans were considered, and they decreased somewhat if only weak partisans were considered.

Although the placement of *nonpreferred* candidate and least-liked party are not derived in the same way for Sweden and the United States, there is no such problem with placing the *preferred* party or candidate. Therefore, it seems reasonable to conclude that subjective agreement between a person and the person's preferred party on the left–right scale in Sweden is *much* stronger than the subjective agreement between a person and the person's preferred candidate in the U.S. on the liberal–conservative dimension.[12]

Unraveling the sources of subjective agreement

As indicated previously, subjective agreement is a relatively gross measure in that there are several processes that can work in the same direction of producing subjective agreement with a preferred party or candidate. Hence, the same level of subjective agreement could be obtained as a consequence of quite different underlying processes. Thus far, it has been shown that the level of subjective agreement is much higher in Sweden than in the U.S. We now try to break down the subjective agreement coefficient into some of its components in order to try to better understand the relative contributions of some of the underlying processes.

Two of the three processes were identified as essentially rational and democratic in nature: when people choose the alternative which stands in the closest proximity to themselves and when people form or alter their self-placement to correspond more closely with that of a preferred party or candidate. To the extent that these two processes occur, voter groups should be divided in terms of how they place themselves on the ideology scale. Thus, the effect of these two processes is reflected in the shared variance between party or candidate preference and self-placement on the ideology scale. This may be called a *rational democratic coefficient*, although we realize we are using the term in a specific and limited sense. In this relationship, perceptions are not involved (except for self-perception). The relative magnitude of the subjective agreement coefficient can be compared to the rational democratic coefficient. The former is presumably the result of all three processes, whereas the latter is the result of only two. A comparison of the two coefficients ought to give an indication of the extent to which subjective agreement is due to rational processes or to the irrational process of assimilation.

To make the comparisons more explicit, two analyses of variance are done. In the first, self-placement on the ideology dimension is the independent variable and placement of preferred party (or preferred candidate) the dependent variable, with the resulting eta coefficient referred to as the *subjective agreement coefficient*. The second uses party or candidate preference as the independent variable and self-placement on ideology as the dependent variable, with the eta coefficient referred to as the *rational democratic coefficient*.

The relationship between party preference and self-placement on the left–right scale was given in table 2.1 for Sweden and that between candidate preference and self-placement on the liberal–conservative scale in table 2.2 for the U.S. In Sweden, each of the party preference groups differed significantly from each other, with the exception of the Liberal and Center parties, and the eta coefficients were robust (.77 in 1979, .79 in 1982, .76 in 1985). In the United States, Mondale and Reagan supporters in 1984 did differ significantly on self-placement, but the eta coefficient was a more modest .43. Ford and Carter supporters in 1976 differed slightly more on self-designated ideology, but the coefficient (.45) was still small in comparison to those for Sweden. The coefficient for 1980, comparing Carter and Reagan supporters, was only .37.

Figure 2.6 compares Sweden and the United States, showing that the subjective agreement coefficient was substantially higher in Sweden than in the United States, that the rational democratic coefficient was also substantially higher in Sweden than in the United States, but the difference between the two coefficients was roughly the same for both countries. By inference, it appears that assimilation, or the tendency toward wishful thinking, when attributing a position to a preferred party or candidate, may have occurred to about the same extent in Sweden and the United States. The much higher level of subjective agreement found in Sweden, in comparison to the United States, appears to be due essentially to stronger rational democratic processes in Sweden.

It is quite likely that self-placement on an ideology scale means different things to different people, depending partially on the extent of their formal education. Figure 2.7 shows that in each country the size of the rational democratic coefficient increases as education increases, although the slope tends to be steeper for the United States, especially in 1980 and 1984. In the U.S. in 1980, there was an especially large percentage of "don't know" and

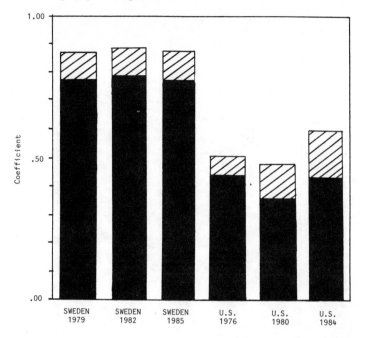

Figure 2.6. Subjective agreement and rational democratic coefficients in Sweden and the United States.
Note. The total height of each bar indicates the size of the overall subjective agreement coefficient based on the relationship between self-placement on the ideology dimension and placement of the preferred party (Sweden) or candidate (United States). The height of the solid portion of each bar indicates the size of the rational democratic coefficient relating candidate or party preference to self-placement on the ideology dimension.

other missing data responses among people with little formal education. Among people with the least amount of formal education who did place themselves on the ideology scale in the U.S. in 1980, the candidate preference groups did not differ significantly in self-placement on the liberal–conservative scale. Also, the rational democratic coefficient was *higher* for the *least* educated group in Sweden than it was for the *most* educated group in the United States.

The large differences between Sweden and the United States in figures 2.6 and 2.7 could be due to the fact that citizens in Sweden are divided into five-party preference groups, while those in the U.S. are classified in only two-candidate preference groups. To check whether our results could be attributed to this basic difference, we recoded party preference in Sweden into two categories: preference for the Communist or Social Democratic Party (regarded in Sweden as the socialist bloc), and preference for one of the other three parties (the bourgeois bloc). Despite this recoding of party

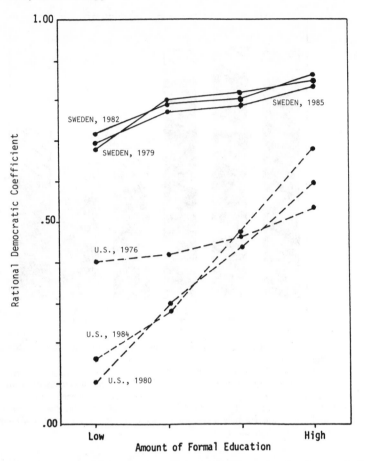

Figure 2.7. Rational democratic coefficient within four educational groups in Sweden and the United States.
Note. The rational democratic coefficient is based on the relationship between candidate or party preference and self-placement on the ideology dimension.

preference, the rational democratic coefficient (between bloc preference and self-placement on the left–right scale) was reduced only slightly (e.g., from .76 to .72 in 1985). Thus, very little of the difference between Sweden and the U.S. in figures 2.5 to 2.7 can be attributed to the fact that the Swedish coefficients are based on five-party preference groups while those for the U.S. are based on only two-candidate preference groups.

Assimilation within party and candidate preference groups

A significant relationship between self-placement and placement of the preferred party or candidate *within* a party or candidate preference group

Table 2.4 *Correlation between self-placement and placement of the five political parties in Sweden on the left–right ideology dimension within five-party preference groups in 1979, 1982, and 1985*

			Correlation between self-placement and placement of					
			vpk	s	c	fp	m	Average N
	vpk	1985	+.53	+.54	+.10	−.06	−.22	
		1982	+.55	+.53	−.11	+.02	−.23	100
		1979	+.54	+.29	−.10	−.17	−.44	
	s	1985	+.26	+.65	−.21	−.16	−.35	
		1982	+.12	+.68	−.15	−.06	−.27	1059
		1979	+.25	+.67	−.12	−.05	+.28	
Party Preference Group	c	1985	−.11	−.22	+.60	+.35	+.16	
		1982	−.12	−.14	+.69	+.32	+.02	322
		1979	−.19	−.07	+.65	+.35	+.15	
	fp	1985	−.19	−.12	+.29	+.73	+.19	
		1982	+.03	−.05	+.28	+.64	+.11	234
		1979	−.05	−.06	+.29	+.66	+.10	
	m	1985	−.27	−.24	+.19	+.47	+.56	
		1982	−.27	−.27	+.31	+.20	+.52	469
		1979	−.26	−.22	+.38	+.33	+.54	

Note: The initials for party preference groups used here are as they are used in Sweden: vpk = Communist Party; s = Social Democratic Party; c = Center Party; fp = Liberal Party; and m = Conservative Party. Row headings indicate the party preference group making the placement judgments. Column headings indicate the party which is being used.

cannot reasonably be attributed to a rational democratic process. A rational democratic process requires variation in party or candidate preference, but when one looks *within* each preference group separately, one is, in effect, controlling preference by holding it constant. Thus, when we look within party preference groups, as we did previously with the 1968 Swedish study, we may be getting relatively "pure" indicators of assimilation and contrast.

Table 2.4 presents the correlations between self-placement and placement of each party within each of the five-party preference groups in Sweden. A positive correlation can be taken to indicate assimilation and a negative correlation contrast.[13] Looking within the party preference categories in table 2.4, Swedish respondents in each party preference group tended to *assimilate* their respective preferred party. Thus, the further to the left their personal self-placement, the further to the left they positioned their preferred party. The range of these assimilative tendencies was from +.52 for the Conservatives in 1982 to +.73 for people preferring the Liberal party in 1985.[14] Also, people in each party preference group tended to assimilate their own party to a greater extent than they contrasted any of the other parties, which is consistent with the asymmetrical results reported previously for specific issues in the United States (Kinder, 1978; Granberg and Brent, 1980). Also evident in table 2.4 is a mild tendency to assimilate when estimating the position of a party ideologically adjacent to one's own or within one's own bloc. Thus, as examples, the Communists assimilate when placing the Social Democratic Party as do Center Party supporters when placing the Liberal Party. It also appears from evidence in that table that there is at least a mild tendency to contrast when making placement judgments of parties in the opposing bloc.

However, the most noteworthy trend in table 2.4 is the strong tendency to assimilate when attributing a position to one's preferred party (highlighted diagonally). This tendency is examined further in figure 2.8, in which the means for placement of one's preferred party are shown *within* party preference categories for each own position group. It is obvious in figure 2.8 that the within-party assimilation tendencies are essentially linear in nature, and some of the differences are rather substantial. For instance, in 1985, Social Democratic supporters who placed themselves at position 1 placed the Social Democratic Party at 1.3, on the average, while Social Democratic supporters who placed themselves at position 5 placed the Social Democratic Party at 3.8. Given the sample's average placement of the Social Democratic Party at 2.8 in 1985, it is quite reasonable to infer that assimilation was occurring.

The comparable results for the United States are shown in table 2.5 and figure 2.8. Although there is some variation from election to election, the results in table 2.5 are rather consistent. Across these three elections, the average correlation between self-placement and placement of one's preferred candidate within candidate preference groups in the U.S. was $+.40$, compared to $-.35$ between self-placement and placement of one's non-preferred candidate. This strongly suggests the occurrence of assimilation and contrast with a hint of asymmetry in the relative strength of these effects.

Once again, some rather substantial tendencies are observed. In 1980, for instance, Carter supporters who placed themselves at position 2 placed Carter at 3.4 and Reagan at 6.1, on the average, while Carter supporters who placed themselves at position 6 placed Carter at 4.9 and Reagan at 3.9. Given the average sample placements of Carter at 3.7 and Reagan at 5.2, these results strongly imply the occurrence of assimilation and contrast. In 1984, Mondale supporters who were themselves at position 2 placed Mondale at 2.7 on the average, while Mondale supporters who were themselves at position 5 placed Mondale at 4.6. Given that the whole sample placed Mondale at 3.4 on the average, it is at the very least not unreasonable to infer that these people were assimilating in their estimates of their preferred candidate's position.

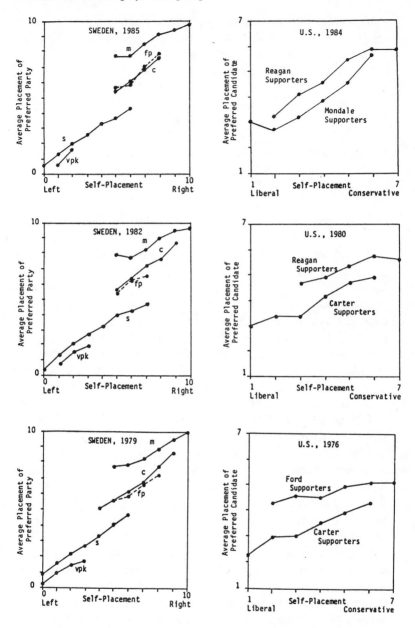

Figure 2.8. Relationship between self-placement and placement of one's preferred party in Sweden on the left–right dimension within five-party preference groups and between self-placement and placement of one's preferred candidate in the United States on the liberal–conservative dimension within candidate preference groups.

Table 2.5 *Correlations between self-placement and placement of the candidates in the United States on the liberal–conservative ideology scale within candidate preference groups in 1976, 1980, and 1984*

People preferring:		Correlation between self-placement and placement of:		
		Democratic candidate	Republican candidate	Average N
Democratic candidate	1984	+.47	−.43	
	1980	+.43	−.32	462
	1976	+.38	−.29	
Republican candidate	1984	−.38	+.49	
	1980	−.37	+.31	612
	1976	−.31	+.30	

Overall, when we look at the relationship between self-placement and placement of the parties in Sweden and placement of the candidates in the United States *within* party and candidate preference groups, we observe strong signs in both countries of systematic displacement effects. In both countries the tendency to assimilate the preferred party or candidate appeared to be somewhat stronger than the tendency to contrast a nonpreferred party or candidate. Within preference groups, the tendency to assimilate one's preferred party appears to be somewhat stronger in Sweden than in the United States. Given that the left–right dimension is more salient in Sweden than the liberal–conservative dimension in the U.S., it follows that it would be more important for people in Sweden to be close to the position of their preferred party.

From the evidence presented thus far, we cannot tell whether the latter is a real difference or a result of the different scales being used. Therefore, we want to consider briefly a comparison from a 1982 survey done by SIFO, the largest commercial polling organization in Sweden, in which people placed themselves and the five parties on a 1–7 left–right scale. The comparison is shown in table 2.6.

There it is evident that using an 11-point scale does result in a higher correlation between self-placement and placement of a preferred party than a 7-point scale in four of five cases (the results for the Communists, the exception, may be unstable due to small numbers of people).[15] However, the average of +.49 for the 1–7 scale in Sweden is still a little higher than the corresponding average for the U.S. (+.40). Thus, our conclusion would be that *within* party and candidate preference groups, there is a substantial tendency to assimilate when placing one's preferred party in Sweden and when placing one's preferred candidate in the United States, and that the former tendency is, if different at all, slightly stronger than the latter.

Table 2.6 *Correlation between self-placement and placement of one's preferred party in Sweden on a 0–10 and a 1–7 left–right ideology scale*

Correlation between self-placement and placement of preferred party on a left–right scale:	Party preference groups in Sweden					
	vpk	s	c	fp	m	Average
0–10 (1982)	+.55	+.68	+.69	+.64	+.52	+.62
1–7 (1982)	+.63	+.49	+.39	+.60	+.32	+.49

Note: The data in the first row (0–10) are drawn from Granberg and Holmberg (1986a), while those in the second row are from Granberg (1987).

Subjective ideology and political perception

The evidence relating to self-placement and political perception on the ideology dimension has already taken us a considerable distance down the path to demonstrating that the political system matters. Differences observed between how things look at the psychological level in Sweden and the U.S. have been large and readily interpretable with reference to the differing political systems. The strong party system in Sweden and the emphasis on qualities of individual candidates in the U.S. are reflected in the political perceptions in many ways.

Although the greater number and range of alternatives in Sweden is an important aspect of the larger picture, we do not think by any means that this is the touchstone that explains all our findings so far. As illustrated in our analysis, compressing the Swedish data from five parties into two blocs may reduce the large differences between Sweden and the U.S., but only slightly. Although it is beyond the scope of our current project, we do not think it would be hard to imagine or find a political system with at least as many alternatives as Sweden but where the alternatives are much less distinct than in Sweden.

Nor does the fact that a nation has only two alternatives or two parties guarantee anything about how similar or different these alternatives will be. As indicated previously, reducing the alternatives in Sweden from five parties to two blocs decreased the strength of some of the effects but only slightly. Within the United States, if a candidate with Barry Goldwater's ideology were to face an opponent with George McGovern's ideology, and if the media were to concentrate on basic issues rather than personalities and personal idiosyncracies, the results might look very different from those for the U.S. in this chapter. Given the experience of the past 25 years, one can hardly gainsay the possibility that people of such relative ideological extremity can win the nomination of large contending parties in a two-party system, Downs' (1957) theoretical implications notwithstanding.

To sum up the major findings in this chapter, we observed first of all that citizens in both countries showed a substantial tendency toward subjective agreement with a preferred party or candidate, though this tendency was much stronger in Sweden than in the United States. Such differences are demonstrably due to the stronger impact of rational democratic processes in Sweden. It was assumed that the tendencies to choose a party or candidate on the basis of proximity or to enhance proximity by altering one's self-placement in the direction of the position of a preferred party or candidate would be captured in the coefficient relating party or candidate preference to self-placement on the ideology scale. According to our results, the rational democratic coefficient was significant in both countries, but much stronger in Sweden.

Secondly, left–right ideology was more stable and coherent in Sweden than liberal–conservative ideology in the United States. Self-designated ideology was also shown to be more strongly linked to attitudes on contemporary issues in Sweden than in the U.S. To fully understand these differences, it would be necessary to take into account many facets of the social, political, and economic histories of Sweden and the United States.

Thirdly, although there was evidence of some degree of perceptual consensus in placement judgments of the parties and candidates on the ideology scale in both Sweden and the United States, the level of consensus was substantially higher in Sweden than in the U.S. This result is likely due to the fact that the ideology dimension is more relevant to Swedish citizens, as is the position of the parties on the dimension and the relationship of most issues to ideology, when compared to the relative lack of interest in political ideology among U.S. citizens.

Fourthly, education appears to be more of a moderating factor in the United States than in Sweden. In the least educated group in the U.S. in 1980, the number of persons who failed to place either themselves or the candidates on the ideology scale was very high, and at the same time for those who did make the placements, the rational democratic coefficient was so low that one can infer that the dimension of liberal–conservative ideology was essentially meaningless for this group of people. However, this was hardly the case for Sweden. Even among the least educated group in Sweden, the rational democratic coefficient was robust, and it was even higher than that for college graduates in the U.S.

Finally, it was also evident that the irrational processes of perceptual distortion, assimilation and contrast, occurred to approximately the same degree in both countries – as reflected in the relative magnitudes of the rational democratic and subjective agreement coefficients. The rationale was that the relative difference between these coefficients reflects the contribution of the irrational process to subjective agreement. Also, when we looked *within* party or candidate preference groups, there was strong evidence of assimilation and contrast. The tendency for assimilation to be stronger than contrast was observed for each of Sweden's five-party preference groups in each year. In the U.S., a similar asymmetry was observed although it was less pronounced.

The numerous differences observed between Sweden and the U.S. cannot be reasonably attributed to differences between the distribution of self-designated ideology in the two countries, since these distributions were similar, though not identical. Nor can the observed differences be attributed to educational differences in Sweden and the U.S. Although difficult to compare, adults in the U.S. may have slightly more formal education, on average, than adults in Sweden.

Instead, the strongest explanation for our findings lies in understanding the operation of social psychological processes within the framework of the political system. Apparently organized and disciplined political parties offer strong anchors by which Swedish citizens make their relatively consistent, consensual, and accurate placement judgments. In the United States, political competition, perhaps especially at the presidential level which has dominated the scene in the twentieth century, is less ideological and more personalized. Americans, it is safe to say, are much less likely to be familiar with the philosophy or ideology represented by specific candidates for the presidency, insofar as they have one, than Swedes are with the philosophy or ideology represented by an established political party. The implication is that there is more ideological and less personalistic voting in Sweden.

For the most part, left–right ideology in the twentieth century has been focused upon domestic questions. One perhaps would expect ideology to be more clear-cut in a neutralist nation that is not preoccupied with global status and pervasive religious concerns, than one in which wars, military intervention, and the arms race have served to distract people from attending to domestic questions embedded in ideological considerations. Also, when political divisions occur along a number of diverse lines – ethnic and racial, regional, rural–urban, religious and moral, as well as class and employment – the multidimensional political picture becomes more difficult for the average citizen to fathom, and ideology becomes less salient and less coherent. Based on our observations and analysis, there is reason to believe that people in Sweden face a political system that is less personalized and less confusing than that facing people in the United States.

3   Partisan political issues

A major criticism of the analyses in the preceding chapter is that they deal with abstract political dimensions pertaining to subjective (left–right and liberal–conservative) ideology. It is possible that these dimensions are so abstract that parties and candidates can be all things to all people. Part of the counterargument has already been given. That is, the high perceptual consensus coefficients for Sweden, the linkages between ideology and specific issue positions, the stability across time, and the connection with party and candidate preference could not be obtained if these ideology dimensions were devoid of meaning. Although the coefficients for the U.S. were lower, the liberal–conservative dimension was hardly empty or devoid of meaning either. Now we turn to some specific political issues and apply the same mode of analysis to political perception on them as we did previously with subjective ideology.

Perception on political issues

Beginning with the early work of Bernard Berelson, Paul Lazarsfeld, and William McPhee (1954), analyzing the impressions people have of the issue positions taken by political parties and candidates has become a rather active area of research (Campbell *et al.*, 1960; Granberg and Brent, 1974, 1980; Holmberg, 1981; Kinder, 1978; King, 1978; Page and Brody, 1972; Sherrod, 1972). The central problems have been how accurate the perceptions are, how people use party affiliation and other cues to draw inferences, and how people engage in systematic perceptual distortions when estimating the issue positions taken by parties and candidates (Conover and Feldman, 1986). This analysis also has been extended to the perceptions of people in leadership positions (Converse and Pierce, 1986; Clausen, 1977; Clausen, Holmberg, and deHaven-Smith, 1983).

As in the prior chapter, a guiding hypothesis, drawn from Heider's (1958) balance theory, is that people would *assimilate* – that is, distort in the direction of their own attitude – when estimating the position of a preferred party or candidate on some specific issue. This notion has been strongly and consistently sustained in empirical analyses. On the other hand, the hypothesis that people would *contrast* – that is, distort in the direction away from their own attitude – when estimating the position of a nonpreferred party or candidate on a specific issue, has received only weak and sporadic support.[1] Incumbent candidates in the United States have been more susceptible to contrast than challengers, but generally assimilation of a preferred candidate has been stronger than contrast of a nonpreferred candidate. This has been referred to as the asymmetry phenomenon in political perception (Kinder, 1978). This, and several other regularities, have been summarized in a set of empirically derived propositions (Brent and Granberg, 1982; Granberg, 1982; Granberg and Seidel, 1976).

However, this line of research has been the subject of some criticism (Conover and Feldman, 1982; Judd, Kenny, and Krosnick, 1983; Shaffer, 1981). First, nearly all relevant studies have used data in which people place themselves and the candidates or parties on 7-point scales with only the two extremes being given explicit verbal designations (e.g., Granberg and Jenks, 1977).[2] On such a scale, it is *not* usually possible to say where on the scale the candidate's or party's true or real position lies.[3] Strictly speaking, one must know a party's real position before one can legitimately infer that distortion (i.e., assimilation or contrast) has occurred. Of course, there are ways around this problem. For instance, it is possible to use the sample mean estimate as an indicator of the party's or candidate's true position (Markus, 1982; Markus and Converse, 1979). To do so has a precedent or analogue in psychometric studies, as pointed out in chapter 6. Nonetheless, this procedure is fraught with danger, and one should do so only very carefully with one eye fixed on political realities. Although the public's perception may, on average and in the aggregate, be generally correct, it is also possible for some rather gross error to occur (Converse and Pierce, 1986; Granberg, 1985b; Page, 1978). Overall, then, not knowing the candidate's or party's real position on an issue is a problem in much of the prior research in political perception.

Secondly, much of the perceptual research on specific political issues has ignored the possibility of reciprocal causation. When a significant relationship has been observed between attitude and perception, it is often assumed that variations in the former cause variations in the latter. If people are motivated to maintain cognitive balance, there are several interrelated ways in which this can be done. Although it is likely that attitudes are more stable than perceptions, more attention needs to be given to trying to discover the various underlying processes.

A third problem, identified by Judd *et al.* (1983), is that of correlated measurement error. When people give, in close succession, their own attitude and perceptions of positions taken by parties and candidates on the same issue, the responses may not be independent of one another, aside from any conceptual or theoretical linkage. For instance, if people use the same portion of a scale to place themselves and the parties, this would bias the actual relationship in the positive direction. Consequently, the inference that assimilation of a preferred party on a political issue is stronger than contrast of a nonpreferred party *could* be due to a methodological artifact.

Subjective agreement and issue voting

We delineated previously three major processes that work together to produce subjective ideological agreement between a citizen and the party or candidate preferred by that citizen. We sought to assess their joint effect, and tried to break it into components. Here we proceed similarly only with respect to specific issues.

In the present context, the three processes are expressed in a slightly different way. First, people could choose a party or candidate on the basis of the objective similarity of positions on some specific issue. Secondly, people may form or alter their own attitude to conform more closely with the issue position taken by a preferred party or candidate. Thirdly, people may be psychologically motivated to perceive similarity between themselves and a preferred party or candidate and to differentiate between themselves and a nonpreferred party or candidate. When this occurs so that the perceived similarity departs systematically from the actual similarity, assimilation or contrast has occurred. This third process is essentially irrational in nature and is distinguished from the first two in that respect.[4]

To get an indication of the degree of *subjective agreement* between people and their preferred candidate or party on a specific issue, we shall examine the relationship between a person's own attitude and that person's perception of the position of the preferred party or candidate, whatever party or candidate that happens to be. Overall, subjective agreement on an issue is derived primarily from (a) rational party or candidate selection, (b) the influence of a preferred party or candidate on a person's attitude, or (c) distorting the preferred party's or candidate's position in the direction of one's own attitude.

We shall also examine issue voting, as reflected in the extent to which voting groups are divided on an issue. This should give an indication of the strength of the first two processes. That is, if people gravitate toward parties or candidates on the basis of issue proximity, or if they form or alter their own attitudes to conform to the position of a preferred party or candidate, this ought to be reflected in a substantial attitudinal difference between voting groups (Abramowitz, 1978).

As with our analyses of subjective ideology, we know of no way of adequately separating the first two processes from each other with cross-sectional data. But it may be more important to separate, by inference, the first two more rational processes from the third more irrational process. Comparing subjective agreement with issue voting gives an indication of the relative contribution of the first two rational processes to the level of subjective agreement. If subjective agreement were high and issue voting were as high or nearly as high, this would imply that the issue is being processed as in a rational democratic model. On the other hand, if subjective agreement were high and issue voting were low, this would suggest that subjective agreement was being brought about by the irrational process of assimilation.

Four issues

The data reported here are from national election studies done in relation to Sweden's parliamentary elections of 1979 and 1982 and the U.S. presidential election of 1980. Toward the end of the chapter, we shall also present some perceptual data from a study done in connection with Sweden's national referendum on nuclear power held in 1980.

In 1979, people in Sweden were presented with four alternatives pertaining to nuclear power plants. Respondents indicated their own attitude by selecting one which best represented their own position, and then indicated which of the four represented the position of each of the five largest political parties. A similar procedure was followed in 1982 in relation to the proposed wage-earner investment funds. Unlike most analyses of U.S. issues using the more vague 1–7 scales, here each alternative represents a different position, and the wording of the alternatives (table 3.1) includes the actual positions of the parties. Both issues were highly salient in Swedish politics at the time.

In 1980, people in the U.S. were presented with four alternatives regarding abortion, an issue on which the parties and candidates had taken explicit positions. Respondents indicated the position they subscribed to themselves, and also gave their perceptions of the positions of the presidential candidates and the two political parties. A similar procedure was followed on the question of a tax cut but with five alternatives. The wording for the tax cut alternatives was brief, but each position had a specific verbal designation and each party and nominee had taken one of the positions (see table 3.2).[5]

Consensus in political perception

Our initial question concerns how much consensus or agreement is represented in the perceptions. The percentages in tables 3.1 and 3.2 are

Table 3.1 Distribution of attitudes and attributions on the nuclear power issue, 1979, and wage-earner fund issue, 1982, in Sweden

Nuclear power issue, 1979	Respondent's own attitude (%)	Placement of political party's position				
		vpk (%)	s (%)	c (%)	fp (%)	m (%)
1 We should refrain from further development of nuclear power and immediately close down the nuclear power plants which are currently operating.	13	71	3	60	2	1
2 We should refrain from further development of nuclear power and phase out those nuclear power plants which are currently operating during the next 10 years.	30	20	14	38	21	5
3 We should utilize nuclear power from the nuclear power plants that are already built or under construction, but no more than these should be brought into operation.	49	5	58	2	69	45
4 We should utilize nuclear power and build more than the 12 nuclear power plants that are now built or under construction.	8	4	25	0	8	49
Nonmissing N	2599	1972	2034	2331	2030	2177
% Attributing/attitude	—	75.9	78.3	89.7	78.1	83.8
$\bar{x}$	2.5	1.4	3.0	1.4	2.8	3.4
S.D.	0.82	0.76	0.71	0.56	0.58	0.66
Consensus coefficient		.32	.37	.50	.48	.41

Table 3.1 (cont.)

Wage-earner fund issue, 1982

1 A societal fund which would give wage earners increased influence and, among other things, be used to create new publicly owned industries.	8	56	23	4	3	1
2 A collective wage-earner fund which would give wage earners increased influence through the purchase of shares in companies, which would provide resources for more investment in Swedish industries.	19	28	69	2	4	1
3 A wage-earner fund with individually owned shares which would give wage earners increased influence and private enterprise more investment capital. Employees would be able, after a certain time, to cash in their shares if they want to do so.	18	7	8	17	22	4
4 We should not have wage-earner investment funds in any form in Sweden.	55	9	0	77	71	94
Nonmissing N	2330	1783	2264	1950	1849	2185
% Attributing/attitude	—	76.5	97.2	83.7	79.4	93.8
$\bar{x}$	3.2	1.7	1.9	3.7	3.6	3.9
S.D.	1.01	0.95	0.55	0.69	0.71	0.39
Consensus coefficient		.15	.51	.38	.37	.65

Note: The percentages in this table are column percentages. The abbreviations used in the column headings are as they are commonly used in Sweden: vpk = Communist Party, s = Social Democratic Party, c = Center Party, fp = Liberal Party, and m = Conservative Party. The row labeled Nonmissing N gives the number of people who answered the question with one of the four provided alternatives. The next row, % Attributing/attitude, gives the percentage of people with an attitude who make the attribution to that political party. $\bar{x}$ indicates average and S.D. the standard deviation.

Table 3.2 Distribution of attitudes and attributions on the abortion and tax cut issues in the United States in 1980

Abortion issue	Respondent's own attitude (%)	Placement judgment			
		Carter (%)	Reagan (%)	Democratic (%)	Republican (%)
1 By law, abortion should never be permitted.	11	11	28	7	20
2 The law should permit abortion only in case of rape, incest or when the woman's life is in danger.	33	38	43	33	49
3 The law should permit abortion for reasons other than rape, incest, or danger to the woman's life, but only after the need for the abortion has been clearly established.	20	28	16	31	18
4 By law, a woman should always be able to obtain an abortion as a matter of personal choice.	36	23	13	29	13
Nonmissing N	2289	1346	1221	1166	1119
% Attributing/attitude		58.8	53.3	50.9	48.9
$\bar{x}$	2.8	2.6	2.1	2.8	2.2
S.D.	1.05	0.95	0.97	0.94	0.92
Consensus coefficient		.15	.13	.16	.17
Tax-cut issue					
1 Do not cut taxes	18	44	9	32	13
2 Cut taxes 10%	21	34	14	38	18
3 Cut taxes 20%	21	13	19	18	24
4 Cut taxes 30%	28	8	51	10	39
5 Cut taxes by more than 30%	12	1	7	2	6
Nonmissing N	1877	1475	1518	976	990
% Attributing/attitude		78.6	80.9	52.0	52.7
$\bar{x}$	3.0	1.9	3.3	2.1	3.1
S.D.	1.30	0.98	1.09	1.04	1.16
Consensus coefficient		.31	.23	.27	.18

Note: The percentages in this table are column percentages. The row labeled Nonmissing N gives the number of people who answered the question with one of the four or five provided alternatives. The next row, % Attributing/attitude gives the percentage of people with an attitude who make the attribution to that political candidate or party. $\bar{x}$ indicates average and S.D. the standard deviation.

informative, but to be more precise we calculated a *consensus coefficient*. As in the prior chapter, the consensus coefficient, with a possible range from .00 to 1.00, is based on the empirically observed standard deviation and the standard deviation that would result if the perceptions had been made randomly.

On most issues in Swedish politics, the positions of parties are quite predictable and can be ordered along a coherent left–right dimension, as discussed in chapter 2 (Holmberg, 1974). That, however, was not true for nuclear power. On this matter, the Center Party and its leader, Thorbjörn Fälldin, took a position against nuclear power. They were joined by the Communist Party. The Social Democrats and the Liberal Party advocated a limited development of nuclear power, while the Conservative Party was more favorable toward producing electricity in nuclear power plants.

In the context of Swedish politics, positions 1 and 2 in table 3.1 were antinuclear power positions, and positions 3 and 4 pronuclear power positions. If we consider responses that way, people with pronuclear attitudes slightly outnumbered those with antinuclear attitudes (57 to 43%). Of those giving their perceptions, fully 98 percent recognized that the Center Party had taken an antinuclear position, and 91 percent that the Communist Party was antinuclear. Fully 94 percent recognized that the Conservative Party was pronuclear, 83 percent that the Social Democrats were pronuclear, and 77 percent that the Liberal Party was pronuclear.

However, when we consider the nuances represented by the differences between positions 1 and 2 and between positions 3 and 4 on nuclear power, the picture changes somewhat. A majority had the mistaken notion that the Center and Communist parties had taken the extreme position (1) opposing nuclear power, whereas, in fact, their position was the more moderate position of opposition (2), calling for phasing out nuclear power within ten years.[6] The modal position chosen for placing the Social Democrats and the Liberal Party (3) was correct, and the perceptions also reflected the fact that the Conservative Party was at least slightly more positive toward nuclear power than the Social Democratic or Liberal Party (Holmberg and Asp, 1984).

The proposal to establish wage-earner investment funds was a divisive issue in Sweden in the 1970s and in 1982 (Åsard, 1986; Gilljam, 1988; Holmberg, 1982; 1984). It is an issue on which the division was in line with the traditional left–right dimension. The Communist and Social Democratic parties both favored wage-earner funds although they differed with regard to details. Alternatives 1 and 2 in table 3.1 were the positions taken by the Communists and the Social Democratic Party, respectively. In the 1982 election, the three bourgeois (nonsocialist) parties all opposed wage-earner funds in any form (alternative 4 in table 3.1). Earlier, the Center and Liberal Parties had considered a wage-earner fund with privately owned shares which could be sold (alternative 3), but they had abandoned this idea by 1982.

Considering positions 3 and 4 as opposing wage-earner funds, the proposal did not have majority support among the public. In fact, 55 percent opposed the idea of wage-earner funds in any form, and only 27 percent supported the proposals of the Social Democrats or the Communists. There was widespread recognition that the bourgeois parties were opposed to the wage-earner funds. Of those giving their perceptions, 98 percent perceived that the Conservative Party was opposed, and nearly as large a percentage recognized that the other two bourgeois parties were also opposed (94 and 93% for the Center and Liberal Parties, respectively). A comparably large percentage recognized that the Social Democrats favored wage-earner funds in some form. When it comes to the nuances of each alternative, the modal response was correct in placing each party. Ninety-four percent recognized that the Conservative Party was unequivocally opposed to the whole idea of wage-earner funds, while 77 percent and 71 percent recognized that the Center and Liberal Parties were similarly opposed. Sixty-nine percent correctly picked out the position of the Social Democratic Party, and 56 percent did so in regard to the Communist Party.

It should be understood that the preceding percentages are based on calculations excluding those who said they did not know the positions of the parties. The response rate can be inferred from table 3.1, and was not the same across parties. On nuclear power, the Center Party was most outspoken in articulating a clear position. On wage-earner funds, the position of the Social Democratic Party was most crucial. Correspondingly, on nuclear power people were most willing to attribute a position to the Center Party, while on the wage-earner fund people were most willing to attribute a position to the Social Democratic Party. Overall, the impression from table 3.1 is that, given the high response rates and the generally accurate impressions, the political parties in Sweden are effective in communicating their issue positions to the public.

On the question of the legal status of abortion, Jimmy Carter and the Democratic Party were best represented in the most permissive alternative 4 in table 3.2.[7] Ronald Reagan and the Republican Party took a position on abortion in 1980 that is best represented by the most restrictive alternative 1.

Considerable diversity in attitudes on abortion is shown in table 3.2. However, respondents choosing the most permissive alternative outnumbered those choosing the most restrictive alternative by more than 3:1. When it comes to perception, the public collectively had the correct notion about the difference between Carter and Reagan and between the Democratic and Republican parties. Among people indicating their perceptions, 71 percent attributed one of the two more restrictive positions to Reagan, compared to 49 percent who attributed one of those two positions to Carter. The percentages for the parties were 69 and 40 attributing one of the two more restrictive positions to the Republican and Democratic Party, respectively. There was, however, considerable variance in these perceptions, and one should bear in mind the relatively low percentage of people who gave their perceptions. This figure hovered near 50 percent.

On the tax-cut issue, Reagan and the Republican Party supported the Kemp–Roth plan to reduce taxes by 30 percent. Carter and the Democratic Party countered that a tax cut was not feasible, given the budget deficit and the need to fund governmental programs. A 30 percent cut was the modal attitudinal response, and most people (82% of those with an attitude) preferred that there be some sort of tax cut. Table 3.2 shows that people correctly sensed that Reagan and the Republican Party supported a tax cut, while Carter and the Democratic Party tended to oppose it. It appears that Reagan's position on the tax-cut issue was more effectively communicated to the public than was his position on abortion.

So our results show that, overall, people in Sweden were more likely to indicate their perceptions and there was a closer correspondence in Sweden than in the U.S. between perceptions and political realities. Consider the consensus coefficients in tables 3.1 and 3.2. The largest consensus coefficient (.65) was in perceiving Sweden's Conservative Party on wage-earner funds. Generally, the perceptions in Sweden imply more consensus than perceptions in the United States. Recall that this is in spite of a considerably higher percentage of people in Sweden giving their perceptions. Had the response rate in Sweden and the U.S. been more similar, the differences between the consensus coefficients, already substantial, would have been even larger.

The perceptions in the U.S. represent significantly more consensus than would occur by chance. But compared to Sweden, the degree of perceptual consensus in the U.S. is relatively low. Variations within Sweden are also coherent. For instance, there was a higher consensus in placing the Center Party on the nuclear power issue than on wage-earner funds, and there was a higher consensus in placing the Social Democratic Party on the wage-earner fund issue than on nuclear power.

We also examined the extent to which the different voting groups agreed or disagreed in their perceptions. If voting groups agree in their estimates of the positions taken by parties or candidates, this would indicate *intergroup consensus in perception*. (This would be indicated by low eta values.) Generally, in both Sweden and the United States, the voting groups differed very little in their average perceptions. For Sweden, the eta averaged .14 across ten comparisons. For the U.S., grouping people according to whether they voted for Carter or Reagan explained very little variance in perceptions, the eta averaging only .10 across eight comparisons. Thus, the main effect of party or candidate preference on perception of issue positions was weak in both Sweden and the U.S. In other words, intergroup consensus in perception was very strong. By itself, this would indicate that these perceptions were stimulus-determined rather than perceiver–determined (Sigel, 1964), but that conclusion must be tempered by subsequent analyses.[8]

Subjective agreement

To get a *subjective agreement coefficient*, for each issue a new variable was constructed called placement of preferred party (Sweden) or placement of preferred candidate (United States). Whatever candidate or party was preferred by the person, perception of that candidate's or party's position was taken as the dependent variable, the person's own attitude position as the independent variable, and the resulting eta is our subjective agreement coefficient.

Overall, subjective agreement between voters' own attitudes and perceptions of their preferred party in Sweden is higher than that between voters' own attitudes and perceptions of their preferred candidate in the United States. Figure 3.1 shows that the regression slopes are stronger for the two Swedish issues than for the two U.S. issues. The eta coefficients in figure 3.1 are the subjective agreement coefficients, indicating the association between a person's own attitude and the perceived position of the preferred party or candidate.

When the two variables of a person's own attitude and the perception of a preferred party or candidate on the same issue are cross-tabulated, one expects a certain amount of agreement by chance. With four alternatives, one would expect about 25 percent agreement by chance, and with five alternatives the chance agreement would be 20 percent.[9] On all four issues, the subjective agreement greatly exceeded the chance level but with substantial variation among the issues. In Sweden, the percentage showing complete subjective agreement between attitude and perception was 68 percent for wage-earner funds and 57 percent on nuclear power. For the U.S., the percentages were 45 percent for abortion and 38 percent for the tax-cut issue.

The subjective agreement coefficient is a relatively gross indicator. Therefore, we also looked within specific voting groups. Table 3.3 shows the

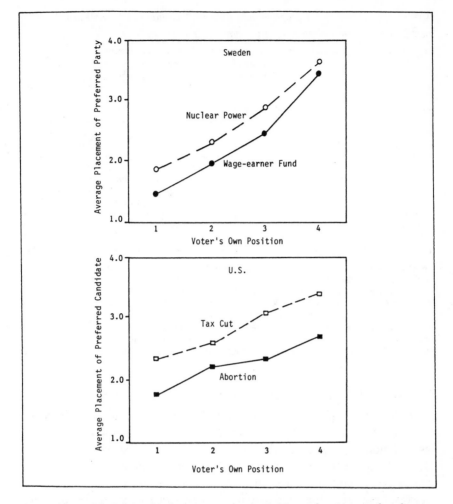

Figure 3.1. Relationship between voter's own position and position attributed to preferred party (Sweden) or to preferred candidate (United States) on four issues. *Note.* The eta values are .69 (wage-earner fund), .49 (nuclear power), .35 (tax cut), and .31 (abortion). As can be observed, the relationships were all essentially linear. Thus, the regression coefficients are only slightly smaller than the eta coefficients. The data point for voter's own position 5 on the tax cut issue (not shown) would be 3.35, about the same as that for own position 4 (3.31).

percentage of people in each voting group who attribute their own attitude to their preferred party or candidate. In Sweden, that percentage ranged between 50 and 90. In the United States those percentages are somewhat lower, but on the tax-cut issue, that may have been due, in part, to the use of five alternatives.

Table 3.3 *Percentage of people whose own attitudinal position and position attributed to preferred party or candidate were the same*

	Percentage in Sweden whose own attitudinal position and position attributed to preferred party are the same					
			Vote			
Issue	vpk	s	c	fp	m	All
Nuclear power	51	57	55	56	61	57
Wage-earner fund	50	50	81	75	90	68

	Percentage in U.S. whose own attitudinal position and position attributed to preferred candidate are the same		
	Carter voters	Reagan voters	All
Abortion	49	42	45
Tax cut	39	38	38

Note: The percentages in this table indicate the percentage of people, in a given voting group and on a given issue, whose own position is the same as they attribute to a preferred party or candidate. The percentage who do not do this would be 100 minus the number given. Thus, for example, 43 percent of the Social Democrats attributed some position other than their own to the Social Democratic Party on the nuclear power issue. Similarly, 58 percent of the Reagan voters attributed some position other than their own to Reagan on the abortion issue. People who said don't know on either the attitude or perception question are excluded from these analyses. The meaning of the symbols for the five Swedish voting groups is given in Table 3.1.

Comparing the subjective agreement and issue voting coefficients

In order to try to separate the effect of rational democratic processes (rational selection and opinion formation) from the irrational process of assimilation, we compared the subjective agreement coefficients in figure 3.1 with issue voting coefficients. An *issue voting coefficient* is the degree to which voting groups differ in their attitudes on an issue, calculated as the eta resulting when the candidate or party selection (who the person voted for) is the independent variable, and attitudinal position on an issue is the dependent variable.

Before turning to the actual issue voting coefficients, however, we want to present the results in percentage terms as that may express the variations across issues in terms easier to understand and closer to "flesh and blood." Table 3.4 reports the degree of voter group differences on the nuclear power and the wage-earner fund issues in Sweden. On each issue, the voters supporting each party tend to be on the same side of the issue as the party they support. The consensus among the bourgeois party voters against wage-earner funds is especially strong. On that issue, a majority of socialist bloc voters with an opinion favored some form of wage-earner funds, although the consensus was nowhere near as strong.

Table 3.4 *Variations in attitude toward nuclear power and wage-earner funds in Sweden as a function of party voting groups*

	Respondent's party choice in election				
	vpk	s	c	fp	m
A *Nuclear power issue, 1979*					
1 Close down now	31	9	22	10	4
2 Close down within 10 years	43	22	59	32	19
3 Utilize nuclear power, no more than 12 plants	22	58	19	51	63
4 Utilize nuclear power, more than 12 plants	4	11	0	7	14
Total	100	100	100	100	100
N	138	1051	413	260	476
B *Wage-earner fund issue, 1982*					
1 Societal fund, new publicly owned industries	33	14	1	0	0
2 Collective fund, increased influence for workers	36	39	3	1	1
3 Individually owned shares	17	27	14	18	11
4 No wage-earner investment funds	14	20	82	81	88
Total	100	100	100	100	100
N	115	908	332	141	556

Note: The numbers are column percentages. The full wording of the alternatives for the two issues is given in Table 3.1. The eta was .41 for the nuclear power issue and .66 for the wage-earner fund issue, using voting group as the independent variable and attitude position as the dependent variable.

The comparable analysis for the two U.S. issues is given in table 3.5. The differences between Carter and Reagan voters on abortion can be seen there to be very small indeed. About 48 percent of the Carter voters took one of the two more anti-abortion positions, compared to 45 percent of the Reagan voters. On the tax-cut issue, the differences between the two voting groups were somewhat larger and, in this case, correspond with the positions of the candidates. Carter voters were less likely than Reagan voters (25 to 43%) to favor a large tax cut of 30 percent or more.

We are now ready to make the more formal comparisons of the subjective agreement and issue voting coefficients for the four issues. The issue voting coefficients, described above, were .66 for the wage-earner funds, .41 for nuclear power, .21 for tax cut, and .03 for abortion. The corresponding subjective agreement coefficients were .69, .49, .35, and .31 for the four issues, respectively (see figure 3.2).

On wage-earner funds, subjective agreement is very high, and issue voting is nearly as high. Thus, on that issue, it may be inferred that most of

Table 3.5 *Variations in attitude toward abortion and a tax cut in the United States as a function of candidate voting groups*

	Candidate choice	
	Carter voters	Reagan voters
Abortion issue		
1 Never permitted	13	11
2 Only extreme circumstances	35	34
3 Other circumstances if need is established	15	23
4 Always allowed	37	32
Total	100	100
N	370	473
Tax-cut issue		
1 No tax cut	33	17
2 10% cut	24	17
3 20% cut	18	23
4 30% cut	18	29
5 >30% cut	7	14
Total	100	100
N	227	343

Note: The numbers are column percentages. The full wording for the alternatives for the two issues is given in Table 3.2. The eta was .03 and .21 for the abortion and the tax-cut issues, respectively, using voting group as the independent variable and attitude position as the dependent variable.

the subjective agreement stems from people choosing a party on the basis of proximity or forming or changing their attitudes to correspond with the position of a preferred party. Since both coefficients are high on wage-earner funds, this strongly suggests the operation of democratic processes. Given that the issue voting coefficient is nearly as strong as the subjective agreement coefficient, the contribution of assimilation to the level of subjective agreement is small on that issue, relative to the contribution of the other two processes.

The nuclear power issue is different in that the level of subjective agreement is somewhat lower than on wage-earner funds, and the issue voting coefficient is also lower. The gap between the two coefficients seems to be slightly larger for the nuclear power issue than for wage-earner funds. However, on nuclear power, issue voting is still contributing very substantially to the level of subjective agreement.

For the two U.S. issues, both coefficients are lower than for the issues studied in Sweden. On the tax cut, the issue voting coefficient was a little more than half as strong as the subjective agreement coefficient. Thus,

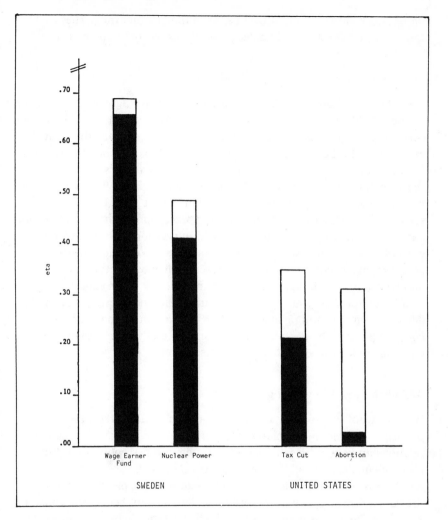

Figure 3.2. Level of subjective agreement and issue voting on four issues.
Note. For each issue, the overall height of the bar is based on the subjective
agreement coefficient and the height of the solid dark portion of the bar is based on
an issue voting coefficient. The actual coefficients are given in the text.

much of the subjective agreement observed on the tax-cut issue was due to
assimilation, but there was at least some difference between the two voting
groups which corresponded to the positions of the two candidates. It is the
abortion issue which provides the most striking comparison to the other
issues. On abortion, the subjective agreement coefficient is relatively low.
But what subjective agreement existed on that issue must have been due
almost entirely to assimilation, in that the issue voting coefficient was not

significantly different from .00 – in spite of the fact that the parties and the candidates took distinctively different positions on that issue in 1980.[10]

Issue importance

It might be thought that the level of both subjective agreement and issue voting would depend directly on the level of involvement in the issue. For each of the issues, there was a measure of the importance the individual ascribed to the issue, although the exact wording was not the same. In Sweden, people were asked directly, with four alternatives, how important the issue (nuclear power in 1979, wage-earner funds in 1982) was in their voting choice in the parliamentary election of that year. In the 1980 U.S. survey, after giving their own attitude and perceptions of the candidates and parties, people were asked to give their impression of the government's current policy on the issue. Then they were asked to rate how important the government's policy on abortion or tax-cut policy was to them. The results for Sweden, shown in figure 3.3, conformed closely to the expectation. The results for the U.S. were much more irregular and are not shown. The differences in the wording of issue importance questions may be larger than could reasonably be accepted in comparative analyses, especially when a large difference was observed as was the case here.[11]

Assimilation within voting groups

We also want to look within voting groups in order to get a more "pure" picture of perceptual displacement. Suppose one observes a significant relationship between a voter's own attitude and perception of a preferred party or candidate on an issue within a voting group. Such an effect *must* be due to perceptual distortion since candidate or party preference (and thus the candidate's or party's position) is for the moment being held constant. Although the party's position is thus held constant, there is still substantial variation in perception of the party's position. The correlations between a person's attitude and that attributed to the parties and candidates *within* voting groups are given in table 3.6 for Sweden and table 3.7 for the U.S.

The displacement tendencies shown in table 3.6 are quite consistent with those in previous analyses (e.g., Brent and Granberg, 1982). People showed a significant tendency to assimilate when attributing a position to a preferred party. It is also evident that the bloc alignments are serving as a cue for Swedish citizens on the wage-earner funds issue. People who prefer one of the bourgeois parties tend to assimilate when estimating the position of the other bourgeois parties, albeit to a lesser extent than they do to their own party. A similar tendency was observed on the ideology scale in chapter

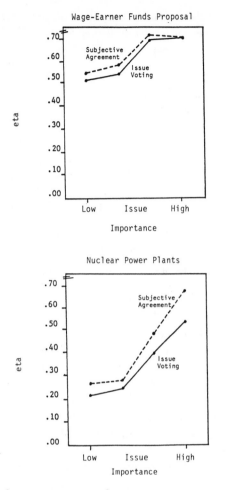

Figure 3.3. Subjective agreement and issue voting on two issues in Sweden as a function of level of importance ascribed to the issues.

2. Here as well, the tendency to assimilate one's preferred party was, in *each* of ten observations, stronger than the tendency to contrast any of the nonpreferred parties (cf. Granberg, 1983). The tendency to assimilate when placing one's preferred party appears to be stronger on the abstract 0–10 left–right scale (table 2.4) than on the partisan issues with explicit alternatives (table 3.6). The foregoing conclusions remain the same if eta values (sensitive to both linear and nonlinear effects) are substituted for the correlation coefficients in table 3.6.

There are, however, a few curious deviations which are quite revealing. The correlation coefficients in table 3.6 would indicate that in 1979, Center

Table 3.6 *Correlation between a person's own attitude and the position attributed to five Swedish political parties within voting groups*

			Party preference groups				
			vpk	s	c	fp	m
	Nuclear power	vpk	.24	−.04	.00	−.22	−.08
		s	.10	.27	.01	−.22	−.15
		c	−.15	−.07	.09	.15	−.01
		fp	−.04	−.04	.03	.37	.07
Correlation between		m	−.13	.00	.04	.16	.30
own and attributed	Wage-earner funds	vpk	.37	.06	.05	.13	.00
position on		s	−.15	.14	.03	.10	.07
		c	−.04	−.03	.33	.26	.23
		fp	.00	−.01	.28	.40	.21
		m	.02	−.06	.00	.30	.47

Note: The meaning of the symbols for the Swedish political parties is given in table 3.1. The boxed-in diagonal, from upper left to lower right, gives the correlations between a person's attitude and the position attributed by that person to a preferred party within each of the party voting groups. The other correlations are between a person's attitude and the position attributed to a nonpreferred party.

Party voters showed no significant tendency to assimilate the position of their preferred party on nuclear power, and that in 1982, Social Democrats showed a significant but quite weak tendency to assimilate when placing their preferred party on wage-earner funds. Moreover, these were the *only* two instances in which the eta values exceeded the r values by an appreciable amount (.30 to .09 for the Center Party voters in 1979 and .26 to .14 for the Social Democrats in 1982). As pointed out previously, the Center Party's position was the focal point on the nuclear power issue as was the position of the Social Democrats on the wage-earner funds (see table 3.1).

When the mean values are plotted in figure 3.4, the results become more clear. The only noteworthy deviations from linearity occur in regard to the Center Party on nuclear power and the Social Democrats on the wage-earner funds. Given that the Center Party's real position on nuclear power was position 2, when Center Party voters whose own position is 1 place the Center party at 1.3, on the average, this is strong evidence of *assimilation*, since the *actual discrepancy* between their own position and that of the party is being *underestimated*. Center Party voters whose own position was the same as that of the party (2) placed the party at 1.7 on the average. But when Center Party voters who took the relatively pronuclear position 3 placed the Center Party at 1.4, this indicates *contrast* since the *actual discrepancy* between their own position and that of the party is being *overestimated*.

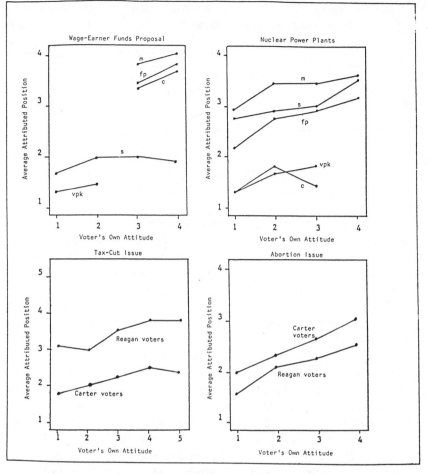

Figure 3.4. Average position attributed by voters to their preferred party or candidate on four issues within voting groups.
Note. The meaning of the symbols for the parties and the wording for the alternatives for the two issues in Sweden are given in table 3.1. The wording for the two issues in the United States are in table 3.2. Only data points which are based on 15 or more people are shown.

The results in table 3.6 and figure 3.4 may be questioned in that the nuclear power scale may be an ordinal scale, but is being treated as if it were an interval scale. If we express the results in percentage terms, however, the conclusions are the same. Among Center voters who themselves take alternative 1, 75 percent placed the Center Party at position 1, compared to only 35 percent of the Center Party voters whose own position was 2. So Center Party voters *did* show assimilation while placing their preferred party but *only* if their own position was on the same side as their preferred party.

Table 3.7 *Correlation between a person's own attitude and the position attributed to the Democratic and Republican nominees for President within voting groups*

			Carter voters	Reagan voters
Correlation between own and attributed position on	Abortion	Carter	.41	−.15
		Reagan	−.19	.24
	Tax cut	Carter	.23	−.08
		Reagan	−.26	.26

The nonsignificant r of .09 in table 3.6 for Center Party voters placing the Center Party is increased to .36 when only the Center Party voters who are on the same side of the issue as their preferred party (positions 1 and 2) are considered.

Similar results appear in the perceptions by Social Democrats of the Social Democratic Party on wage-earner funds. Social Democrats who took position 1 placed their preferred party at 1.6, on the average. This indicates assimilation since the position of the party is being displaced toward the respondents' own position. However, perception of the party by Social Democrats who were themselves at positions 2, 3, and 4 was basically accurate and showed little variation. Thus, Social Democrats who were on the other side of the issue from their preferred party did not show assimilation of their preferred party. Among Social Democrats whose own position was 1, 50 percent placed the party at position 1, compared to only 8 percent of the Social Democrats whose own position was 2. When only the Social Democrats whose own position was on the same side of the issue as their preferred party (1 or 2) are considered, the correlation of .14 for Social Democrats in table 3.6 changes to a relatively robust .47.

Thus, the erstwhile exceptions in table 3.6 provide an additional insight under closer scrutiny. Overall, people tended to assimilate when placing a preferred party, and this tendency is stronger than the tendency to contrast any of the nonpreferred parties. But when the party under consideration has taken a strong, well-publicized position on the issue, only the supporters whose own position is on the same general side of the issue as that of their preferred party will show the tendency to assimilate.[12] The evidence of assimilation and contrast here is strengthened by the use of issues on which the actual positions of the parties are known and represented among the alternatives explicitly provided.[13]

The corresponding analyses for the two U.S. issues are summarized in table 3.7. On abortion, Carter voters showed somewhat more assimilation of their preferred candidate than did Reagan voters. Both voter groups, however, showed considerable assimilation. For instance, if Carter's real position was permissive alternative 4, when Carter voters who were themselves at position 1 perceived Carter at 2.0, on the average, and when Carter voters at position 2 perceived Carter at 2.3, this is *very strong* evidence of assimilation – especially in comparison to the perception of Carter by Carter voters who were themselves at positions 3 (2.7) and 4 (3.0).

On the tax-cut issue, each voter group showed a weak but significant trend toward assimilation of the preferred candidate. There is a mild anomaly on this issue, as Carter voters showed a stronger tendency to contrast Reagan than to assimilate their preferred candidate. But the difference was slight and, considered in relation to the bulk of the evidence elsewhere (Brent and Granberg, 1982), may not be especially noteworthy. Once again, the more abstract 1–7 liberal–conservative scale appears to have been somewhat more conducive to assimilation and contrast (table 2.5) than the issues with explicit alternatives (table 3.7).

In the perceptions of Carter and Reagan by Carter voters and Reagan voters, we do not observe deviation from linearity as occurred in placements of the Center Party on nuclear power and the Social Democratic Party on wage-earner funds. Recall that the positions of these U.S. candidates were rather vaguely known by the electorate. Reagan's position on the tax cut was better known to people than his position on abortion, but even on the tax cut his position remained relatively obscure to the citizenry in comparison to the knowledge of the positions of the parties held by people in Sweden. To produce the sort of effects observed in the case of Sweden's Social Democratic Party on the wage-earner funds and the Center Party on nuclear power, it may take a rather sustained effort on the part of political parties and the mass media to see to it that the positions of the parties are accurately transmitted. Without such an effort, people who take a position on the opposite side of an issue from their preferred party or candidate may well persist in assimilation when giving their political perceptions.

Perceptions of party positions in the nuclear power referendum

We now turn to a consideration of political perception in the special context of the national nuclear power referendum held in Sweden in 1980. Once again we are dealing with a situation in which the parties have taken explicit positions represented directly in the alternatives included in questions answered by people in the study. Nuclear power and energy sources followed by employment and taxes had been the three most important issues in the 1979 election in the eyes of the voters (Holmberg, 1981, p. 63). In the referendum held in March, 1980, the *sole* issue under consideration was the future of nuclear power in Sweden (Holmberg and Asp, 1984). The referendum study was described in chapter 1. For present purposes, it is

Table 3.8. *Percentage placing five parties as supporting Line 1, 2, or 3 in the context of the 1980 nuclear power referendum in Sweden*

Percentage	Party which is being placed					
	vpk	s	c	fp	m	Combined
A Placing the party	90	93	93	88	91	91
B Placing party correctly	85	86	90	76	86	85

Note: In this table, the percentages are based on the number of people who did place the party in relation to the three lines plus the people who said they didn't know the party's position.

sufficient to note that in the referendum, people chose from among three alternatives. Line 1 was endorsed by the Conservative Party and was the most pro-nuclear alternative. Line 3, the most anti-nuclear alternative, was supported by the Center and Communist parties. It called for no new nuclear plants and for those currently in use to be phased out within 10 years. Line 2, the moderately pro-nuclear alternative was endorsed by the Social Democratic and Liberal parties. Although intermediate to the other two options, it was generally understood that Lines 1 and 2 were much more similar than Lines 2 and 3. An estimate is that the interval between Lines 2 and 3 was about four times as large as that between Lines 1 and 2.[14]

The period before the referendum involved an intense campaign by the parties and other interest groups to inform and persuade the Swedish people. One of our interests here is how accurate political perceptions can become in the context of such an intensive campaign. In the pre-referendum surveys people were asked which of the three lines came closest to their own view on nuclear power and which line they intended to vote for in the referendum. They were also asked to place or estimate the position of each of the five parties in relation to the three options in the referendum. These data are of special interest here because the number of alternatives is constrained to only three, and it was widely publicized what the actual position of each party was.

Some results pertaining to these perceptions are summarized in table 3.8. There it is evident that most people had an impression of what the positions of the parties were. On average, only about 9 percent said they did not know a party's position. Moreover, of those who did place the party's position as favoring Line 1, 2, or 3, the accuracy level was very high indeed, averaging about 93 percent. If we include the "don't know" people, about 85 percent of those interviewed were able to accurately associate the parties with particular options.

There was some variation in the degree of accuracy across parties, as seen in table 3.8. Given what has been said previously about the Center Party taking the lead in opposing nuclear power, it is not surprising that this party elicited the highest level of accuracy in perception with 90 percent of the sample correctly stating that the Center Party favored Line 3. The Liberal Party's position was least well known, with an overall accuracy of 76 percent.

It seems reasonable to ask whether, in such a context, the influence of such social psychological factors as one's attachment to a party and one's attitude toward nuclear power, would still be evident to some degree. Or is this influence, which almost certainly operates when the situation is more ambiguous, now reduced to zero? The results indicate that even here the accuracy level of political perception depends to some degree on whether it is one's preferred party whose position is being estimated and whether the party under consideration has taken a position that is congruent with one's own position. Theoretically, one might expect the greatest accuracy to occur when one's preferred party is being placed *and* that party's position coincides with one's attitude. When these conditions hold, the accuracy level increases to 98 percent. People placing a discrepant preferred party were 89 percent accurate, while those placing a consonant nonpreferred party were 90 percent accurate. People placing a discrepant nonpreferred party were 93 percent accurate. Although these differences are not large, they indicate that even in this context, social psychological factors still exert some discernible interactive effect.

In the same 1980 pre-referendum survey, people were asked to place the five parties, themselves, and spokespersons for the three options in the referendum on a −5 (very negative toward nuclear power as an energy source) to +5 (very positive) scale. This 11-point scale may be more conducive to systematic displacement effects than asking people which party supported which line and is also roughly comparable to the 0–10 left–right scale used in the previous chapter.

On this 11-point nuclear power scale, the parties were placed quite similarly to the options they supported in the referendum. Line 3 was placed at −4.6, on the average, the Center Party at −4.4 and the Communist Party at −4.3. Line 2 was placed at +2.9, the Social Democratic Party at +2.8, and the Liberal Party at +2.4. The Conservative Party was perceived to be at +4.4, the same as the position attributed to Line 1. Thus, we see the strong link between perceptions of the parties' positions and the options in the referendum. More people placed themselves on the positive than on the negative side, but owing to the greater intensity of the anti-nuclear people, the average self-placement was slightly negative (−0.2).

The perceptual consensus coefficients on this 11-point nuclear power scale were in the same general range as on the left–right scale. On the nuclear power scale, the perceptual consensus coefficients were .55, .51,

.47, .42, and .41 for the Conservative, Center, Communist, Social Democratic and Liberal parties, respectively. The options in the referendum were placed on this scale with a similar, perhaps slightly higher, level of perceptual consensus: .58, .50, and .65 for Lines 1-3, respectively.

When the subjective agreement and rational democratic or issue voting coefficients were calculated for this 11-point nuclear power scale, the resulting eta values were .58 (subjective agreement) and .53 (issue voting). These are both considerably lower than for the left–right scale in chapter 2. Evidently, the subjective agreement between where people place themselves and where they perceive their preferred party to be on the left–right scale is considerably higher than on the nuclear power scale.

The reason behind this difference is that in the referendum, many people (roughly 29%) voted for an option other than the one endorsed by their preferred party.[15] These people quite closely resemble cross-over voters in that they departed in their voting from their party but retained, in most instances, their party preference. People who supported the option endorsed by their preferred party may be said to be in a state of cognitive balance, while those departing in their line preference from the option endorsed by their preferred party are in a state of imbalance. Figure 3.5 shows the subjective agreement relationship for the sample as a whole (upper portion) and for people in balanced and imbalanced situations considered separately (lower portion). For people in a balanced situation, the subjective agreement coefficient is very strong and about as strong as that for the left–right scale. On the other hand, the subjective agreement for the people in an imbalanced state between where they place themselves and where they place their preferred party on nuclear power was very weak and irregular.

This is shown further in a correlational analysis in table 3.9. Generally, the correlations between where people place themselves and where they place their preferred party are quite weak, considerably weaker than the comparable coefficients for the left–right scale. In the case of the left–right scale, these within party assimilative correlations averaged +.61 compared to only +.22 for the nuclear power scale. As shown in table 3.9, these nuclear power assimilative coefficients increase to +.42 among people in a balanced state (still not as strong as on the left–right scale) and decrease to an average of −.01 among people in an imbalanced state.

Taking these analyses together, the following conclusions can be drawn. People in Sweden show a strong tendency to assimilate when placing their preferred party on the left–right dimension. They also show a tendency, though considerably weaker, to assimilate in their perceptions of their preferred party on nuclear power. This tendency, in turn, has been shown to be confined completely to people who selected the same option in the

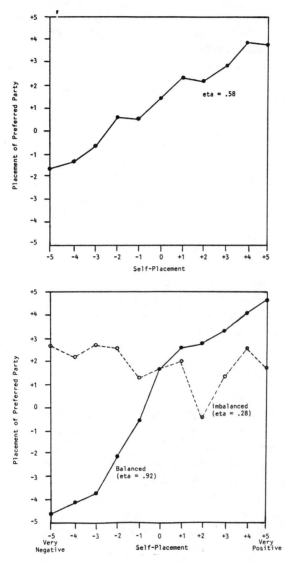

Figure 3.5. Average placement of preferred party on the − 5 (very negative to nuclear power as an energy source) to + 5 (very positive) scale as a function of the person's self-placement.

Note. The upper graph shows the results for the sample as a whole. The lower graph shows the relationship separately for people in states of balance and imbalance. A balanced state is defined as intending to vote for the alternative in the 1980 nuclear power referendum endorsed by one's preferred party. An imbalanced state is intending to vote for an alternative other than that endorsed by one's preferred party.

Table 3.9 *Correlation between self-placement and position attributed to the preferred party on the* − 5 *to* + 5 *nuclear power scale overall and within party preference groups in Sweden, 1980*

	Party preference group					Overall
	vpk	s	c	fp	m	
All	+.39	+.28	+.16	+.14	+.15	+.57
Balanced	+.57	+.48	+.23	+.35	+.48	+.91
Imbalanced	+.06	+.01	−.22	+.14	−.02	−.03

Note: The entries in this table are correlations between where people place themselves and where they place their preferred party on the 11 point (− 5 to + 5) scale used to measure attitudes and perceptions regarding nuclear power as an energy source. The right-hand column gives the correlation for the sample as a whole, and the other five columns give the correlations within party preference groups. A balanced state is intending to vote for the alternative endorsed by one's preferred party. An imbalanced state is intending to vote for an alternative in the referendum other than the one endorsed by one's preferred party.

referendum as that endorsed by their preferred party. People who crossed over and voted for an option in the referendum other than that endorsed by their preferred party did not assimilate when attributing a position on nuclear power to their preferred party.

The study of political perception

We must acknowledge that there was something special about the nuclear power issue in 1979–1980 and the wage-earner funds issue in 1982 in Sweden. They were the most controversial issues in Sweden at the time, and therefore were given rather intensive scrutiny in the election studies. At the same time, abortion was certainly a controversial and well-publicized issue in the United States in 1980 and the preceding years. It was an issue about which some people felt very strongly, so much so that they were willing to become politically active for the first time and, in a few instances, go so far as to engage in illegal activities such as trespassing, harassment, and even bombing and arson. The tax-cut issue in 1980 was, of course, less emotional, but it was a central issue in the campaign of that year.

Our analyses have served to clarify several considerations pertaining to political perception. The consensus coefficient provides a quantitative measure of the degree of perceptual agreement within a group. Comparing the subjective agreement and issue voting coefficients provides a basis for inferring approximately how much the processes of rational selection and opinion formation are contributing to subjective agreement. There can be little doubt that these three coefficients are stronger in Sweden than in the U.S.

Consensus in political perceptions as to the position of a candidate or party reflects the clarity of the position that has been taken and the degree to which this position has been effectively communicated to the people. Perceptual consensus of this sort is generally much higher in Sweden than in the U.S.

Overall, voting groups show little systematic variation in perception of the position of a party or candidate. In order to observe substantial systematic variance in perceptions, it is usually necessary to take into account simultaneously the voter's candidate or party preference *and* the voter's own attitude on the issue.

People show far more subjective agreement with their respective preferred candidate or party than would occur by chance. However, in Sweden, subjective agreement is due more to rational democratic processes, while in the United States, it may be due more to the irrational process of assimilation. In Sweden at least, both subjective agreement and issue voting increase systematically as the ascribed importance of the issue under consideration increases.

People tend to assimilate, that is, distort in the direction of their own attitude, when perceiving the position of a preferred party or candidate. This was thought to be true previously, but our analyses strengthen this conclusion in that we used, in addition to the relatively abstract 11-point left–right and nuclear power scales, issues and scales with explicit alternatives on which the positions of the parties or candidates were known and represented in the alternatives used in the surveys.

When a party's position on an issue has been well articulated and publicized and has been the focus of controversy, assimilation by the party's supporters occurs only among those who are on the same general side of the issue as their preferred party. The tendency of people to assimilate when perceiving the position of a preferred party or candidate is stronger than the tendency to contrast when perceiving the position of a nonpreferred party or candidate. Our impression is that this asymmetry is a reflection of political and social psychological realities rather than a methodological artifact.

When an intensive campaign has been conducted, such as the referendum on nuclear power in Sweden, which includes communicating in unambiguous terms the positions of political parties, political perception can become very accurate. The highest level of accuracy in such a context is achieved when a preferred party's position is being estimated and that party's actual position coincides with the position of the person doing the estimating. In such a context, assimilation when placing a preferred party appears limited to those people who support the alternative endorsed by their preferred party.

4   Mass attitude systems

A little more than twenty years ago Philip Converse (1964) published an influential and widely cited paper on "The nature of belief systems in mass publics." In this treatise, shrewdly reasoned and grounded in empirical data, Converse developed the thesis that most people in the U.S. are incapable, or at least not inclined, to think ideologically about political and social issues. Attitudes were simply not constrained in the sense of being sufficiently correlated with each other as one might have expected on logical or ideological grounds. Moreover, responses to the same attitude questions answered at different points in time by people participating in the 1956–1958–1960 U.S. election study panel were so unstable as to call into question the very idea that many people even have attitudes on social issues in any meaningful sense. It appeared that many people were really expressing "nonattitudes" to attitude questions, that is, giving an answer more or less at random to be cooperative and to get through the interview. The image of the average citizen implied in Converse's analysis was not a favorable one, to put it mildly, especially in reference to the notion of what the citizen should be like in democratic theory.

The reaction of many U.S. political scientists to Converse's thesis was intense, even visceral in some instances, and sustained. The response calls to mind the reaction which legend tells us occurred after the initial publication of Darwin's theory with its implications about the origin of the human species, namely "Let us hope that this is not true. If true, let us hope it does not become widely known."

The more analytical and grounded responses have centered mainly on two issues. First, some have acknowledged that Converse may have been right about U.S. citizens in the quiescent 1950s, but perhaps things changed subsequently in the more turbulent and polarized 60s and 70s (Stimson, 1975; Nie, Verba, and Petrocik, 1976; Bishop, Oldendick, Tuchfarber, and Bennett, 1978). The second main line of criticism has questioned Converse's methods. That is, if only Converse had used other questions or techniques, unstructured in-depth interviews (Lane, 1962; 1973), cluster analysis (Fleishman, 1986), Lisrel (Judd and Milburn, 1980), or Q-sort (Conover and Feldman, 1984), then perhaps his conclusions would have been different.

Although we shall not review these arguments and the associated evidence in depth, Converse may generally have been correct about attitudes and a lack of attitudinal organization among adults in the U.S. (Converse and Markus, 1979; Kinder and Sears, 1985; Sniderman and Tetlock, 1986; Sullivan, Piereson and Marcus, 1978). What seemingly has escaped most people appears to us as a rather obvious possibility. Why not take a comparative approach to see how things look in a democratic system that is substantively different from that of the United States? More specifically, in a country with a strong, disciplined party system such as that in Sweden, perhaps one can observe signs of attitudes hanging together more strongly than in a more loosely structured system such as the U.S. In a system such as Sweden's, parties and the principles for which they stand provide reliable and enduring anchors for individual citizens.

The possibilities addressed in this chapter have been alluded to already in the two previous chapters. In chapter 2, it was shown that self-designated ideology is more stable, much more strongly correlated with attitudes on specific issues, and much more strongly connected with voting behavior in Sweden than in the U.S. In chapter 3, it was shown that, at least on the four issues considered there, the voting groups in Sweden were much more neatly divided in their attitudes on contemporary issues than voting groups in the United States. Also, in regard to one of Converse's main points, Niemi and Westholm (1984) have already shown that political attitudes of people in Sweden are much more stable across time than comparable attitudes of people in the U.S. Thus, the "nonattitude" argument may pertain much more to the U.S. than to Sweden.

Overall, Converse's analysis may have been quite revealing in that most people in the U.S. may tend not to think very abstractly or ideologically about political matters, and may tend to express attitudes in an unstable and, at most, a loosely organized manner. But one should not assume that this exhausts the possibilities or that there is anything inevitable or inexorable about such a state of affairs. We tend to believe that Converse's results are quite system-specific, or pertain at most to people within a certain type of system. As we have argued throughout this book, we expect to observe at the individual level some social psychological reflections, counterparts, or consequences of the political system in which the person is living.

The remainder of this chapter reports data relevant to these matters. First, we look at recent Swedish and U.S. election studies in terms of how closely constrained or correlated the responses are to issue questions. Secondly, if the parties are anchoring the attitudes in Sweden the way we think they are, it follows that the voting groups should be rather sharply divided on a variety of (though not all) political issues, especially in comparison to the relative lack of division over issues between the voting groups in the U.S. Thirdly and finally, we shall briefly examine some evidence from Sweden in the context of offering yet another alternative approach to the question of attitude organization, involving tests for transitivity of attitudes rather than relying on correlations or other measures of association.

Constraint among issue attitudes

In this chapter, we are working mainly with the U.S. election studies of 1980 and 1984 and the Swedish election studies of 1982 and 1985. In each of those surveys, there are many questions asking people their attitudes on current social and political issues. Rather than examining and averaging correlations between all possible pairs of items as was done by Converse (1964), we began by doing a series of factor analyses with different specifications, in an exploratory manner looking for naturally occurring clusters of issues that belong together. We shall not report the details of these factor analyses, but they were used to locate the strongest attitudinal factors in each country, and to select the best items within each of these factors. We were also interested in identifying politically relevant variables such as strength of partisan identification, political activity, and political interest, that might intervene in the determination of how closely attitudes are linked to each other. Our approach suggests that attitudes ought to be more constrained among voters than nonvoters, and that constraint should increase as the strength of partisan identification increases, as political interest increases, and as political activity increases. We may also presume that one's cognitive resources increase as education increases. Thus, we also examine education and level of political information as possible intervening variables in the relationships among attitudes.

Table 4.1 summarizes the analyses of the U.S. data. In both 1980 and 1984, the strongest factor was a domestic *social welfare* factor in which the key question was whether the government should guarantee citizens a job and an adequate standard of living. This issue has been a pivotal issue for the Democrats at least since the "New Deal" programs, including Social Security, were formulated in the 1930s. The other items in this factor in 1980 pertained to the level of social services provided by the federal government and to the preferred trade-off between inflation and unemployment. In 1984, the items in the social welfare factor included once more the guaranteed jobs and social services questions, and also questions pertaining to aid to minority groups and the government's role in improving the socioeconomic status of women. In 1980, the second factor consisted of questions pertaining to the role of women in society, the Equal Rights Amendment, abortion, and prayer in the schools, and can be named a

Table 4.1 Constraint correlations within the United States, 1980 and 1984

	Social welfare items		Average correlations between Traditional–modern items	Environmental items	Foreign-policy items
	1980	1984	1980	1980	1984
All	.39	.35	.29	.29	.25
Strength of partisanship					
Strong	.45	.41	.23	.34	.32
Not strong	.35	.32	.33	.26	.21
Lean	.38	.36	.30	.32	.27
None	.26	.30	.25	.22	.14
Political interest					
High	.49	.42	.31	.25	.36
Medium	.35	.31	.29	.36	.24
Low	.26	.34	.23	.13	.13
Validated voter					
Yes	.44	.39	.30	.29	.30
No	.32	.29	.27	.30	.19
Respondent tried to influence others					
Yes	.50	.44	.32	.37	.38
No	.29	.33	.26	.24	.20
Respondent joined national organization, member political organization					
Yes	.40	.46	.29	.35	.59
No	.38	.36	.29	.29	.23
Number of political actions taken					
2 or more	.53	.50	.34	.35	.45
1	.45	.35	.29	.34	.32
0	.28	.33	.27	.24	.17
Education					
High	.42	.41	.33	.36	.38
Medium	.35	.32	.25	.29	.18
Low	.31	.28	.16	.17	.13
Level of information					
High	.49	.41	.30	.36	.39
Medium	.30	.31	.27	.29	.19
Low	.29	.33	.24	.14	.11

traditional–modern factor. A third factor in 1980 consisted of questions dealing with nuclear power and *environmental* regulation. In 1984, the second factor consisted of three *foreign policy* items dealing with relations with Russia, the military budget, and Central America.[1] Table 4.1 shows the average correlation between the pairs of items within each of these factors for the 1980 and 1984 samples as a whole and also within several subsamples. It is our position that such a selection gives a more appropriate estimate of the degree of constraint than if we were to consider all possible correlations among all issue items regardless of the topic or content. There are noticeably different dimensions in political attitudes, and it is not

Table 4.2 *Constraint correlations within Sweden, 1982 and 1985*

	Average correlations between					
	Public–private economy items		Social welfare items	Environmental items		Moral items
	1982	1985	1985	1982	1985	1982
All	.48	.52	.42	.33	.30	.29
Strength of partisanship						
Strong	.54	.58	.47	.30	.25	.28
Not strong	.46	.50	.39	.34	.29	.29
Lean	.42	.46	.41	.33	.34	.30
None	.27	.28	.30	.36	.29	.25
Political interest						
Much	.61	.62	.56	.46	.36	.24
Quite a lot	.53	.56	.42	.32	.30	.29
Not especially	.37	.43	.39	.30	.28	.31
Not at all	.27	.32	.39	.19	.37	.24
Validated voter						
Yes	.49	.53	.43	.34	.30	.29
No	.38	.37	.27	.21	.36	.29
Respondent tried to influence others						
Yes	.60	.61	.49	.43	.41	.26
No	.46	.47	.40	.30	.28	.30
Political party or organization						
Active Member	—	.68	.52	—	.45	—
Inactive Member	—	.56	.44	—	.31	—
Nonmember	—	.49	.41	—	.29	—
Education						
High	.61	.60	.47	.40	.43	.29
Medium	.47	.51	.42	.39	.27	.27
Low	.41	.44	.37	.24	.21	.28
Level of information						
High	—	.63	.49	—	.36	—
Medium	—	.51	.40	—	.29	—
Low	—	.34	.40	—	.26	—

Note: The questions regarding membership in a political party and level of information were not asked in 1982.

realistic to expect items in one dimension to be highly constrained by items in another dimension.

The comparable analyses for Sweden, shown in table 4.2, pertains to three factors. The first set consists of four items, available in both 1982 and 1985, which deal with attitudes toward a socialist society, a market-oriented society with more free enterprise, the wage-earner funds, and the size of the public sector. These items comprise a *public–private economy* factor in that they deal with fundamental considerations regarding economic arrangements in society. In 1985, three items are used which pertain to *social welfare* programs, one dealing with sick-leave policy and the other two with the general level of government spending on social welfare programs.[2] In both years, two questions comprising an *environmental* factor were used. These questions dealt with attitudes toward nuclear power, and moving toward "a more environmentally oriented society even if this means low or no economic growth." Finally, the 1982 survey included four items measuring attitudes toward abortion, pornography, alcohol, and developing a "society in which Christian values play a more important role." These items can be labeled as a *moral* factor in Sweden.

When we consider the results in tables 4.1 and 4.2 in relation to each other, several observations seem warranted. First, considerably more constraint can be observed within the public–private economy factor in Sweden than within any other factor in either country. The items in the public–private economy factor are closely related to the basic left–right dimension which is known to be strong, coherent, and closely related to the vote, as shown in chapter 2. There is no comparable factor in U.S. politics.

Items in the social welfare factor appear to hang together somewhat more in Sweden than in the U.S., but here the difference is small enough so that it could be due to such considerations as what questions were asked. We would also point out, however, that there is *much* more missing data in the U.S. surveys than in the Swedish surveys. Other things being equal, this would suggest that the attitude correlations ought to actually be higher for the United States, whereas generally the reverse is true. Stated differently, if the amount of missing data were as low in the U.S. as in Sweden, the constraint correlations for the U.S. would almost certainly be lower than what they are in table 4.1.

We can simulate this equalizing condition by assigning a middle value to each person who said "don't know," "haven't thought much about it," or gave some other answer outside the prescribed range. If people have missing data on two or more of the items under consideration, this could actually increase the size of the constraint correlations. In fact, however, the constraint correlations in tables 4.1 and 4.2 are reduced somewhat if the people with missing data are included in this way. For example, the average constraint correlations for the social welfare items are thereby reduced from .39 to .29 for the U.S. in 1980, from .35 to .32 for the U.S. in 1984, and from .42 to .39 for Sweden in 1985. Thus, with this control, the differences between Sweden and the U.S. on constraint among the social welfare items may become even larger.

The two environmental questions correlate slightly more strongly in Sweden than in the U.S. In the U.S., items in the foreign policy and traditional–modern factors show less constraint than the social welfare items. In Sweden, the morality items are constrained at a moderate level, but the degree of constraint is unrelated to political factors including voting.

As an intervening variable, strength of partisan identification works in the expected manner within Sweden in the public–private economy and social welfare factors. On the environmental and moral factors in Sweden, degree of constraint among items is quite unrelated to strength of partisan identification. On the public–private economy and social welfare factors, constraint is noticeably higher among the strong party identifiers than among those who lack a party identification, with the weak identifiers and those who lean toward a party being intermediate. In the United States, the same trend is evident except on the traditional–modern factor.

The various measures of political involvement and activity work about as anticipated. That is, those who voted, those with greater political interest, those who tried to influence others to vote a particular way, and those who are politically active generally show more constraint among their attitudes than nonvoters, those with less interest, those who did not try to influence others, and those who are not politically active.

Education and amount of political information also appear to exert an intervening effect on degree of constraint, an effect which in some cases is rather strong. The more formal education people have, and the more politically informed they are, the higher the correlations between their attitudes.[3] Education appears to be especially important in determining how closely related attitudes toward the environment are correlated. The moral factor in Sweden forms an interesting exception to the foregoing observations. The four items in this factor are correlated at a significant level, but the level of these correlations does not appear to be related to any of the erstwhile intervening variables in table 4.2. This indicates that people in Sweden do have relatively organized views on matters of morality, but they are basically not on the current political agenda. Moral issues are not the source, nor do they reflect political divisions within Sweden of the 1980s.

It follows from the preceding analyses that constraint should continue to increase as one shifts the focus toward political elites. The Swedish parliamentary study of 1985 provides an opportunity for a mass–elite comparison similar to that reported by Converse (1964) for the U.S. public and the United States Congress, using data from 1958, and by Converse and Pierce (1986), using data from France in the late 1960s. The Swedish parliamentarians were asked some of the same questions that were posed to the Swedish electorate in the 1985 election study. Here we concentrate on answers to nine different questions (Items A–I in table 4.4 give the topics covered in the questions), all of which are correlated significantly with the left–right dimension. They all pertain to either the public–private or the social welfare dimensions, factors which are not independent in Sweden. In order to compare the Members of Parliament to different segments of the

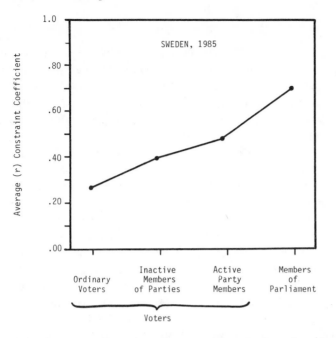

Figure 4.1. Average level of constraint among voters and Members of Parliament in Sweden, 1985. Each data point is based on an average of 36 correlations, correlating each of nine issue attitudes with each of the other attitude items.

public, we divided the public into three groups consisting of those who are active members of a political party (6%), inactive members of a political party (10%), and nonmembers (84%). For each of these groups and the parliamentarians, 36 correlations were calculated, thus examining the link between each possible pair of these nine items.

Similar to what Converse found in the U.S. and France (Converse, 1964; Converse and Pierce, 1986), the average constraint correlation was considerably higher for the Swedish parliamentarians (.72) than for members of the Swedish public (.30). As shown in figure 4.1, when the public is divided, it is easy to see a steady increase in the degree of constraint as one moves from ordinary voters (.27) to inactive party members (.40) to active party members (.49). This is certainly supportive of our view that within Sweden, the political parties provide strong anchors to stabilize people's issue attitudes and increase the constraint among them. At least this is true of contemporary issues that have been on the political agenda and which are related in some degree to the basic left–right dimension.

Issue attitude differences among voter groups

If the parties in Sweden offer a readily available anchor for people in relation to which attitudes can be formed and maintained, then we ought to observe substantial differences among the party preference groups in their attitudes on contemporary political issues. On the other hand, insofar as the parties are less prominent in the United States and the personal qualities of the candidates play a more significant role, it is expected that differences between the voting groups on the contemporary social and political issues will be weaker.

Our method of analysis in this context is basically the same as in the corresponding portion of chapter 3, although here we are considering many more issues. Specifically, we are looking at the degree of association (eta) between voting group as the independent variable and attitude position as the dependent variable. The resulting coefficient was called the "issue voting coefficient" in chapter 3, although we recognize that the observed level of association could be due to rational selection or to a persuasion effect, or, more likely, some combination of the two. We are not interested here in trying to unravel those two possible effects (Abramowitz, 1978). Nor is it our intent to do a thorough or comprehensive analysis of issue voting in all its nuances. We recognize that if voting groups are observed to differ on an issue, this is not sufficient proof to know for certain that issue voting occurred. On the other hand, if voting groups do not differ on an issue, it is most unlikely that issue voting did occur. That is, it is probably true that for all practical purposes, a difference on an issue between voting groups constitutes a necessary, though not a sufficient, condition for issue voting. Moreover, the larger the difference between voting groups on an issue, the more probable it is that issue voting occurred (Holmberg and Gilljam, 1987).

The two main voting groups in the United States were compared in their attitudes on the same issues as were used in table 4.1. In 1980, the average eta for the social welfare items was .39. For the environmental items, it was .16, and for the traditional–modern items, it was .12.[4] In 1984, the eta averaged .35 for the social welfare items and .33 for the foreign policy items. Although these eta coefficients are rather modest in size, they indicate that there was probably at least some issue voting in these two U.S. elections.

The comparable coefficients for the four public–private economy questions in Sweden averaged .62 in 1982 and .64 in 1985. These are based on comparing the five main voting groups in Sweden. If these five voting groups are collapsed into the two voting blocs, these average coefficients are reduced, but only slightly, to .60 in 1982 and .62 in 1985. Thus, the strength of these coefficients is not due primarily to the fact that we are comparing five voting groups in Sweden and only two in the United States. The average issue voting coefficient for the three social welfare questions in the 1985 Swedish survey was .47, somewhat larger than that for the social welfare questions in the U.S. (.39 and .35 in 1980 and 1984, respectively). The issue voting coefficient for the two environmental questions in Sweden averaged .29 and .26 in 1982 and 1985, respectively. Finally, on the four morality questions in the 1982 Swedish study, the issue voting coefficient averaged only .19. Thus, it is clear that the voting groups in Sweden are rather sharply divided on some issues, while on others they differ but not so much, and on still others they differ very little. In the early and middle 1980s, the voting groups in Sweden differed most in regard to questions pertaining to public–private economy, substantially but not quite as much on questions about social welfare, only somewhat on environmental matters, and very little on the morality items.

This pattern is shown rather clearly in figure 4.2 in which strength of partisan identification is used as a moderating variable in determining the level of issue voting. In each country, we observed the degree to which the voting groups differed on the issues within each of four levels of party identification. The results strongly support the view that the parties in Sweden are anchoring people's attitudes on the public–private economy and social welfare questions and also, though to a lesser degree, the environmental questions. At the same time, strength of party identification does not modify the degree to which the voter groups in Sweden are divided over the morality issues, as can be seen in the lower left hand portion of figure 4.2.

The results for the U.S., also in figure 4.2, are more irregular. On the social welfare items, one can observe some increase in the issue voting coefficients as strength of partisanship increases, especially in 1980. However, the results for the foreign policy, environmental, and traditional–modern items are weak and irregular. This provides further support for the thesis that parties and partisanship are more closely linked with particular issue attitudes in Sweden than in the U.S.

In order to provide a more complete picture of the degree of issue voting in these two countries, we want to show some results for issues beyond those which were strongly embedded in the factors used in tables 4.1 and 4.2 and figure 4.2. In addition to providing more concrete evidence, it will also show that our results are not biased or limited to the issues we have thus far considered.

Table 4.3 shows the results of comparing Mondale and Reagan voters in 1984 on a rather wide range of issues. The largest differences between the two groups were over the level of government-provided social services (eta = .39), the government guaranteeing jobs and a standard of living (.38), and the level of military spending (.37). On all the comparisons in

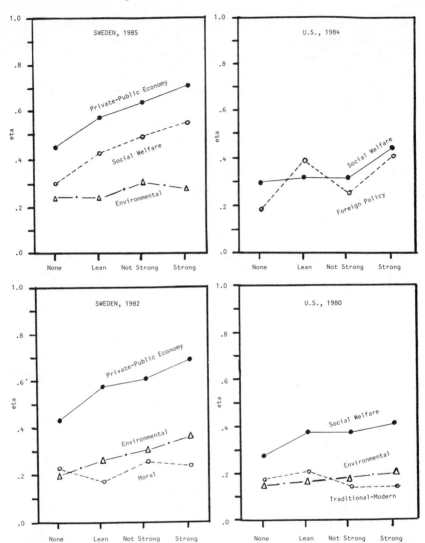

Figure 4.2. Degree of division of voting groups on issue attitudes as a function of degree of partisanship and type of issue in Sweden (1982 and 1985) and the United States (1980 and 1984).

table 4.3, the difference between the two voting groups is statistically significant, although in one instance (abortion), it is quite small.

Table 4.3 also gives, in the right-hand column, the correlation between attitude position on each issue and the respondent's position on the liberal–conservative scale. Note that there is no one issue on which the voting

Table 4.3 *Relationship between issue position, voting and ideological self-placement in the U.S., 1984*

Attitude issues	eta comparing Mondale and Reagan voters	r with liberal–conservative self-placement
A Government provided social services	.39	.26
B Government guarantees jobs and living standard	.38	.28
C Military spending	.37	.28
D Aid to minority groups	.32	.26
E Relations with Russia	.32	.26
F Socioeconomic status of women	.31	.28
G Central America	.30	.22
H Abortion	.11	.23
I Liberal–conservative self-placement	.44	—

groups in 1984 were as divided as much as they were on the liberal–conservative scale (eta = .44). Secondly, all of the specific issues in table 4.3 were slightly and similarly correlated with the liberal–conservative scale with relatively little variation in the magnitude of this correlation (the range being only between .22 and .28).

In addition to the eight issues in table 4.3, people in the 1984 U.S. survey were asked whether they thought federal spending should be increased, kept about the same, or decreased on a series of ten spending areas (e.g., crime, science, public schools). Mondale and Reagan voters did not differ more on any of these ten issues than on the issues in table 4.3. The spending questions on which the voting groups differed the most were social welfare programs, specifically food stamps (eta = .37), government programs designed to help blacks (.35), and government programs to create jobs for the unemployed (.32).

The attitudinal differences between voting groups might be expected to increase as one moves from the politically inactive or inert citizens to the political activists. The 1984 U.S. survey included a series of six questions asking people whether they had participated in politics in a variety of ways. A majority (56%) said they had done none of the six, but a substantial number reported having done one (27%) or more (17%). The issue voting coefficients for the eight issues in table 4.3 were recalculated separately for people who reported no actions, those who reported having done one (but no more) of the actions, and those who reported having done two or more of the actions. As shown in figure 4.3, the average issue voting coefficients varied substantially from .24 for those who had done no actions, .31 for those who had done one, and .44 for those who had done two or more of the actions. This indicates that the degree to which the voter groups are divided

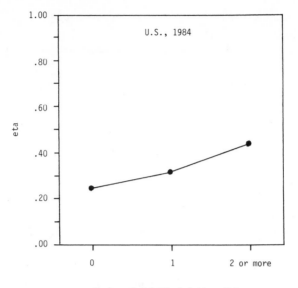

Figure 4.3. Average degree of issue voting in the United States in 1984 as a function of the level of political activity. Each data point is an average issue voting coefficient comparing Reagan and Mondale voters on eight separate issues.

or polarized over the issues does indeed increase as political activity increases in the U.S.

The results of the comparable breakdowns for Sweden are summarized in table 4.4. Here, however, we have an additional intriguing feature which is not available for the U.S. in the 1980s, namely the study of the Members of the Swedish Parliament. Table 4.4 shows eta coefficients for both citizens and Members of Parliament on 11 issue attitudes and 7 more abstract societal values. One can see that there is no specific issue which divides the voting groups in Sweden as much as the wage-earner funds question (eta = .73). The voter groups, however, also differ rather substantially over the size of the public sector (.53) and privatizing health care (.56). The voting groups in Sweden seem to differ over defense spending (.37) about as much as the voting groups in the U.S. differ over the size of the military budget. Overall, there seems to be a much broader range in the Swedish coefficients than the comparable coefficients for the United States. The proposal to forbid pornography once again serves as a good example of an issue which is not approached in a partisan manner in Sweden.

On each of the issues in table 4.4, the party groups in the Parliament differed more than did the corresponding groups of voters. Generally, the differences among the voter groups and the parliamentarians were in the

Table 4.4 Relationship between attitude and value position, voting and ideological self-placement in Sweden, 1985

	eta comparing five party preference groups		eta comparing two blocs		Correlation with left–right self-placement	
	Voters	Members of Parliament	Voters	Members of Parliament	Voters	Members of Parliament
Issue attitudes						
A Wage earner funds	.73	.97	.73	.97	.66	.81
B Privatize health care	.56	.97	.54	.90	.52	.83
C Size of public sector	.53	.91	.50	.87	.48	.86
D Government control of private business	.52	.87	.49	.83	.52	.79
E Social reform programs	.49	.84	.47	.79	.47	.82
F Daycare centers	.41	.75	.39	.66	.35	.70
G Six-hour workday	.39	.73	.36	.63	.38	.68
H Defense spending	.37	.76	.29	.66	.34	.74
I Advertising on TV	.34	.86	.26	.80	.34	.79
J Nuclear power	.30	.72	.03	.36	.11	.56
K Pornography	.15	.35	.05	.13	.07	.21
L Left–right self-placement	.75	.90	.71	.82	—	—
Value dimensions						
1 Socialist society	.68	.89	.66	.87	.65	.79
2 Market economy	.63	.91	.60	.88	.63	.84
3 Industrial democracy	.40	.58	.39	.54	.40	.62
4 Christian values	.27	.66	.24	.63	.22	.59
5 Economic growth society	.26	.60	.13	.21	.17	.40
6 High tech society	.26	.45	.21	.24	.20	.36
7 Environmentally oriented society	.19	.51	.08	.15	.12	.38

same direction. The third and fourth columns in table 4.4 show that the coefficients are reduced, but usually no more than slightly, when the five party groups are collapsed into the two blocs.

The two right-hand columns of table 4.4 give the correlations between where people place themselves on the 0–10 left–right scale and their response to each of the attitude and value items. Once again, the parliamentarian correlations are larger than those of the electorate. This is to be expected since one only becomes a Member of Parliament in Sweden by being politically active and working one's way up through the party. One can also see a rather substantial range in the link between an issue and the left–right dimension from the wage-earner fund and public sector questions which are strongly correlated with the left–right dimension all the way down to the pornography item which is essentially unrelated to the left–right dimension among the public and only mildly related to the left–right dimension among Members of Parliament.

The lower portion of table 4.4 presents the results of the same type of analysis done with regard to seven more abstract proposals or values. Each of these items presents a concept or direction in which society could develop in the future, and people are asked to evaluate the concept on a 0–10 scale on which 0 is labeled a very bad idea, 10 a very good idea, and 5 an idea which is neither good nor bad (Holmberg, 1984; Holmberg and Asp, 1984; Holmberg and Gilljam, 1987).

The largest differences to be seen among the party preference groups on the value items in table 4.4 are in relation to the concepts of a market economy and a socialist society. These were among the items in the public–private economy factor discussed earlier in this chapter. The remaining items produce coherent differences among the party groups, but these differences reflect a lesser degree of division or polarization. Once again, the correlations between each of these value items and self-placement on the left–right scale are given in the two right-hand columns. All of the value items are correlated with the left–right dimension in some degree but with considerable variation in magnitude, ranging from the items pertaining to socialism and a market economy which are very strongly linked to the left–right dimension all the way down to the items pertaining to economic growth and the environment, which are no more than slightly correlated with the left–right dimension. The latter items may even comprise a new non-left–right dimension in Sweden, but thus far it is not a strong factor in that it lacks internal coherence on the mass level (Holmberg and Asp, 1984).

The Swedish electorate in 1985 was again divided in terms of political activity, differentiating among those who are active members of a political party, inactive party members, and nonmembers. Within each of these

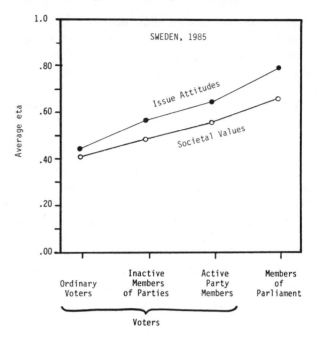

Figure 4.4. Average degree of division of party preference groups on eleven issue attitudes and seven values among voters and Members of Parliament in Sweden, 1985.

levels of political activity, people in the five voting groups were compared to see how differently they responded to the seven value items and the 11 attitude items in table 4.4. The resulting eta coefficients were then averaged for the value and attitude items. In addition to the three groups of voters (active, nonactive, and nonmembers), the Members of Parliament comprise a fourth group for the sake of comparison. The results of these analyses are summarized in figure 4.4.

As political activity increases, division among voter groups increases in a rather orderly manner. On both the issue attitude and value measures in Sweden, inactive party members are more divided on the issues than nonmembers, active members more than inactive members, and the Members of Parliament are more divided than active party members. It can also be seen that within each of these four categories the party preference groups are slightly more divided over the attitude items than over the value items.

Overall, we have seen evidence in this section that strongly implies issue voting in both countries. Moreover, we observed a steady increase in issue voting as level of activity increases in both countries, but more issue voting anchored by the stronger party system in Sweden.[5]

Taking the results of the last two sections together, it can be said with considerable confidence that the degree to which attitudes hang together and the extent to which voting groups differ over issues depends in good measure on the nature of the political system and the issues under consideration. If we add in the rather convincing demonstration of Niemi and Westholm (1984), who used panel data to show that attitudes are more stable in Sweden than in the United States, things start to add up to a coherent picture.

It seems reasonable to suppose the strong party system in Sweden lies behind these differences. That is, because the political party system in Sweden is relatively stronger than that of the U.S., people in Sweden have attitudes that are more stable, more constrained, and more closely linked to voting behavior. Certainly, the picture one would derive about the "belief systems of mass publics" would be quite different were one to focus solely on a system like the United States *or* solely on a system like that of Sweden. This strongly implies the importance, perhaps even the necessity, of taking into account the nature of the political system when analyzing such topics as constraint among attitudes and issue voting.

Transitivity of attitudes

Finally, in the last section of this chapter, we consider briefly an alternative approach to the question of whether people really have attitudes that are ordered in a coherent manner. This approach focuses attention on the criterion of logical transitivity. If a person prefers X over Y and Y over Z, and if the three elements exist in the same dimension, then logically the person ought to prefer X over Z. In the context of politics, suppose in the late stages of the 1984 Democratic primary election campaign, people had been asked in a series of three paired comparisons whether they liked Jesse Jackson or Gary Hart better, whether they liked Jackson or Walter Mondale better, and whether they preferred Hart or Mondale. Those who preferred Jackson over Hart and Hart over Mondale ought to have also preferred Jackson over Mondale by the criterion of logical transitivity, provided the judgments are unidimensional. Given any answers to two of the questions, the logical answer to the third can be determined. Hence, the patterns shown by people in their answers can be compared to what would be demanded by this standard of logical coherence and also to what would be expected if people gave answers at random reflecting "nonattitudes." The problem is that a complete set of such questions is rarely included in surveys. It is far more common, for instance, to ask people to evaluate one party or one candidate at a time, using a rating scale of some sort – what psychologists call the method of single stimulus.

Such a set of paired comparison questions, however, was included in the surveys of the Swedish electorate in 1968 and 1985 and also in the survey of the Members of Parliament in 1985. The issue under consideration was the representational role of the Members of the Swedish Parliament, and the importance or priority members should accord to different sources of influence in deciding how to cast their votes. This is a classical question in democratic theory which is often posed in terms of delegate versus trustee roles (Miller and Stokes, 1963; Holmberg, 1974; Converse and Pierce, 1979). In the delegate role, a legislator would ascertain what the constituents want and vote accordingly. The trustee role calls for a Member of Parliament to exercise an individually determined judgment. To capture the realities of the European political context, it is essential to add a third possibility, the party role. That is, legislators often (perhaps even most often, depending on the country) vote in line with the preferences of the party which nominated them. In practice, these three sources of influence may often reinforce each other. However, it is also easy to imagine other instances in which the behavior implied by these roles would be in conflict with each other. Answers which specify how a person thinks the various conflict situations should be resolved can reveal an underlying normative orientation.

The questions in the Swedish studies successively posed conflicts between (a) the party and individualistic roles, (b) the delegate and individualistic roles, and (c) the party and delegate roles. In addition to these three normative questions, the public (but not the parliamentarians) was also asked a more cognitive question about how they think Members of Parliament usually do resolve a conflict between party and individualistic roles. The wording of the four questions together with the marginal percentages are given in table 4.5. Question 1 shows that a majority of the Swedish public prefers the individualistic role over the party role, and the size of this majority increased between 1968 and 1985 (from 59 to 69%). The perceptions of the Swedish people show a rather strong consensus that this dilemma is usually resolved in favor of the party role, and the size of this perceptual consensus increased from 1968 to 1985 (from 79 to 88%). If we consider these two questions together, the results indicate a growing disparity between preference and perception at the aggregate level. That is, while Swedish voters increasingly expressed a preference for the individualistic role, their perceptions of what Members of Parliament were doing indicated an increased impression of party role behavior.

Answers to the second item in table 4.5 show a majority of the public preferring the delegate over the individualistic role with some increase in the margin of this preference between 1968 and 1985 (from 56 to 65%). Finally, only a minority prefer the party role over the delegate role, and the

Table 4.5 *Four questions pertaining to the roles played by Members of Parliament in Sweden*

	Swedish public, 1968 (%)	Swedish public, 1985 (%)	Members of Swedish Parliament, 1985 (%)
1 *Party role preferred over individualistic role* "Sometimes it happens that a Member of Parliament has a different opinion from that which his/ her party in the Parliament has. What do you think the member should do in such a case? Should he/she vote the party's position or vote according to his/her own opinion?"	41	31	61
2 *Individualistic role preferred over delegate role* "If a member of Parliament believes that most of the people who voted for him/her have a different view on a certain matter from his/her own opinion, what do you think he/she should do? Should he/she vote according to the voters' views or according to his/her own attitude?"	44	35	67
3 *Party role preferred over delegate role* "What do you think a Member of Parliament should do if his/her party in the Parliament has a position and most of the people who voted for him/ her have another view? Should he/she vote the party's position or according to the opinion of his/ her voters?"	42	27	67
4 *Percent perceiving party role over individualistic role* "[In regard to the dilemma in question 1 above], What do you think that Members of the Parliament usually do?"	79	88	—

Note: The above percentages are based only on people who answered the question with one of the two provided alternatives, excluding "don't know" and other missing data. Thus, the percentage giving the other answer, e.g., preferring the individualistic over the party role in question 1, would be 100 minus the number given.

size of this minority decreased significantly from 1968 to 1985 (42 to 27%).[6] Among the Swedish citizens, there was relatively little variation in attitudes and perceptions as a function of party preference. As might be expected, preference for the party role did vary somewhat as a function of the strength of party preference, but the difference was not large. The percentage preferring the party role increased slightly as one moves from those with no party preference to those who identify strongly with a party. The largest difference, however, is only 16 percent. In 1985, 38 percent of the strong identifiers preferred the party role over the individualistic role, compared to 22 percent of those with no party preference.

It is not surprising that orientations of the Members of Parliament

Table 4.6 *Patterns of attitudes toward the role of Members of Parliament among Swedish citizens and Members of the Swedish Parliament*

	Swedish public 1968 (%)	Swedish public 1985 (%)	Members of Swedish Parliament 1985 (%)
Attitude patterns			
I Transitive types			
A *Party role preferred*	21	13	47
1 Party, individualistic, delegate	8	4	26
2 Party, delegate, individualistic	13	9	21
B *Delegate role preferred*	39	52	14
3 Delegate, individualistic, party	21	36	5
4 Delegate, party, individualistic	18	16	9
C *Individualistic role preferred*	32	28	32
5 Individualistic, delegate, party	15	19	11
6 Individualistic, party, delegate	17	9	21
II Intransitive types			
7 I>P, P>D, D>I	5	5	1
8 P>I, I>D, D>P	3	2	6
Total	100	100	100
N	2197	1985	240

Note: In describing the two intransitive types in this table, I indicates individualistic role, D the delegate role, and P the party role, and the preference ordering is indicated by a greater than sign. The wording of the questions is in Table 4.5.

regarding their own roles differ substantially from that of the electorate. As can be seen in table 4.5, Members of Parliament were more favorable toward the party role and less favorable toward the delegate role than was the citizenry in 1985.

For present purposes, however, it is of greater interest to examine the pattern of answers to the three preference questions at the individual level. When people answer three dichotomous questions, there are eight possible ways or patterns of answering the questions. Six of these patterns, as shown in table 4.6, are of the transitive type and two are intransitive. Thus, if people gave answers at random, about 25 percent of the people should show answers of the intransitive type. This percentage may change somewhat once the marginals are known. As shown in table 4.6, the large majority of the public in 1968 (92%) and 1985 (93%) and of the Parliament in 1985 (93%) give answers that fit one of the six transitive patterns. In each case, answers to these role questions approximate much more closely the rational transitive pattern than the intransitive random answer pattern. It is thus reasonable to conclude that most of the people held a logically ordered set of attitudes in regard to these rather abstract issues. Although some of the people may have been giving random answers to the questions, it does not seem to have been very common to do so.

As to content, it appears that the Swedish public was most favorable to one of the patterns emphasizing the delegate role and least favorable to the party role. Parliamentarians, on the other hand, were generally most favorable to the two patterns emphasizing the party role and least favorable to the delegate role.[7]

Overall, it deserves to be emphasized that most of the people in these studies gave what appear to be logically ordered sets of answers to the three attitude questions pertaining to the role of parliamentarians. In spite of the fact that this may be a rather remote set of questions for the average citizen, it is of interest that members of the electorate were about as likely as parliamentarians to give a logically transitive set of answers. For both groups, the results in table 4.6 depart dramatically from what would be expected if they did not have attitudes on these questions and merely gave answers at random. Thus, a rather high level of constraint was observed using this method.

Constraint varies by political system

Philip Converse (1964) certainly can be credited with raising a series of intriguing and significant questions regarding citizens in democratic systems. However, by focusing on people in a loosely structured system such as the U.S., Converse, together with his critics and supporters, may have tacitly and unintentionally led to an underestimation of what voters can be like and what they can do. Even within the U.S., there are signs that higher levels of constraint and issue voting can be observed among those who more strongly identify with a political party and those who are more actively involved in political matters. Based on our comparisons of Sweden and the U.S., the level of constraint, issue voting, and attitude stability that can be observed at the individual level may be presumed to vary as a direct function of the extent to which the people are living in a political system which has strong parties with well-known positions on an ideological dimension encompassing most contemporary issues on the political agenda.

Serious democratic theorists, such as V. O. Key (1949) and Giovanni Sartori (1976), have stressed the vital importance of the party and have argued forcefully that "pure candidate-domination of elections is a recipe for irresponsible, unaccountable performance in office ..." (Burnham, 1986, p. xiii). We have seen in this chapter some social psychological counterparts or consequences of the different political systems found in Sweden and the U.S. In the country with the stronger political parties, Sweden, we observed more constraint among attitudes. In addition to attitudes hanging together more strongly, we also observed in Sweden more stability of attitudes across time, and more evidence of issue voting. These differences are due to the way in which parties in Sweden provide stronger and more clear cues that are relevant to the attitude-formation process.

5 Parties, leaders, and candidates

Attitudes which people express regarding political parties, party leaders, and people nominated by parties can tell us a great deal about the condition of the political landscape of a country. Since the 1930s, especially, many resources and much energy have gone into systematic measurement of these attitudes. Such studies are read with considerable interest both in the higher circles and by average citizens. The intangible power and influence exerted by people in political office may derive, in some degree, from their standing in recently published polls.

Provided that people feel free to tell the truth when asked to evaluate parties, candidates, and office holders, the results can be used to help interpret how well the political system is operating. Attitudes on such matters can be interpreted in regard to questions pertaining to trust and confidence. They also may be used in considering the possibility that people are casting negative votes, choosing the least undesirable alternative.

Here we shall consider the attitudes expressed by people in Sweden and the U.S. toward political parties, the leaders of the parties, and people nominated by the parties for high office. In addition to the intrinsic interest which these data hold for describing the situation in these two countries, certain theoretical questions will be addressed. First, we want to examine the possibility that people in either or both countries show some general tendency toward positivity or negativity in their evaluative judgments. Do people show a trend toward making predominantly positive or negative judgments? Within the United States, David Sears and his colleagues have identified what they called the "positivity bias in evaluation of political figures," which referred to the tendency to make predominantly favorable assessments when asked to evaluate each of several people on a list of contemporary politicians (Rook et al., 1978; Sears, 1969). The occurrence of this tendency or bias is widely thought to be true, real rather than a methodological artifact (Lau, Sears, and Centers, 1979), and sufficiently important to be controlled when attempting to analyze individual attitudes for other purposes (Knight, 1984).

Secondly, in addition to a general positivity bias in the political realm, Sears (1983) later identified what he termed the "person positivity bias," which refers to the tendency to evaluate attitude objects favorably to the degree they resemble individual human beings. Both of these ideas provide guidance to our analyses. If correct or applicable to our contexts, we would expect attitudes toward parties, leaders, and candidates to be predominantly favorable and for the attitudes toward leaders and candidates to be more favorable than attitudes toward parties.

Although useful as a source of ideas, the observation of the positivity and person positivity biases cannot be taken for granted. Much of Sears' (1983) evidence is drawn from intensive studies of college students at UCLA, and there is no reason to think that they typify all people. One attempt to replicate Sears' studies on Swedish students and how they evaluated political parties and party leaders on semantic differential scales came up with, at best, mixed results relative to the positivity and person positivity biases (Nilsson and Ekehammar, 1987). Sears' positivity concepts are also a little counter-intuitive, given the widespread assumption that many people in modern societies are quite negatively disposed toward politics, political parties, and politicians. Gant and Sigelman (1985) have observed at least some evidence of anti-candidate voting in the U.S. – which in our context would be indicated by people rating both the major candidates negatively and then voting for the one rated less negatively (i.e., "the lesser of two evils").

Our third major question concerns how well the attitudes toward leaders, nominees, and parties "hang together." Insofar as people really have attitudes, one would expect that they would cohere in a reasonably orderly manner. Attitudes toward a party and the leader or nominee of that party can be thought of in Gestalt terms as a part–whole relationship. Given the unit relationship, it is reasonable to expect the two attitudes to be positively linked in some degree. The attitudes also would be expected to be at least somewhat stable across time (Converse, 1964). On the other hand, if people are just answering the attitude questions to be cooperative and to get through the interview, we would expect the answers to be related in a relatively more random or haphazard manner, and to be unstable across time.

As in other chapters, our analyses focus on recent Swedish and U.S. election studies. In 1979, 1982, and 1985, people in the Swedish studies were asked to rate each of the five largest political parties and the leaders of those parties on an 11-point dislike–like (*ogillar–gillar*) scale. On the numbered scale, going from -5 to $+5$, three points were given a verbal designation, -5 (strongly dislike), 0 (neither like nor dislike), and $+5$ (strongly like). In each survey, the questions pertaining to the five parties were asked first and in the same random order, followed by the questions pertaining to the five current leaders of those parties, asked in a corresponding order.

The U.S. national election studies have used a 0–100 degree affective feeling thermometer to measure people's attitudes. First used in 1964 to measure attitudes toward groups, it was then used in 1968 and in each study since, to measure people's attitudes toward the presidential and vice-presidential candidates, as well as political groups and the political parties (Weisberg and Rusk, 1970). Although technically this is a 101-point rating scale, most people (well over 90%) express their feelings by choosing one of the nine designated points on the scale shown to the respondent (0, 15, 30, 40, 50, 60, 70, 85, or 100). Thus, for all practical purposes, we are dealing with a 9-point scale (albeit with unequal intervals). In our analyses, the scale is transformed into a −5 to +5 scale on which judgments of 100 converted to +5, 50 to 0, 0 to −5, and so forth.[1]

Unfortunately, the timing and sequence with which the feeling thermometer questions have been asked in the U.S. studies are complex and inconsistent. For example, attitudes toward the presidential candidates were measured only in the postelection interview in 1968, only in the pre-election wave in 1976, and on both pre- and postelection waves in 1972, 1980, and 1984. Attitudes toward the parties were not measured until 1980.

Attitudinal lay of the land

Tables 5.1 and 5.2 give the overall average ratings for Sweden and the U.S., respectively. Of the 30 mean values in the Swedish case, 20 are positive overall, which could indicate some trend toward positivity. This, however, depends largely on which party or leader is being evaluated and by whom, as can be seen in the rest of table 5.1 which breaks down the Swedish samples into the five main voting groups. It is the ideologically extreme parties, the Communist and Conservative Parties, that receive negative overall ratings. Note that in each instance the leader of these two parties is rated more positively (or less negatively) than the party.

Table 5.2 shows that of 44 averages calculated for the U.S. samples to describe their attitudes toward the presidential and vice-presidential candidates, the parties, and the party groups, all but five of these averages are positive. The exceptions were George McGovern and Sargent Shriver in 1972 and Spiro Agnew in 1968, none of whom received an overall positive evaluation by U.S. adults. Ratings of these people and others (e.g., George Wallace) indicate that people in the U.S. are not incapable of making negative evaluations, but the results in table 5.2 show that by and large they are disinclined to do so – at least in regard to politicians and parties within the mainstream or "vital center" of U.S. politics.

It is not difficult to see in table 5.2 what lies behind the overall positive

Table 5.1 *Average overall ratings of the five parties in Sweden and their respective leaders*

Average attitudinal ratings of		Overall	Voter groups					
			vpk	s	c	fp	m	eta²
Parties								
vpk	1985	−1.3	+3.4	+0.4	−3.0	−2.8	−3.8	.48
	1982	−1.6	+2.8	−0.1	−3.3	−3.5	−3.9	.45
	1979	−1.4	+3.7	+0.1	−2.8	−3.1	−3.8	.45
s	1985	+1.3	+2.7	+3.9	−0.7	−0.2	−1.7	.61
	1982	+1.2	+2.6	+3.7	−1.2	−0.6	−1.7	.63
	1979	+1.2	+2.0	+3.9	−1.1	−0.7	−1.9	.65
c	1985	+0.5	−1.0	−0.5	+3.5	+1.1	+0.9	.30
	1982	+0.4	−1.4	−0.9	+3.4	+1.4	+1.2	.40
	1979	+0.7	−1.0	−0.8	+3.7	+1.4	+1.3	.41
fp	1985	+1.3	−0.8	+0.1	+2.0	+3.4	+2.2	.34
	1982	−0.1	−1.8	−1.1	+1.1	+2.6	+0.6	.28
	1979	+0.7	−1.3	−0.3	+1.6	+3.3	+1.5	.32
m	1985	−0.2	−3.9	−2.6	+1.3	+1.3	+3.9	.62
	1982	−0.2	−3.9	−2.5	+1.3	+0.9	+3.8	.62
	1979	−0.4	−4.1	−2.9	+1.2	+1.0	+3.7	.63
Party leaders								
Lars Werner (vpk)	1985	+0.4	+3.6	+1.5	−0.9	−0.1	−1.3	.26
	1982	−0.1	+2.9	+0.9	−1.2	−1.3	−1.7	.25
	1979	0.0	+3.2	+1.0	−1.1	−1.1	−1.3	.22
Olof Palme (s)	1985	+1.1	+2.4	+3.5	−0.8	−0.4	−1.4	.45
	1982	+1.2	+2.9	+3.5	−1.2	−0.4	−1.3	.49
	1979	+0.9	+1.7	+3.5	−1.5	−0.8	−1.9	.53
Thorbjörn Fälldin (c)	1985	+0.1	−1.2	−1.0	+2.8	+0.6	+0.6	.22
	1982	+0.3	−1.7	−1.2	+3.2	+1.1	+1.2	.32
	1979	+0.1	−1.5	−1.4	+3.1	+0.6	+0.7	.31
Bengt Westerberg (fp)	1985	+1.9	+0.1	+0.9	+2.4	+3.5	+2.9	.25
Ola Ullsten (fp)	1982	−0.1	−1.9	−0.9	+1.2	+2.0	+0.2	.20
Ola Ullsten (fp)	1979	+1.2	−0.8	+0.4	+2.0	+3.1	+1.9	.23
Ulf Adelsohn (m)	1985	+0.3	−2.9	−1.7	+1.7	+1.8	+3.6	.47
Ulf Adelsohn (m)	1982	+0.6	−2.0	−1.2	+1.9	+2.0	+3.5	.43
Gösta Bohman (m)	1979	+0.5	−2.4	−1.8	+2.2	+2.3	+4.0	.48

Note: Each eta² value in the right-hand column is based on a one-way analysis of variance with voter group as the independent variable and rating of a party or party leader as the dependent variable. The symbols for the five parties follow the customary usage in Sweden: vpk = Communist, s = Social Democratic, c = Center, fp = Liberal, and m = Conservative. The leaders are given in the same order as the parties.

ratings. Considering the evidence from ratings of presidential candidates, people, of course, tend to rate their preferred candidate positively and their nonpreferred candidate negatively. But the preferred candidate is rated more positively than the nonpreferred candidate is rated negatively. When both voting groups show such an asymmetry, the result is an overall positive

Table 5.2 *Average overall ratings of the two parties, party groupings, and the presidential and vice-presidential nominees of those parties in the United States*

Average rating of	Overall	Democratic voters	Republican voters	eta²	Average rating of	Overall	Democratic voters	Republican voters	eta²
Democratic Party					*Republican Party*				
1984 Pre	+1.1	+2.6	0.0	.33	1984 Pre	+0.7	−0.9	+2.1	.35
1984 Post	+0.8	+2.5	−0.4	.34	1984 Post	+0.9	−0.9	+2.3	.39
1980 Pre	+1.0	+2.6	−0.2	.32	1980 Pre	+0.6	−0.4	+1.7	.22
Democrats					*Republicans*				
1980 Post	+1.3	+2.7	+0.4	.31	1980 Post	+0.8	+0.1	+1.7	.19
1976 Post	+1.2	+2.0	+0.4	.21	1976 Post	+0.7	+0.1	+1.4	.14
1972 Post	+1.6	+2.6	+1.0	.15	1972 Post	+1.2	+0.2	+1.9	.16
1968 Pre	+0.9	+2.2	+0.2	.22	1968 Pre	+0.8	+0.2	+1.8	.18
Democratic presidential candidate					*Republican presidential candidate*				
1984 Pre	+0.7	+2.6	−0.8	.48	1984 Pre	+1.0	−1.3	+3.1	.55
1984 Post	+0.2	+1.9	−1.0	.36	1984 Post	+1.5	−0.9	+3.4	.54
1980 Pre	+0.6	+2.6	−0.9	.38	1980 Pre	+0.5	−1.0	+2.2	.39
1980 Post	+0.5	+2.4	−1.1	.45	1980 Post	+0.9	−0.6	+2.6	.42
1976 Pre	+1.2	+2.7	−0.5	.41	1976 Pre	+1.0	0.0	+2.3	.28
1972 Pre	−0.1	+2.3	−1.6	.39	1972 Pre	+1.5	−0.6	+2.9	.39
1972 Post	−0.4	+2.3	−1.9	.46	1972 Post	+1.5	−1.0	+3.0	.49
1968 Post	+1.1	+3.5	−0.3	.53	1968 Post	+1.6	+0.5	+3.1	.34
Democratic vice-presidential candidate					*Republican vice-presidential candidate*				
1984 Pre	+0.7	+2.4	−0.5	.31	1984 Pre	+0.5	−0.7	+1.5	.27
1984 Post	+0.3	+2.0	−0.7	.27	1984 Post	+0.6	−1.1	+2.0	.35
1980 Pre	+0.4	+1.4	−0.4	.18	1980 Pre	+0.4	−0.1	+1.1	.10
1976 Pre	+0.3	+1.1	−0.6	.19	1976 Pre	+0.1	−0.7	+0.9	.16
1972 Pre	0.0	+1.6	−1.0	.24	1972 Pre	+0.4	−1.3	+1.5	.25
1972 Post	−0.3	+1.6	−1.3	.28	1972 Post	+0.5	−1.4	+1.6	.29
1968 Post	+1.1	+2.6	+0.4	.25	1968 Post	0.0	−0.7	+0.8	.13

Note: Each eta² is based on a one-way analysis of variance with voter group as the independent variable and rating of the party, party grouping, or nominee as the dependent variable. The nominees of the Democratic Party for President and Vice-President, respectively, were Walter Mondale and Geraldine Ferraro in 1984, Jimmy Carter and Walter Mondale in 1980 and 1976, George McGovern and Sargent Shriver in 1972, and Hubert Humphrey and Edmund Muskie in 1968. The nominees of the Republican Party for President and Vice-President, respectively, were Ronald Reagan and George Bush in 1984 and 1980, Gerald Ford and Robert Dole in 1976, and Richard Nixon and Spiro Agnew in 1968 and 1972.

rating for each candidate. Another consistency is that people voting for each candidate show significantly less variance in rating that candidate than do people voting against him. There are no exceptions to this at the presidential level.

The results for Sweden are quite similar. The two largest parties during these years, the Social Democrats and Conservatives, both show a tendency to rate their own party and its leader more positively than a tendency to rate the nonpreferred party and its leader negatively. Although the standard deviations are not shown, in each instance the Social Democrats showed much more variance than the Conservatives when the Conservative Party and its leader were being rated. Conversely, the Conservatives displayed more variance in their attitudes than the Social Democrats when the Social Democratic Party and its leader were being evaluated. Nilsson and Ekehammar (1985) obtained results similar to these and interpreted them by suggesting that attitudes toward a nonpreferred object are more complex than attitudes toward a preferred object. While we cannot advance or refute that particular interpretation, it certainly does appear that people rating a nonpreferred party, leader, or nominee show much more variability in their attitudes than when the same object is being rated by people who prefer it. This finding appears highly reliable and seems to work in basically the same way in Sweden and the United States.

Overall, tables 5.1 and 5.2 do contain evidence of positivity in evaluation of political figures in both countries. When we look at the averages for different voting groups, however, we see that people do make negative evaluations, but in the aggregate they tend to be outweighed because preferred parties are rated more positively than nonpreferred parties are rated negatively.

There is another generalization that can be extracted from these tables. As the eta^2 values in the right-hand column of table 5.1 show, voting groups in Sweden differ more in their attitudes toward the parties than they do in their attitudes toward the party leaders. This holds true in *all* of the 15 possible comparisons in table 5.1, the average eta^2 value being .48 for the parties and .34 for the leaders, so this undoubtedly represents a reliable result. The results for the U.S. in table 5.2, as would be expected from a knowledge of the two systems, are in the opposite direction. That is, the voting groups in the U.S. are more divided in their attitudes toward the presidential candidates (average eta^2 = .45) than they are in regard to the political parties (average eta^2 = .32). Here is an instance where a difference is observed at the attitudinal level between the two countries which corresponds closely to differences that are known to exist at the level of political system.[2]

Is there a person positivity bias?

In spite of evidence published by Sears (1983), which seems quite strong, we did not presume that we would necessarily observe a person positivity bias in either country but rather regarded it as an interesting possibility. First, our analyses of the U.S. data show, to our surprise, little evidence of person positivity. The person positivity hypothesis leads one to expect that the nominee of a party would be rated more favorably than the party. The detailed rationale for this thesis has been spelled out elsewhere (Sears, 1983), but the implication is rather clear that if this effect were to occur, Walter Mondale, for example, should be rated more favorably than "Democrats" as a group, which, in turn, should be rated more favorably than the Democratic Party. As noted earlier, the questions about attitudes toward the parties were not asked prior to 1980, so the number of tests is rather limited. As can be seen in table 5.2, Ronald Reagan was rated more favorably than the Republican Party in 1984, but not in 1980. Walter Mondale in 1984 and Jimmy Carter in 1980 were both rated less favorably than the Democratic Party. Moreover, in each of six comparisons, the party was rated more favorably than its vice-presidential nominee.

To look more closely at this, a person positivity index was devised for each individual respondent by adding together the respondent's attitudes toward the presidential and vice-presidential candidates and dividing by four, and subtracting from that the sum of the attitudes toward the two parties (or party groups, prior to 1980) divided by two. The average scores on the positivity indexes for the U.S. are shown in table 5.3. In 1968, people voting for Humphrey showed a slight person positivity tendency, and, in 1984, people voting for Reagan showed essentially no tendency in either direction on the postelection survey. In all the other instances, people overall and within each of the voting groups were more positive toward the parties than toward the individuals nominated by these parties. Thus, when we consider the U.S. electorate as a whole, Sears' person positivity hypothesis was not supported.

The data for Sweden were analyzed similarly. First, the average ratings of the parties and party leaders in table 5.1 can be reconsidered with Sears' person-positivity concept in mind. If we examine first the aggregate ratings by the sample as a whole (left-hand column in table 5.1), the results are mixed. Eight instances are observed (six of which involve the ideologically extreme parties, the Communist and Conservative parties) in which the leader is rated more positively or less negatively than the party, but there are also five instances in which the party is rated more favorably and two instances in which the two are rated essentially the same.

Altogether there are 15 cases in table 5.1 in which people are rating a

Table 5.3 *Average positivity and person positivity for evaluations of individual candidates, parties, and party groupings in the United States*

		A — Average attitude toward presidential and vice-presidential candidates			B — Average attitude toward political parties or political groupings			C — Person positivity tendency (A–B)		
		Overall	Democratic voters	Republican voters	Overall	Democratic voters	Republican voters	Overall	Democratic voters	Republican voters
1984	Pre	+0.7	+0.7	+0.8	+0.9	+0.9	+1.0	-0.2	-0.1	-0.2
1984	Post	+0.7	+0.5	+0.9	+0.8	+0.8	+1.0	-0.2	-0.3	0.0
1980		+0.5	+0.7	+0.4	+0.8	+1.1	+0.8	-0.4	-0.4	-0.3
1976		+0.6	+0.8	+0.5	+0.9	+1.1	+0.9	-0.3	-0.3	-0.4
1972		+0.3	+0.4	+0.3	+1.4	+1.4	+1.5	-1.1	-1.0	-1.1
1968		+1.0	+1.5	+1.0	+1.0	+1.3	+1.1	-0.3	+0.3	-0.3

Note: The stimuli for B (columns 4–6) were the Democratic and Republican Parties in 1980 and 1984 and Democrats and Republicans in 1968, 1972, and 1976. The derivation of the indexes reported here is explained in the text. The values for C are calculated at the individual level, and therefore, due to rounding, the difference between the corresponding averages under A and B does not always exactly match that reported under C.

Table 5.4 *Average positivity and person positivity tendencies for evaluations of party leaders and parties in Sweden*

		A Average of attitudes toward party leaders	B Average of attitudes toward parties	C A–B person positivity
All	1985	+0.8	+0.3	+0.4
	1982	+0.4	+0.0	+0.4
	1979	+0.5	+0.2	+0.4
Voter groups				
vpk	1985	+0.4	+0.1	+0.3
	1982	0.0	−0.3	+0.4
	1979	0.0	−0.1	+0.2
s	1985	+0.6	+0.2	+0.4
	1982	+0.2	−0.2	+0.4
	1979	+0.3	0.0	+0.3
c	1985	+1.1	+0.6	+0.4
	1982	+0.8	+0.3	+0.5
	1979	+0.9	+0.5	+0.4
fp	1985	+1.1	+0.5	+0.5
	1982	+0.7	+0.1	+0.6
	1979	+0.8	+0.4	+0.5
m	1985	+0.9	+0.3	+0.6
	1982	+0.4	0.0	+0.4
	1979	+0.7	+0.2	+0.5

Note: The derivation of the indexes reported here is explained in the text. The values for C are calculated at the individual level and, therefore, the difference between the corresponding averages under A and B does not always exactly match that reported under C.

preferred party and its leader. In 1979 and 1985, Communist voters rated Lars Werner, the Communist leader, more favorably than the Communist Party. In 1985, Liberal Party voters rated Bengt Westerberg more positively than they rated the Liberal Party, and, in 1979, Conservative voters rated Gösta Bohman higher than they rated the Conservative Party. However, in each of the other 11 cases, people rated their preferred party more favorably than its leader. So although there are exceptions, it would appear that in Sweden it is somewhat more likely that people rate their preferred party more favorably than they rate the leader of their preferred party.

There are also 60 possible comparisons in table 5.1 in which people are rating a nonpreferred party and its leader. In these comparisons, there does appear to be some evidence of a person positivity tendency. In 38 instances, the leader is rated more favorably than the party, while 19 instances are observed in which the party is rated more favorably than the leader, and in three cases the two receive essentially the same average rating. It is of interest to note here that in each instance involving ideologically extreme and opposing parties (Communist and Conservative), the leader is rated less negatively than the party.

We also analyzed the Swedish data by deriving a person positivity index for each respondent. This was done by adding together the attitudinal ratings for the leaders and dividing by five, and then subtracting the sum of the party attitudes divided by five. The results are shown in table 5.4. In each year, people in the Swedish surveys show a significant tendency toward person positivity by this measure.

Here, however, we must be sensitive to the political realities of Sweden. Respondents voting for a party in the bourgeois bloc are, in effect, asked to rate three parties and their leaders which are essentially on the "same side of the fence" as themselves, while those voting for a party in the socialist bloc are rating only two parties on their own side of the fence. Thus, it is of some importance to look at these indexes as they occur within each of the voting groups. That is also shown in table 5.4. While there is some variation in these indexes as a function of voting group, with the Communists being least positive and the Social Democrats next, nonetheless each voting group showed a tendency in each year toward person positivity. Thus far, it appears that the person positivity hypothesis is generally supported in Sweden but not the U.S.

Patterns of attitudes

Another mode of analysis was to consider the various combinations or patterns of attitudes people hold. In Sweden, with people rating five parties on an 11-point scale, there are 161,051 possible ways of answering the five questions, obviously an unmanageable number.[3] If we disregard for the moment the intensity of their attitudes and focus only on whether the attitude is negative, neutral, or positive, the number of attitudinal patterns is reduced to 243, a considerable reduction but still not a manageable number to consider. However, these 243 patterns can be reduced further down to 21 basic patterns provided we are willing to ignore which party was evaluated which way and consider only the overall pattern of attitudes, that is, focus on the form while temporarily disregarding the content. These 21 patterns, together with the percentage showing each pattern in ratings of the five parties and the five party leaders, are shown in table 5.5.

Several observations can be made regarding the results. The two most common patterns were to hold three positive and two negative attitudes or two positive and three negative attitudes. These two modal patterns are to be expected, given the tradition of bloc politics in Sweden. Yet it is also true that these two modal patterns account for only about a third of the cases. So

Table 5.5 *Patterns of attitudinal ratings toward five parties and five party leaders in Sweden in 1979, 1982 and 1985*

Number of ways the pattern can occur	Attitudinal pattern	Parties			Party leaders		
		1979 (%)	1982 (%)	1985 (%)	1979 (%)	1982 (%)	1985 (%)
1	+++++	2	2	3	7	7	8
5	++++0	2	2	2	4	5	6
5	++++−	8	6	9	12	9	14
10	+++00	3	2	3	3	4	4
20	+++0−	10	8	13	10	10	11
10	+++−−	24	19	23	21	16	21
10	++000	2	2	1	2	2	2
30	++00−	5	5	6	4	5	5
30	++0−−	11	13	14	10	11	9
10	++−−−	13	15	11	12	14	10
5	+0000	1	2	1	1	2	1
20	+000−	2	2	2	1	1	1
30	+00−−	4	4	3	3	2	2
20	+0−−−	4	7	4	3	4	2
5	+−−−−	6	7	3	4	5	2
1	00000	2	3	2	2	2	2
5	0000−	0	0	0	1	0	0
10	000−−	0	1	0	0	0	0
10	00−−−	0	0	0	0	0	0
5	0−−−−	0	0	0	0	1	0
1	−−−−−	1	0	0	0	0	0
243		100	100	100	100	100	100
	(N)	(2613)	(2649)	(2595)	(2607)	(2632)	(2590)

Note: This table is based on ratings on the 11-point like–dislike (*gillar–ogillar*) scale (−5 to +5) used to measure people's attitudes toward the five largest political parties in Sweden and their respective leaders. For the purpose of this table, only the direction of the attitude is considered (+, 0, or −) and not the intensity. Thus, for instance, the value of 10 in the fifth row and the left-hand column indicates that 10% of the people had positive attitudes toward three parties, were negative toward one party, and neutral toward one party. The zeroes in the bottom five rows do not mean that no one in the sample had this pattern. Rather, each zero is the result of rounding to the nearest whole percentage. Thus each zero was obtained when some, but less than 0.5% showed a particular attitudinal pattern.

that leaves about two-thirds showing the diverse patterns summarized in table 5.5.

It can also be seen that most of the Swedish respondents (97%) have a positive attitude toward at least one of the political parties. These data also show some signs of positivity. People were more likely (12 to 6%) to have positive attitudes toward four or five parties than they were to have negative attitudes toward four or five parties. An even stronger trend in this direction is observed in regard to attitudes toward leaders. About 24 percent of the Swedish respondents have favorable attitudes toward four or five of the leaders, while only about 4 percent hold negative attitudes toward four or five party leaders. Thus, there is evidence of person positivity in that people were about twice as likely to hold positive attitudes toward four or five of the leaders as they were to hold positive attitudes toward four or five of the parties.

With only two parties and candidates, the patterns of attitudes in the U.S. are somewhat simpler to analyze (cf. Weisberg and Grofman, 1981). Disregarding intensity, one can get nine different patterns of attitudes toward the two nominees and the two parties, as shown in table 5.6. The most remarkable result there is that regardless whether one considers the sample as a whole or only the people who voted for one of the two leading presidential candidates, the double positives (+ +) vastly outnumber the double negatives (− −). By this measure at least, the percentage of people in the U.S. who vote for a candidate they do *not* like because he is less disliked than the other must be very small, perhaps only about 2 percent. That the + + pattern is so much more common than the − − pattern can be taken as further evidence of a positivity trend in evaluative judgments. However, notice that this occurs both in regard to candidates *and* parties. In fact, the ratio of + + to − − is higher for the two parties (21.6 for all respondents and 40.6 for two-party voters, averaging across years) than it is for the candidates in the same years (10.6 for all respondents and 28.9 for the two-party voters). This is further evidence *against* the occurrence of a person positivity tendency within the U.S.

A roughly comparable analysis can be done for Sweden if we consider only the two largest parties in Sweden and the people who voted for one of them. These results, shown in table 5.7, indicate that in Sweden also, the number showing the + + attitude pattern greatly outnumber the − − pattern. This holds true both with regard to leaders and parties, and for both the sample as a whole and for the two-party voters. It can also be seen in that the + + pattern is about twice as likely to occur in regard to the leaders as it is to the parties, when one focuses on the two-party voters (25 and 12%, respectively, averaging across years). The results are in the same direction for all respondents, though not so pronounced. This is a further indication of person positivity occurring in evaluative judgments in Sweden.

To sum up, we have observed considerable evidence of positivity in evaluating political "actors" in both Sweden and the U.S. The main source of this positivity tendency is that people tend to rate a preferred alternative more positively than they rate a nonpreferred alternative negatively. This tendency toward positivity occurs both in regard to individual leaders and nominees and to political parties and groups. In fact, in the U.S., there appears to be somewhat more positivity toward the parties than toward the individuals nominated by these parties. On the other hand, in Sweden more

Table 5.6 Patterns of attitudes toward the political parties, party groupings, and presidential candidates in the United States

| Democratic Party/Democrats | + | + | + | 0 | 0 | 0 | - | - | - | | | |
Republican Party/Republicans	-	0	+	-	0	+	-	0	+	Total	Ratio ++/--	N
All												
1984 Pre[a]	16	9	32	0	13	7	2	0	21	100	19.8	2127
1984 Post[a]	21	12	24	2	9	9	3	2	18	100	8.4	1863
1980 Pre[a]	19	9	33	0	12	5	4	1	17	100	8.6	1509
1980 Post[b]	12	12	37	1	17	8	2	1	10	100	22.7	1341
1976 Post[b]	13	12	34	1	24	5	1	1	9	100	25.3	2246
1972 Post[b]	11	8	49	1	15	6	1	0	9	100	47.7	2058
1968 Pre[b]	8	12	36	1	20	10	2	1	10	100	18.9	1148
Two-party voters only												
1984 Pre[a]	22	7	32	0	8	9	2	0	20	100	19.1	1328
1984 Post[a]	20	9	23	2	6	12	2	1	25	100	13.5	1330
1980 Pre[a]	20	9	34	0	8	5	2	1	21	100	13.5	832
1980 Post[b]	12	12	40	0	13	9	1	1	12	100	56.2	849
1976 Post[b]	14	12	36	1	19	6	1	1	10	100	38.2	1577
1972 Post[b]	12	8	49	0	13	6	1	1	10	100	90.0	1458
1968 Pre[b]	8	11	40	0	15	11	1	2	12	100	54.0	673

Table 5.6 (cont.)

Democratic candidate Republican candidate		+/−	+/0	+/+	0/−	0/0	0/+	−/−	−/0	−/+	Total	Ratio ++/−−	N
All													
1984	Pre %	22	6	26	2	4	13	1	1	25	100	21.3	2171
1984	Post %	16	6	22	3	4	14	3	2	30	100	6.9	1896
1980	Pre %	21	11	29	1	2	4	6	2	24	100	5.0	1521
1980	Post %	18	10	27	1	4	7	4	3	26	100	6.0	1370
1976	Pre %	18	9	39	1	3	7	2	1	20	100	18.4	2727
1972	Pre %	14	5	24	2	4	12	3	2	34	100	7.6	2575
1972	Post %	15	4	20	2	3	11	4	2	39	100	5.0	2116
1968	Post %	11	11	40	1	3	10	3	2	19	100	14.6	1302
Two-party voters only													
1984	Pre %	24	4	25	1	2	12	1	1	30	100	42.4	1354
1984	Post %	18	6	22	2	2	14	2	1	33	100	10.7	1337
1980	Pre %	21	10	30	1	1	4	3	1	29	100	11.0	832
1980	Post %	17	9	28	1	2	7	2	2	32	100	12.8	862
1976	Pre %	18	9	39	1	2	6	1	1	23	100	37.1	1603
1972	Pre %	15	5	24	1	2	11	2	1	39	100	12.9	1547
1972	Post %	17	4	19	1	2	9	3	1	44	100	6.7	1491
1968	Post %	11	11	45	1	1	10	0	1	20	100	97.7	865

Sources: [a] Stimuli were the Democratic and Republican Parties.
[b] Stimuli were Democrats and Republicans.

Note: This table is based on ratings on the 0–100 affective feeling thermometer used to measure people's attitudes toward the political parties, political groupings, and individual candidates.

Table 5.7 Patterns of attitudes toward the two largest parties in Sweden and their leaders for the entire sample and for people who voted for one of these parties

Ratings of

Social Democratic Party Conservative Party	+ −	+ 0	+ +	0 −	0 0	0 +	− −	− 0	− +	Sum	N	Ratio ++/−−
Ratings made 1985	39	7	16	1	4	6	2	2	23	100	2612	7.4
by entire 1982	39	7	15	1	4	5	2	2	25	100	2663	5.8
sample 1979	40	6	12	2	4	6	3	2	25	100	2624	8.8
Ratings made 1985	51	7	13	1	2	4	0	0	22	100	1535	51.0
by s and m 1982	47	8	14	1	2	5	0	0	23	100	1682	34.3
voters only 1979	53	7	10	0	2	4	1	0	23	100	1571	10.8

Ratings of

Olof Palme Ulf Adelsohn/Gösta Bohman	+ −	+ 0	+ +	0 −	0 0	0 +	− −	− 0	− +	Sum	N	Ratio ++/−−
Ratings made 1985	31	5	25	2	3	6	4	1	23	100	2614	6.3
by entire 1982	27	8	27	1	3	6	3	2	23	100	2645	11.3
sample 1979	31	5	21	2	3	6	3	1	28	100	2623	6.3
Ratings made 1985	41	7	24	1	2	5	1	0	19	100	1529	21.6
by s and m 1982	34	9	28	1	3	4	1	0	20	100	1669	33.7
voters only 1979	42	7	22	1	2	4	1	0	21	100	1566	21.4

Note: For the purpose of this table, the −5 to +5 like–dislike scale has been collapsed to − (−1 to −5), 0 (0), and + (+1 to +5).

positivity was observed in relation to the individuals chosen to lead the parties than toward the parties. This person positivity tendency in Sweden occurred especially in ratings of the ideologically more extreme parties and also when people were rating a nonpreferred party. Thus, somewhat ironically given that the idea was developed by a U.S. social psychologist (David Sears) working with U.S. data, our analyses indicate support for the person positivity concept in Sweden but not in the United States.

How can we account for the facts that in Sweden, individual leaders are rated more favorably than parties, while in the U.S., parties are rated more favorably than nominees? Our explanation, which is sensitive to the realities of the two political systems, can be called the "principal actor" thesis. Being a parliamentary system with proportional representation, political parties are more salient in Sweden than in the U.S. In fact, one could say that over the years the political parties are the major or "principal actors" in the Swedish political system.[4] On the other hand, within the U.S., the nominees of the parties clearly play the dominant role, and could be labeled the "principal actors" in that political system.[5] This interpretation draws support from the finding in tables 5.1 and 5.2 that in Sweden, attitudes toward the parties differentiate the voter groups more than attitudes toward the party leaders, while in the U.S., attitudes toward the candidates differentiate the voter groups more successfully than do attitudes toward the parties. Thus, our view is that a positivity tendency will be extended especially to that political "actor" (party in the U.S., leader in Sweden) which is *not* the principal actor in that system.

Linkages between attitudes

Knowing the attitudes of people toward A, can we predict their attitudes toward B? This matter was considered in the previous chapter in regard to attitudes on contemporary social and political issues. Here we are concerned with the correlations between attitudes toward parties, leaders, and candidates. Our primary focus is on the part–whole problem of attitudes toward an individual leader or nominee and toward the party that person represents. It seemed reasonable to hypothesize that such correlations would be positive. However, given that Sweden has a stronger party system than the United States, it was expected that there would be a stronger link between party and party leader in Sweden than between party and party nominee in the U.S. The results, shown in tables 5.8 and 5.9, are in that direction, but the difference is not pronounced. The average correlation between attitudes toward a party and toward the leader of that party was .76 in Sweden. The comparable correlations in the U.S., available for 1984 and 1980 only, averaged .69 for attitudes toward a party and toward the presidential

Table 5.8 *Correlations between attitudes toward parties, party groups, and nominees in the United States when the stimuli are within the same party*

		Presidential candidate and party/party grouping		Vice-presidential candidate and party/ party group		Presidential and vice-presidential candidates	
		Democrat	Republican	Democrat	Republican	Democrat	Republican
1984	Pre[a]	.70	.74	.57	.62	.65	.68
1984	Post[a]	.67	.77	.56	.67	.68	.73
1980	Pre[a]	.65	.59	.50	.38	.52	.39
1980	Post[a]	.54	.62				
1976	Pre[c]					.54	.58
1976	Post[bc]	.48	.47	.40	.38		
1972	Pre					.64	.64
1972	Post[b]	.45	.60	.40	.51	.69	.70
1968	Pre[bc]						
1968	Post[c]	.49	.40	.32	.32	.59	.58
Average Correlation		.54	.57	.44	.45	.60	.58
Average N		1750	1766	1655	1676	1839	1872

Sources: [a] Stimuli were the Democratic and Republican Parties.
[b] Stimuli were Democrats and Republicans.
[c] The correlations for attitudes toward the candidate and party group involved one of the attitudes measured on the pre- and the other on the post-election survey.

Note: The correlations reported in this table are for all the people in the sample who answered the questions under consideration. That is, the correlations are not reported separately for the different voting groups. All the correlations in this table are positive and signficantly different from .00. The row giving the average correlation counts each year as a single case and splits the difference if two indicators are available for a given year.

nominee of that party, and .55 for the attitudes toward a party and toward the vice-presidential nominee of that party.

It can also be seen in table 5.9 that while the average party–leader correlation in Sweden was the same in each year (.76), within each year there was considerable variation by party. The party–leader correlation was especially strong for the two largest parties, averaging .82 for the Social Democrats and .81 for the Conservatives. This correlation was somewhat lower for the two centrist parties, averaging .74 for the Liberal Party and .75 for the Center Party. Finally, the relationship was weakest for the Communist Party and its leader, averaging .68 across years.

It also appears that in the United States, the correlation between attitudes toward a presidential nominee and his party tends to be stronger than that between attitudes toward a presidential nominee and supporters of his party. Table 5.8 shows that there is no more than a moderately strong correlation (averaging .61) between attitudes toward the presidential and vice-presidential nominees of the same party – in spite of the fact that one must vote for both or neither of them in the election. Notice that the weakest

Table 5.9 *Correlations between attitude toward a political party and attitude toward that party's leader in Sweden*

				Attitudes toward			
	Communist Party & Lars Werner	Social Democratic Party & Olof Palme	Center Party & Thorbjörn Fälldin	Liberal Party & Bengt Westerberg/ Ola Ullsten	Conservative Party and Ulf Adelsohn/ Gösta Bohman	Average correlation	Average N
1985	.67	.83	.71	.76	.83	.76	2597
1982	.68	.82	.77	.70	.79	.76	2647
1979	.69	.81	.76	.76	.80	.76	2607

Note: All the correlations in this table are positive and signficantly different from .00. Bohman was the leader for the Conservative Party in 1979 and Adelsohn in 1982 and 1985. Ullsten was the leader of the Liberal Party in 1979 and 1982 and Westerberg took over that position in 1985.

of the presidential–vice-presidential nominee correlations (.39) occurred in 1980 in relation to attitudes toward Ronald Reagan and George Bush, who had been opponents during the primary election campaign earlier that year. Four years later, after having served a full term in office together, that same relationship increased dramatically to a robust .73.

We also examined the correlations between attitudes toward the competing parties, leaders, and nominees. A simple conflict model would lead to the prediction that the more one likes X, the more one dislikes Y. Bloc politics in a multiparty system immediately complicates such an analysis. In fact, the correlations between attitudes toward parties and leaders in the same bloc were invariably positive, and those involving two parties or leaders in opposing blocs were invariably negative. The salience of the parties in Sweden was again evident in that in each of 30 comparisons, the party–party correlation is higher (average, disregarding the sign = .48) than the corresponding leader–leader correlation (average = .36). It is safe to conclude that within Sweden, attitudes toward the parties are linked more strongly than are attitudes toward the party leaders. The strongest correlation occurred in regard to attitudes toward the Conservative and Social Democratic parties (−.66).

Within the U.S., just the opposite was observed, as expected given the focus in the system on individual candidates for president. In every comparison, attitudes toward the opposing presidential nominees were linked more strongly than attitudes toward the opposing parties or party groups.[6]

Given the focus of the two systems, an appropriate comparison may be between the party–party correlations in Sweden (.48) and the presidential candidate–presidential candidate correlations in the U.S. (.33). So it appears that attitudes at this level may be more strongly linked in Sweden than in the U.S.

Attitude stability

Attitudes toward the parties and party leaders in Sweden are measured in panels with a three-year interval. It was expected that in Sweden, attitudes toward parties would be more stable than attitudes toward the party leaders. In each of eight possible comparisons in two panels (1979–1982 and 1982–1985), this expectation was sustained. The three-year auto-correlations for parties averaged .69, compared to .62 for the party leaders.

The U.S. panel correlations are more scattered and varied. Some involve only the time interval between the preelection and postelection interviews which can be estimated at about six weeks. Other correlations, using the 1972–1974–1976 panel cover a two- or four-year interval. Although the stimuli were varied, the autocorrelations for attitudes toward individual persons averaged .70 for the six-week interval, .56 for the two-year interval, and .53 for the four-year interval. The corresponding correlations for groups averaged .66 for the six-week interval involving parties, .50 for the two-year interval involving party groups, and .43 for the four-year interval involving party groups. Overall, we can tentatively conclude that within Sweden, attitudes toward the parties are more stable than attitudes toward the party leaders while in the U.S., attitudes toward the presidential nominees are more stable than attitudes toward the parties or party groups. Also, it appeared that attitudes toward parties and party leaders may be somewhat more stable in Sweden than are the corresponding attitudes in the U.S.

Attitudes toward the political actors

The evaluative judgments of the major political actors, the parties, leaders, and candidates, were predominantly favorable, on average, in both Sweden and the U.S. Most people find at least some of the parties and individual politicians attractive and appealing. Further evidence of a general positivity tendency was found when the double positives vastly outnumbered the double negatives.

Although we cannot rule out the possibility that these findings could be influenced by methodological factors, it is also quite plausible that the results say something about the way the two systems are operating. It is not difficult to imagine a political context in which such attitudinal judgments would be predominantly negative and in which the double negatives outnumber the double positives.

Similarly, in both Sweden and the U.S. much more variance in attitudes is evident when the party or individual being evaluated is not preferred than when it is a preferred party or candidate. This is because people's attitudes toward preferred political actors in Sweden and the U.S. are predominantly positive, while people's attitudes toward nonpreferred actors are a curious mixture of negative, neutral, and mildly positive attitudes. If one were to find some other system in which attitudes toward nonpreferred actors were predominantly negative, while attitudes toward preferred actors were a mixture of positive, neutral, and negative, then our finding with regard to variance in attitudes could be reversed.

We expected to find evidence of a person positivity bias in the U.S. but were less sure of what would be observed for Sweden. Instead, we found rather strong evidence of a person positivity tendency for Sweden, but in the U.S. individuals tended to rate the parties more favorably than the individual candidates nominated by these parties. This calls into serious question Sears' (1983) hypothesis about person positivity as a general human tendency. Therefore, we offered an alternative, the principal actor thesis, that is more compatible with our results. The principal actor hypothesis is that people will hold less positive attitudes toward the principal actor in a political system, whether it be individual candidates in the U.S. or political parties in Sweden.

Several of our findings reinforce our attempt to understand social psychological phenomena relative to the political context in which they occur. Within Sweden, the strength of the party system and the focus on parties are reflected at the social psychological level when attitudes toward parties are more stable, more highly correlated with each other, and more predictive of voting behavior than attitudes toward the leaders of these parties. This becomes more noteworthy in light of the demonstration that in the U.S. the differences were in the opposite direction. Finally, the fact that in the U.S. there is a looser coupling between candidates and parties has its correspondent finding at the social psychological level of analysis. We observed a somewhat weaker correlation between attitudes toward parties and candidates nominated by those parties in the U.S. than between attitudes toward parties and party leaders in Sweden.

6 Ideology and proximity voting

One of the more well-established principles in social psychology is that attraction varies as a direct function of similarity. This principle is thought to hold true when the object under consideration is either a person or a group. In practice, other considerations play a role in determining liking or disliking, but similarity is regarded as a rather fundamental factor.

Within social psychology, Donn Byrne (1971) has advanced this view through a variety of experimental studies. For instance, in one field experiment college students participated in a computer-aided dating event. Unbeknownst to the subjects, they were assigned randomly to be in an experimental condition in which their partner had been selected deliberately, based on earlier measures, to be at a certain level of similarity with regard to attitudes and beliefs. The dependent variable, measured by a number of indicators, was the level of attraction the dating partners felt toward each other following an initial date. In this study attraction varied as a direct function of manipulated similarity, i.e., similarity caused attraction (Byrne, Ervin, and Lamberth, 1970).

In another study, less realistic but more germane to politics, people were provided a description of a hypothetical politician whose alleged views were manipulated to be at different levels of similarity for different subjects. Again, the dependent variable of attraction varied directly as a function of manipulated similarity (Byrne, Bond, and Diamond, 1969). Both of these studies varied actual similarity through manipulation by the experimenter.

For several years, a rather lively dispute occurred over whether racial identity or attitude similarity was more significant in interpersonal judgments. Some social scientists (e.g., Harry Triandis) argued that race was so basic that social distance norms would often prevent people from associating closely enough to even know whether their values and attitudes were similar. Others, notably Milton Rokeach, argued that belief similarity was actually the more fundamental consideration, implying that people would prefer to associate with someone whose race was different but whose beliefs were similar over someone whose race was similar but who held different beliefs.

Some cross-national comparisons in this research tradition show that people in different countries accord different weight to different criteria when making social distance judgments. Thus, in one study it appeared that race was the most salient criterion in the United States, while religion was the most important in Greece, and occupation was the most important in Germany and Japan (Triandis and Triandis, 1965). For our purpose, it should be emphasized that in such studies, the potency of similarity is not being compared to that of other factors. Rather, what is being considered is the relative importance of different types of similarity (e.g., similarity in religion, socioeconomic status, ethnic origin, and beliefs). The underlying, though often unstated, assumption is that similarity of whatever kind will enhance attraction to another person or group.

Within political science, there is a close parallel in the tradition that has ꞈnphasized proximity and looked for evidence of proximity voting and developed models that pertain to it (e.g. Upton and Särlvik, 1981). This is closely linked to the rational democratic model. In it, citizens would be well informed about the policies advocated by different parties and candidates and would select the one that best represented their interests and goals. Knowing this, parties would formulate policies and strategies so as to maximize their support from the electorate (Downs, 1957).

Much of the research in this tradition utilizes some objective *or* subjective definition of proximity – but usually not both. For example, Rabinowitz, Prothro, and Jacoby (1982) used proximity measures based on the difference between a person's attitude and the position that same person attributed to a presidential nominee, "how close the respondent's stance is to the perceived stance of the candidate" (p. 46).[1] On the other hand, Luttbeg and Gant (1985) used, as a measure of spatial proximity, the absolute distance between the respondent's position on an issue scale and where the sample placed the candidate on that scale, on the average. They justified their usage of the mean to represent the candidate's true position by saying that this was done "to avoid the contaminating effects of such selective mechanisms as projection and persuasion" (p. 87).

Our analysis seeks to clarify the relationships among actual similarity, perceived similarity, and attraction. We presume that the relationship between actual similarity and perceived similarity is problematical and may be illuminating in that it may significantly modify the interpretation that is placed upon any relationship that might be observed between perceived similarity and attraction. The effect of actual similarity on attraction, both direct and as mediated through perceived similarity, may reflect the operation of a rational democratic process. That is, in the rational democratic model, perceived similarity should correspond to actual similarity since that is a question of accurate and undistorted perception. If that is true, then a relationship between perceived similarity and attraction can be interpreted as a rational proximity-oriented judgment.

From the view of social psychology, and more specifically the Lewinian tradition of field theory within social psychology, it is plausible to suppose that similarity, to produce its effect, would have to be perceived and experienced. That is, it would have to be within the individual's "life space." In social psychology, it is more or less axiomatic that what is real in people's minds is real in its consequences (Merton, 1948; Sherif and Sherif, 1969b; Thomas and Znaniecki, 1919). However, this classical axiom begs the question whether what is objectively real can also be consequential, even though it may not be real in people's minds.[2] The only way to answer this is to have measures of both objective and subjective reality within the same study.[3]

One can easily imagine a strong, weak, or even no relationship between actual and perceived similarity.[4] If actual similarity were unrelated, or only weakly related to perceived similarity and attraction, this would hardly fit our conception of a rational democratic situation. On the contrary, the rational democratic model requires that actual similarity be either directly linked with attraction or linked to attraction indirectly through perceived similarity.

Proximity voting

First, let us take a look at the overall relationship between ideological self-placement and voting behavior in Sweden and the U.S. This provides an initial impression of the degree of proximity-oriented behavior in these two countries. Once again, as in chapter 2, we use the left–right, liberal–conservative ideological dimension as a summary measure to which political issues (more or less) cling. Given the evidence in chapter 2, people in Sweden who place themselves to the right of center "ought" to vote, on proximity grounds, for one of the bourgeois parties, while people to the left of center ought to vote for the Communist or the Social Democratic Party.

It is evident in table 6.1 that these expectations are met in a very sizeable majority of cases. Proximity voting is also far from absent in the U.S. In each instance in table 6.1, a majority of people at every position to the left of center voted for the Democratic candidate, and a majority of people to the right of center voted for the Republican candidate. The size of this majority varied from 56 to 95 percent, depending to a considerable extent on the degree of departure from the center. This would be implied in a proximity model that takes into account the degree of proximity as a factor that increases the probability of voting a particular way. When the data for

Table 6.1 *Voting behavior as a function of self-placement on the 0–10 left–right scale in Sweden and on the 1–7 liberal–conservative scale in the United States*

	Percentage voting socialist bloc in Sweden										
	Left				Self-placement					Right	
	0	1	2	3	4	5	6	7	8	9	10	Eta
1985	98	99	98	97	94	54	18	4	2	7	7	.71
1982	100	99	99	98	92	53	15	5	3	7	1	.73
1979	98	99	98	97	83	44	9	5	3	2	6	.71

	Percentage voting Democratic in United States						
	Liberal			Self-placement		Conservative	
	1	2	3	4	5	6	7	Eta
1984	91	75	67	45	22	14	23	.46
1980	91	92	59	39	30	16	27	.45
1976	88	83	73	53	26	20	14	.45
1972	83	83	56	31	15	10	5	.49

Note: Each percentage in this table is the percentage of the people at a given ideological position who voted for a party in the socialist bloc (Sweden) or for the Democratic candidate for President (United States). Only those who voted for a party in the socialist or bourgeois bloc or for the Democratic or Republican candidate are included in these calculations. Thus, the percentage who voted for a party in the bourgeois bloc or for the Republican candidate would be a 100 minus the percentage given in this table. The eta values result from analyses in which bloc choice in Sweden or candidate choice in the U.S. is the independent variable and self-placement on the ideology scale is the dependent variable.

Sweden and the U.S. were averaged across years, the results for Sweden appear to be stronger and somewhat more nonlinear (see figure 6.1).

When it comes to supporting particular parties in Sweden, the proximity model becomes somewhat more exacting in its demands. For example, people at positions 0 or 1 on the 0–10 left–right scale ought to vote, on the sole grounds of proximity, for the Communist Party, but in each year a majority of them vote for the Social Democratic Party. Table 6.2 gives a percentage breakdown of the vote by party in Sweden for people at each of 11 ideological positions in three recent elections. People at positions 2, 3, and 4 ought to vote for the Social Democratic Party and a very substantial majority of them do. At the other end of the scale, people at positions 8, 9, and 10 ought to vote for the Conservative Party, and a majority in each case do so. People at positions 6 and 7 ought to vote for the Center or Liberal Party, and a majority of them did.

Figure 6.2 takes the Swedish bloc vote and breaks it down into four parties. Support for the Center Party peaks at ideology position 6 (just to the right of center), and decreases as one moves toward the extreme right position 10. The probability of voting for the Conservative Party increases

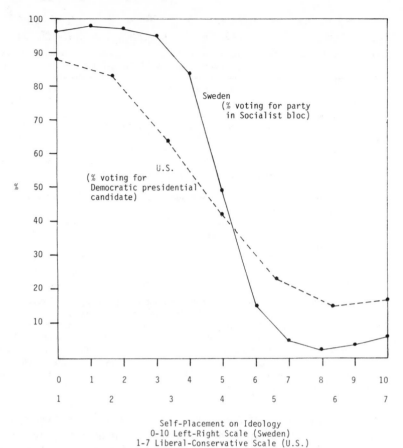

Self-Placement on Ideology
0-10 Left-Right Scale (Sweden)
1-7 Liberal-Conservative Scale (U.S.)

Figure 6.1. Percentage voting for a party in the socialist bloc in Sweden as a function of self-placement on the 0–10 left–right scale (average across four elections, 1976–1985), and percentage voting for the Democratic candidate in the United States as a function of self-placement on the 1–7 liberal–conservative scale (average across four elections, 1972–1984).

substantially as one moves from the center of the ideology scale toward position 10. At the other extreme, support for the Communist Party is strongest among those who place themselves at position 0 and decreases steadily as one moves toward the center of the scale. The likelihood of voting for the Social Democratic Party is highest among those who place them-selves at position 3 – exactly what would be expected in a simple proximity model given that the actual position of the Social Democratic Party is believed to be somewhere between 2.5 and 3.5. Moving in either direction from 3, the probability of voting for the Social Democratic Party decreases, although the drop is more precipitous as one moves toward the right.

Table 6.2 *Percentage voting for each of five parties in Sweden as a function of self-placement on the 0–10 left–right scale*

		Left				Self-placement						Right
		0	1	2	3	4	5	6	7	8	9	10
Party												
vpk	1985	22	18	21	9	10	3	0	0	0	0	0
	1982	27	24	15	8	5	3	1	0	0	0	0
	1979	32	24	17	12	3	1	0	1	0	0	0
s	1985	76	81	76	88	84	51	18	4	2	7	6
	1982	73	75	84	91	87	49	14	5	3	7	1
	1979	67	75	81	85	80	43	9	4	3	2	6
c	1985	0	0	1	2	3	16	23	18	13	5	12
	1982	0	0	1	1	4	27	37	26	18	22	10
	1979	1	1	1	1	7	30	38	19	20	19	11
fp	1985	0	1	2	1	2	23	39	36	21	15	9
	1982	0	0	0	0	2	11	18	15	3	2	2
	1979	0	0	1	1	7	17	26	20	14	7	2
m	1985	2	0	0	0	1	7	20	42	64	73	73
	1982	0	1	0	0	2	10	30	54	76	69	87
	1979	0	0	0	1	3	9	27	56	63	72	81

Note: The percentages in this table are column percentages giving the percentage of people at each of 11 positions who vote for the five largest political parties. Only those who voted for one of the five parties are included in these calculations.

So once again we see a picture of very considerable, though obviously not perfect or complete, proximity voting. An alternative approach is to take into account people's perceptions in calculating the degree of proximity voting. This would be a measure of subjective proximity. Do people vote for the party which seems closest to their own position? Table 6.3 gives the results of such an analysis of three recent Swedish elections. About 75 percent vote for a party which seems closest, or as close as any other party, to their own position. Over 90 percent vote for the bloc which has the party which seems closest to their own position. There also appears to have been a slight decrease in proximity voting in Sweden between 1979 and 1985 (Holmberg and Gilljam, 1987).

In the U.S. the comparable percentage supporting a candidate who was seen as closest, or as close as the other candidate, was 88 percent in 1976, 86 percent in 1980, and 86 percent in 1984. In interpreting these results, two things should be borne in mind. A much higher percentage of people in the U.S. did not place themselves on the ideology scale, as mentioned in chapter 2, and these people are not included in the measures of subjective proximity voting. Also, the chance level of subjective proximity voting would be about 20 percent in Sweden with five parties and 50 percent in the

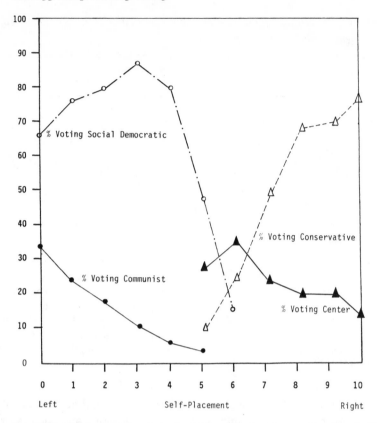

Figure 6.2. Percentage voting for each of four political parties as a function of self-placement on the 0–10 left–right scale (based on an average over four elections, 1976–1985).

U.S. with two candidates. Nonetheless, by this standard, we see that in each country, there is a relatively small minority who depart from the principle of subjective proximity in their vote.

Regardless of how the analysis is done, the most interesting and politically significant departure from simple proximity voting occurs among people who place themselves ideologically in the center. In the Swedish surveys this position is explicitly labeled "neither to the left nor the right." In the U.S. in 1984, the people who were at the center position 4 themselves should have voted by the criterion of objective proximity for Mondale, but a majority of them voted for Reagan, as shown in table 6.1. Estimates of Mondale's and Reagan's positions were given in chapter 2. Similarly, in 1980, the centrists (people who place themselves at position 4 on the 1–7 liberal–conservative scale) should have voted for Carter, but a majority of them voted for Reagan. In Sweden, the people who place themselves neither

Table 6.3 *Percentage of voters in Sweden who selected the party and bloc which was subjectively the closest to their own position on the 0–10 left–right scale*

		Percentage proximity voting on party			Percentage proximity voting on bloc		
		1979	1982	1985	1979	1982	1985
Party	vpk	81	76	74	99	100	98
	s	82	79	73	88	86	80
	c	77	79	75	98	99	98
	fp	83	81	78	99	98	97
	m	66	65	60	100	100	100
	Combined	78	76	71	94	92	90

Note: The analysis in this table is based on people who placed themselves and the five parties on the 0–10 left–right scale. The three left-hand columns give the percentage of people who placed their chosen party closer, or as close, to their own position than any other party. The three right-hand columns give the percentage of people who placed a party in the bloc they voted for closer, or as close, to their own position than any other party in the opposing bloc (cf. Holmberg & Gilljam, 1987, p. 301).

to the left nor the right (position 5 on the 0–10 left–right scale) ought to vote for the Center or the Liberal Party by the criterion of objective proximity. However, in the two more recent elections, a majority of these people actually voted for one of the socialist parties. We shall return in a later section to a further consideration of these centrists. For now, suffice it to say that there is considerable evidence of subjective and objective proximity voting in Sweden and the U.S. but also some rather interesting departures from it.

Measures of actual similarity, perceived similarity, and attraction

In our discussion of prior studies, we have already alluded to how perceived similarity and actual similarity are to be measured. The measure of perceived similarity is derived as the absolute difference between a person's own position on the ideology scale and placement by that same person of the party or candidate on the same scale. The result of that computation is then inverted (reverse-coded) to provide a measure of perceived similarity. Lacking a direct indicator of the party's or candidate's "real" position, we used the sample's average placement of the party or candidate under consideration and calculated the absolute difference between the sample average and a person's self-placement. This was also inverted to provide a measure of actual similarity.

Our measures of attraction are affective ratings of the five parties in Sweden on a −5 to +5 like–dislike scale and ratings of the candidates in the U.S. on a 0–100 degree affective feeling thermometer. As in the prior chapter, we converted the 0–100 U.S. scales directly to a −5 to +5 scale. The only consequence of doing this is that the unstandardized regression coefficients for the two countries are then based on scales that are similar. These measures of attraction are closely linked to actual voting with well over 90 percent in each country voting for the party or candidate liked best (i.e., rated most highly).[5] Not only are these measures of attraction virtually a surrogate for the vote, they also have certain advantages beyond their close operationalization of the theoretical construct of attraction. Because they provide for a range of possible responses, they measure not only the general direction but also the intensity of a person's feelings toward a party or candidate. The affective ratings also permit a separate analysis of attitudes toward each candiate or party whereas the vote by itself makes it difficult to separate attitudes toward the various alternatives. As shown in chapter 5, especially with regard to the United States, there is not necessarily a simple or strong relationship between these attitudes (e.g., the more people like one candidate, the more they dislike the other).

Table 6.4 presents the correlations among actual similarity, perceived similarity, and attraction for recent elections in Sweden and the U.S. In examining the results for Sweden, one is struck by the strength of these relations and the remarkable stability of the coefficients across years. Note also that in each year the three variables are somewhat more strongly related for the Communist, Social Democratic, and Conservative parties than for the Center and Liberal parties.

For the U.S., the correlations, while generally significant, are consistently weaker than those for Sweden. The average correlation between actual similarity and perceived similarity was .81 for Sweden and .60 for the United States. One can infer from this that political realities are more correctly apprehended in Sweden, which is consistent with the differences in the perceptual consensus coefficients reported in chapter 2. The correlation between actual similarity and attraction averaged .55 for Sweden but only .30 for the United States. Finally, the average correlation between perceived similarity and attraction was .62 in Sweden and .52 in the U.S. The latter relationship must be interpreted somewhat differently for Sweden and the U.S., given that actual similarity and perceived similarity are more closely linked in Sweden. We shall consider this more closely in regression analyses, but first let us pause and consider a measurement problem.

The "slender reed" problem

There are those who may question our reliance on the sample mean perception as an estimate of the candidate's or party's real position, which is

Table 6.4 *Correlations between perceived similarity, actual similarity, and attraction to five parties in Sweden and to the presidential candidates in the United States.*

Political party in Sweden being considered	Perceived similarity and actual similarity			Perceived similarity and attraction			Actual similarity and attraction		
	1979	1982	1985	1979	1982	1985	1979	1982	1985
Communist	.89	.90	.89	.67	.65	.67	.63	.61	.64
Social Democratic	.81	.83	.81	.70	.73	.71	.62	.65	.65
Center	.75	.75	.76	.52	.51	.44	.39	.40	.31
Liberal	.74	.73	.76	.51	.46	.52	.36	.33	.41
Conservative	.86	.87	.85	.74	.75	.75	.74	.76	.75
Average	.81	.82	.81	.63	.62	.62	.55	.55	.55

Presidential candidate in the United States being considered	Perceived similarity and actual similarity	Perceived similarity and attraction	Actual similarity and attraction
Walter Mondale (1984)	.55	.49	.30
Ronald Reagan (1984)	.53	.59	.34
Jimmy Carter (1980)	.47	.45	.11
Ronald Reagan (1980)	.66	.52	.37
Jimmy Carter (1976)	.61	.48	.28
Gerald Ford (1976)	.63	.49	.25
George McGovern (1972)	.72	.56	.41
Richard Nixon (1972)	.62	.56	.38
Average	.60	.52	.30

Note: Derivation of the three variables in this table, perceived similarity, actual similarity, and attraction, is described in the text.

then used, together with the person's self-placement, to derive the actual similarity variable. Is this not a rather "slender reed" on which to base one's analysis? Since the preceding section and those which follow hinge on this usage, it seems advisable to consider it with some scrutiny.

First, knowing what we know about politics in Sweden and the U.S., the mean placements have a certain face validity. For example, in the U.S., Reagan was perceived as being somewhat to the right of the other Republican candidates and George McGovern somewhat to the left of other Democratic candidates. Overall, the average placements in both countries seem to correspond to the prevailing understanding of the political situation in the two countries in several ways. This is not unimportant in our judgment. If the means are off, they are probably not off by much. Moreover, these estimates of the real positions of the parties and the candidates do not need to be precisely accurate. As we shall see in a moment, the results we report would not change much if these position indicators were changed somewhat in one direction or the other.

Secondly, the logic involved in using the mean placement judgment by the sample as an estimate of the party's or candidate's real position is quite similar to that used in deriving scale values for attitude measuring instruments. Thurstone (1928) advocated having "judges" sort attitude statements into 11 piles or categories based on the degree of favorability or unfavorability expressed in the statement. A measure of central tendency could then be used to derive the scale value for a given statement. When the same attitude statements were used in subsequent research, attitudes of respondents could be measured rather precisely using these empirically derived scale values. Although subsequent research and analyses questioned the veracity of Thurstone's assumption that the scale values thus derived would be independent of the attitudes of the "judges" (Granberg, 1982; Hovland and Sherif, 1952; Sherif and Hovland, 1961), it is nonetheless true that the scale values derived from judges with opposing attitudes are very similar and highly correlated (over .90). The point here is that our usage follows a customary logic used in psychometric studies – except perhaps the scale values should be derived from a different set of people than those included in the final analysis.[6]

Thirdly, there is ample precedent within political science for our use of the mean sample placement as an indicator of actual position. In addition to the usage of Luttbeg and Gant (1985), already described, a similar procedure has been utilized by Inglehart and Klingemann (1976, p. 256), Markus (1982, p. 558), and Sani and Sartori (1983). That these people have done so does not indicate that it is beyond reproach, but rather that our method has seemed reasonable to some respected political scientists.

There is also the practical consideration that often, for several U.S. presidential candidates, there is no better way that is readily available for estimating the true ideological position of the candidates.[7] However, for Sweden, we do have an alternative, and we turn now to a brief consideration of that evidence.

In the 1985 study of the Swedish Parliament, members were asked to place themselves and the five political parties on the same 0–10 left–right scale used in studies of the Swedish voters. If we were to choose our single most preferred indicator of the real position of each party's left–right position, it would be where members representing that party in the Parliament place themselves. These people after all have been selected and nominated by the party to be the representatives of the party, and therefore, where they place themselves should be a strong and rather direct indicator of the party's actual position. The results on that measure are shown for each party in figure 6.3, together with three other possible indicators of

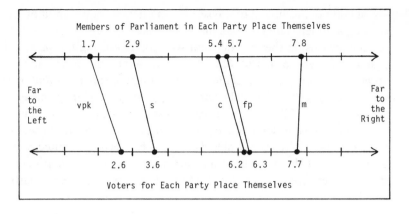

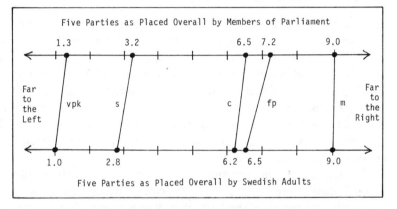

Figure 6.3. Four alternative ways of placing the five Swedish political parties on the left–right scale, based on studies of the Swedish electorate and Members of the Swedish Parliament in 1985.

each party's position. In four of five cases (the Conservative Party being the exception), members of a party in parliament place themselves somewhat to the left of where the people who voted for that party place themselves.

The lower portion of figure 6.3 shows how the overall placement of the parties by Members of Parliament compares with the overall placement of the parties by the representative sample of Swedish adults. These means are quite similar, varying by no more than 0.7 on a 0–10 scale. The parties are ordered in the same manner by both samples, albeit with somewhat different mean values. It is apparent that the results in figure 6.3 could only be obtained if there was general agreement as to where on the left–right dimension the various parties are positioned.

In any case, we are primarily interested in what the likely consequences are of operationalizing actual position, and hence actual similarity, in one way or another. The correlations for Sweden in 1985 in table 6.4 were recalculated using the four different ways of measuring the party's actual position shown in figure 6.3. Although some minor variations were observed, the average correlations between actual similarity and perceived similarity (range of .77 to .81), and between actual similarity and attraction (range of .48 to .57), are similar regardless of which of four ways is used to ascertain the real position of the party. Thus, it is our view that the results in table 6.4, especially the sizeable differences between the United States and Sweden for all three relationships, are valid and are not dependent on a suspect procedure for operationalizing the actual positions of the parties and candidates.

Modeling similarity and attraction

The next step was to analyze how attraction varies as a function of actual similarity and perceived similarity. The rational democratic model, shown at the top of figure 6.4, can be thought of as a contingently rational model. That is, the interpretation of a strong relationship between perceived similarity and attraction is contingent on the relationship between actual similarity and perceived similarity. The rational democratic model is contrasted to the more irrational assimilative model in figure 6.4. In the latter, perceived similarity is linked to attraction, but perceived similarity is not grounded in actual similarity.

The regression analyses show that in comparison to the results for the United States, results for Sweden indicate a strong link between actual similarity and perceived similarity as well as a stronger link between actual similarity and attraction. The link between perceived similarity and attraction is about the same in both countries when the effect of actual similarity is controlled. However, this link between perceived similarity and attraction must be interpreted differently for the two countries in relation to the contingently rational model. Inasmuch as perceived similarity is more closely tied to actual similarity in Sweden than in the United States, the link between perceived similarity and attraction in Sweden is more indicative of a rational democratic process than is the link between perceived similarity and attraction in the United States. Overall, the results for the United States more closely resemble the irrational assimilative model. The same conclusion is implied by a comparison of the effect (direct and indirect) of actual similarity on attraction, which can be estimated at .55 for Sweden and .32 for the United States.

Figure 6.4 is based on cross-sectional analyses with all three variables measured at the same time. From a methodological point of view, it would

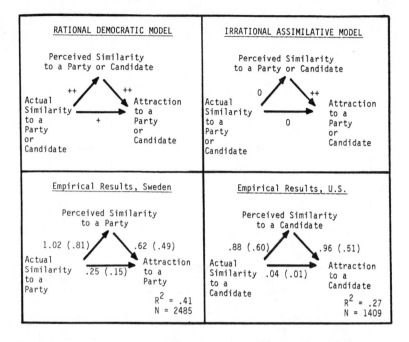

Figure 6.4. Modeling the relationships among actual similarity, perceived similarity, and attraction.
Note. The empirical analyses are based on the correlations in table 6.4. The coefficients for Sweden are based on an average on 15 regression analyses, done separately for each of five parties in three different elections. The results for the United States are based on an average of eight regression analyses, done separately for each of two candidates in four different elections. The coefficients given in the figure are unstandardized regression coefficients with the corresponding standardized coefficients given beside them in parentheses.

be preferable that the dependent variable (attraction) be measured with a time lag. This can be done for both the United States and Sweden with available panel data. The problem is that the time lag may not be the most appropriate, and it is not the same for the two countries. The Swedish panels analyzed in this respect involve perceived similarity and actual similarity assessed at one time (1979 or 1982) and attraction measured three years later (1982 or 1985). The U.S. data involve a shorter lag, within campaign lags (from pre- to postelection) for the two major candidates in 1980 and 1984 and from 1974 to 1976 for Gerald Ford. These results, though the comparisons are imprecise, are shown in figure 6.5. The relationships between similarity and attraction are, not surprisingly, weakened somewhat with the time lag. They nonetheless continue to appear significant, and the earlier observations, about the United States results bearing a closer resemblance to the irrational assimilative model with those for Sweden

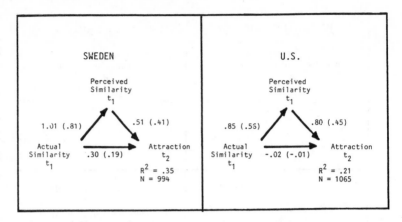

Figure 6.5. Modeling the relationship among actual similarity, perceived similarity, and attraction using panel data.
Note. The results shown here are based on an average of ten regression analyses of Swedish panel data in which perceived similarity and actual similarity to a party are measured at Time 1 (t_1) and attraction to the party is measured three years later (t_2). The results for the United States are based on an average of five regression analyses of panel data in which perceived similarity and actual similarity are measured at t_1 (1974, and prior to the 1980 and 1984 elections) and attraction to the candidates at t_2 (1976, and after the 1980 and 1984 elections). The coefficients in the figure are unstandardized regression coefficients with the corresponding standardized coefficients given beside them in parentheses.

more closely resembling the rational democratic model, appear to be sustained. In spite of the longer time lag for the Swedish panels, more variance in attraction is explained as a function of similarity for Sweden than is true for the United States (35 to 21%).

Another test considers the possibility that changes across time in attraction can be related to similarity. This entails including attraction at both times in the analysis. Thus, we are asking whether similarity measured at Time 1 can predict attraction at Time 2, even after we control for attraction at Time 1. Stated differently, can similarity predict future changes in attraction? The lower portion of figure 6.6 shows a fully specified model. It assumes that actual similarity can have a direct effect on attraction, even when the effect of perceived similarity on attraction is taken into account. The model in the upper portion of figure 6.6 is a more social psychological model in the sense that actual similarity is presumed to have only an indirect effect on attraction. Given that the two models explain about the same amount of variance, the simpler one (upper portion of figure 6.6) is to be preferred by the criterion of parsimony.

The results are compatible with the view that similarity has a substantial impact on attraction. Perceived similarity at Time 1 appears to have both a direct effect on attraction at Time 2 and an indirect effect on attraction at

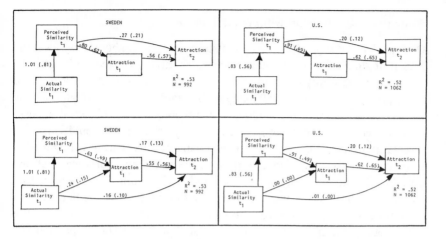

Figure 6.6. Modeling the effect of actual similarity, perceived similarity, and attraction at Time 1 (t_1) on attraction at Time 2 (t_2) using panel data.
Note. The results shown here are based on an average of ten regression analyses of Swedish panel data in which actual similarity and perceived similarity are measured at t_1 and attraction to a party at both t_1 and t_2. The results for the United States are based on an average of five regression analyses of panel data in which actual similarity and perceived similarity are measured at t_1 (1974, before the 1980 and 1984 elections), and attraction is measured at both t_1 and t_2 (1976, and after the 1980 and 1984 elections). The coefficients in the figure are unstandardized regression coefficients with the corresponding standardized coefficients given beside them in parentheses.

Time 2 through attraction at Time 1. The effect of actual similarity on attraction may be entirely indirect, but is, nonetheless, rather substantial, especially in the case of Sweden. The results indicate that the direct effects of actual similarity are negligible for the United States and marginal for Sweden. Thus, the direct effects of actual similarity on attraction can be removed from the model – in the interest of parsimony – without any substantial loss in explanatory power relative to the dependent variable, attraction.

In the models in figure 6.6, roughly the same amount of variance in attraction at Time 2 is explained in the Swedish and U.S. data. This is because attraction appears to be more stable in the United States than in Sweden, which, in turn, is almost surely because of the shorter time lag in the case of the U.S. panel data. We consider our parsimonious model to be a reasonably sound picture of how actual similarity and perceived similarity have an impact on attraction to a party or candidate – so long as one holds in mind the provision that the magnitude of the regression coefficients and the R-squared value will be affected by, among other things, the amount of time in the lag.

Similarity and attraction within voting groups

Our results in the previous section sustain at a reasonably strong level the idea that similarity and attraction are substantially related. This could be due to the anchoring effect of party preference. What happens if we hold party preference constant by looking within each group? Although this may be viewed as a more demanding test, theoretically it follows that even within a party or candidate preference group, attraction should vary as a direct function of similarity. Of course, when one looks within voting groups in Sweden or the U.S., one is restricting the range and variance of all the variables in the similarity–attraction model. Thus, one would expect that the relationships would weaken, but they still ought to be significant.

Figures 6.7 and 6.8 present some evidence in that regard for the 1984 U.S. election and the 1985 Swedish election. For the sake of comparison, the results are presented for the U.S. sample as a whole and then for Mondale and Reagan voters separately. The upper portion of figure 6.7 shows that attraction to Mondale and Reagan does vary significantly as a function of self-placement on ideology for the sample as a whole. Theoretically, one might expect that people at position 5 would feel the most attraction to Reagan since they may be in the closest objective proximity to Reagan. In fact, however, it was the people at position 7 (the extreme right position) who liked him the most.

When we look at how attraction to one's preferred candidate varies as a function of self-placement on the 1–7 ideology scale in the United States, the results, shown in the upper portion of figure 6.7, are rather strange. Walter Mondale was placed with almost equal frequency at positions 2, 3, and 4 with his average placement being at 3.4 (see chapter 2). Yet, among Mondale voters, it was those who placed themselves at position 6 (N = 29) who liked Mondale the most. We shall not belabor this point, but it appears that among Mondale voters, the relationship between self-placement on ideology and liking for Mondale is weak and irregular. Among Reagan voters who place themselves at positions 4 to 7 on the liberal–conservative position, attraction to Reagan increases as the degree of self-designated conservatism increases. But the Reagan voters who place themselves at positions 2 and 3 (to the liberal side of the center) do not like Reagan any less than Reagan supporters who are in the center. Thus, the relationship between self-placement on ideology and attraction to Reagan among Reagan voters is also slightly nonlinear.

The lower portion of figure 6.7 shows that when attraction to the U.S. candidates in 1984 is analyzed as a function of perceived similarity, rather than the respondent's self-placement on ideology, the observed relations become stronger and more linear. Here we observe attraction to a candidate

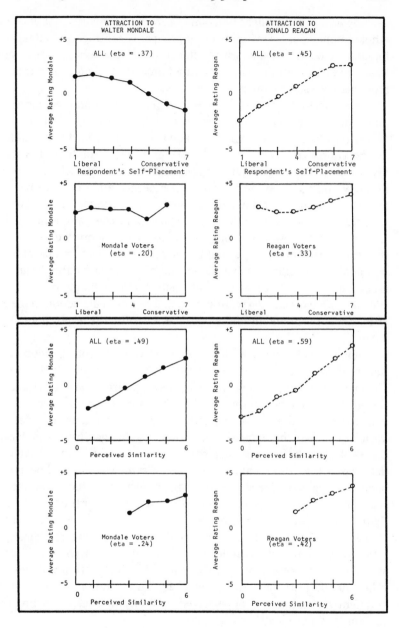

Figure 6.7. Average attraction to Walter Mondale and Ronald Reagan in 1984 as a function of self-placement on ideology and of perceived similarity among all respondents and people preferring that candidate.
Note. Only means with an N of 15 or more are shown.

varying as a positive linear function of perceived similarity not only for the whole sample, but also within voting groups. The attraction to Reagan as a function of perceived similarity to Reagan was somewhat stronger among Reagan voters than the corresponding function involving the attraction of Mondale voters to Mondale.

The results for Sweden in figure 6.8 are more robust and regular. Here we limit ourselves to a consideration of results from the 1985 election study and to results for Social Democratic and Conservative Party voters, the two largest voting groups in Sweden.[8] The upper portion of figure 6.8 shows a very strong and slightly nonlinear relation between self-placement on ideology and attraction to the Social Democratic and Conservative Parties for the 1985 sample as a whole. Hypothetically, attraction to the Conserva- tive Party should peak for those who place themselves at position 9 – since they are in the closest proximity to the party's position. Figure 6.8 shows that this expectation is borne out by the data. On the left, people at position 3 should hypothetically have shown the most liking for the Social Demo- cratic Party. In fact, it was those at position 1 who were most attracted to the Social Democratic Party. However, differences in attraction to the Social Democratic Party among those who place themselves at positions 0–4 are trivial.

Among Social Democratic and Conservative Party voting groups, attrac- tion to their preferred party also varies as a function of self-placement on ideology. The within-voting group relationships are somewhat weaker than those for the sample as a whole, but this was anticipated because of the constriction in the variation in both the independent and dependent variables. When the independent variable is changed from self-placement on ideology to perceived similarity, about the only change that can be detected is that the relationships become somewhat more linear for the sample as a whole. The similarity of the coefficients in the lower and upper portions of figure 6.8 stand in sharp contrast to those for the United States in figure 6.7. If one wanted to predict attraction to the Social Democratic or Conservative Party in Sweden, among all voters or among only those people who voted for the party under consideration, self-placement on ideology would do about as well as perceived similarity. For the United States on the other hand, attraction was shown to vary more strongly and more coherently as a function of perceived similarity than as a function of self- placement on ideology.

In summary then, we can say that we have observed that the relationship between perceived similarity and attraction can be observed within voting groups, as well as for the sample as a whole. The picture changed from blurry to quite clear when we shift from self-designated ideology to perceived similarity for the United States, while for Sweden this shift made

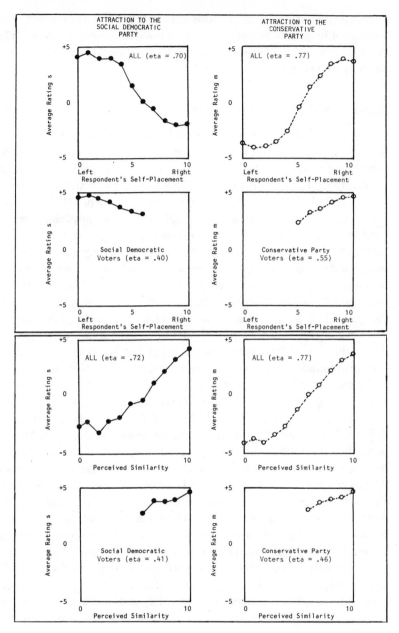

Figure 6.8. Average attraction to the Social Democratic and Conservative parties in Sweden as a function of self-placement on ideology and of perceived similarity among all respondents and among people preferring that party.
Note. Only means based on 15 or more people are shown.

very little difference. As in previous analyses, the results here indicate that within voting groups as well as for the sample as a whole, similarity is linked to attraction in both Sweden and the United States, but somewhat more strongly in Sweden.

Similarity and attraction across time

Throughout this chapter, we have made the somewhat simplistic assumption of a recursive relationship between similarity and attraction. To do so suited our purposes, even though we have never explicitly denied the possibility that attraction could also be a cause of similarity (Granberg and King, 1980). In fact, it is very difficult to sort out these possibilities even with the excellent sets of panel data available to us. One possibility sometimes used to try to sort out such matters is two-stage regression (e.g., Page and Jones, 1979). However, to use this method convincingly, one would have to have exogenous variables that predict attraction but are unrelated to similarity and/or other variables that predict similarity but are unrelated to attraction. We do not have such variables, nor can we readily imagine what they would be. Such a lack has not deterred other people from using two-stage regression, but perhaps it should have. One could, of course, ignore such requirements or act as if one had them, but that does not strike us as a very firm foundation on which to build knowledge or test ideas.

We could also have concentrated on doing cross-lagged analyses with the panel data. However, the earlier enthusiasm with which this method was greeted seems to have waned (Kahle and Berman, 1979; Kenny, 1975; Rogosa, 1980). Nonetheless, because of the possibility that some light could be shed on our problem and it may serve to help to complete the picture, we consider here briefly the results of some cross-lagged panel analyses. Altogether we did 13 cross-lagged panel analyses between perceived similarity and attraction, 10 for Sweden and 3 for the United States. For Sweden, the cross-lagged correlations from perceived similarity at Time 1 to attraction at Time 2 and from attraction at Time 1 to perceived similarity at Time 2 both averaged .57. These results offer no clue that the causal flow is predominantly in one direction or the other. The results for the United States were similar. The correlations from attraction at Time 1 to perceived similarity at Time 2 averaged .45, practically identical to the average of the correlations going from perceived similarity at Time 1 to attraction at Time 2 (.44).

The lagged regression analyses compare the effect of perceived similarity on attraction, controlling for the stability of attraction with the effect of attraction on perceived similarity, controlling for the stability of perceived similarity. If one uses the magnitude of the unstandardized regression

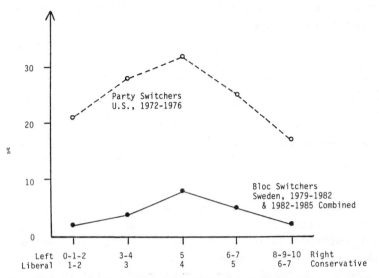

Figure 6.9. Percentage of party switchers in the United States (based on the 1972–1976 panel) and bloc switchers in Sweden (based on the 1979–1982 and 1982–1985 panel studies) as a function of the respondent's self-placement on ideology among people who voted in both elections.

coefficients as the criterion, then the effect of perceived similarity on attraction would appear to be the stronger, but not by a decisive margin. A plausible inference is that there is in fact a nonrecursive (bidirectional) relationship between perceived similarity and attraction. This does not invalidate the model in figure 6.6, since that model did not include perceived similarity or actual similarity at Time 2. It implies rather that a more complete model could include the effect of attraction at Time 1 on perceived similarity at Time 2.

A closer look at the centrists

One of the most interesting deviations from proximity voting involves the people who place themselves precisely in the middle of the left–right or liberal–conservative scale. Inasmuch as this is the modal position for self-placement in both countries, the actual number of these people in the electorate is rather substantial.[9] In Sweden in 1982, 27 percent placed themselves at position 4 on the 1–7 left–right scale, and in the United States in 1984, 34 percent placed themselves at position 4 on the 1–7 liberal–conservative scale (Granberg, 1987). It can also be shown that the behavior of these people can be quite pivotal in either electoral system. Figure 6.9 shows how across-election volatility varies as a function of where people

Table 6.5 *Distribution of self-placement on a 0–10 left–right scale among Social Democratic Party voters in Sweden*

	Left				Self-placement						Right		
	0	1	2	3	4	5	6	7	8	9	10	Total	N
1985 (%)	4	7	12	22	21	27	4	1	1	0	1	100	1011
1982 (%)	4	7	15	24	20	24	3	1	1	1	0	100	1072
1979 (%)	4	8	17	20	21	26	2	1	1	0	0	100	1048

Note: The percentages in this table are row percentages giving for each year the percentage of Social Democratic voters who place themselves at each of the 11 positions on the 0–10 left–right scale.

place themselves on the ideology scale. In both the United States and Sweden, people in the center of the ideological spectrum are more likely to switch from one bloc to the other, followed in turn by people near the center, with people near either extreme being less likely to switch. This greater bloc volatility of people at the center position means that they are the most significant people in attempts at political influence in a campaign.

It is also demonstrable that in both countries the votes of these centrists are crucial for electoral success. As shown in table 6.1, at least in the years for which we have appropriate data, no candidate has won the U.S. presidency without carrying a majority of the vote of the centrists who place themselves at position 4 on the 1–7 liberal–conservative scale – even though it would be possible to do so.

In Sweden, the situation is similar. Table 6.5 shows how voters for the largest party in Sweden, the Social Democratic Party, are distributed when they place themselves on the 0–10 left–right scale. Relatively few Social Democratic voters place themselves to the right of center. Those who do may misunderstand the dimension or have other reasons for voting as they do. But they are both small in number and are roughly balanced by the corresponding small percentage of people to the left of center who vote for one of the bourgeois parties. What is not small is the percentage of Social Democratic voters who place themselves in the middle at position 5, which is explicitly labeled "neither to the left nor the right." Over the past three elections, an average of about 26 percent of the Social Democratic voters place themselves in the middle position on the left–right scale. Given that these elections have been close, it can easily be argued that these people provide a winning margin for the Social Democrats (when they win) and comprise an essential element in the implicit strategy of the Social Democratic Party for electoral success. Given the distribution of self-designated ideology in Sweden, the vote of these centrists becomes crucial. If the Social Democrats do well among these centrists, they can be a governing party. If the Social Democratic Party does poorly among the centrists, it would be only a large party of the left.

Yet, as was pointed out earlier, if these people at the ideological midpoint were to vote solely on the grounds of objective proximity or actual similarity, they would vote for the Liberal or Center Party. Similarly, in the last two U.S. elections, the people in the middle of the ideological continuum should have voted for the Democratic candidate on the grounds of objective proximity or actual similarity, but a majority of them in both 1980 and 1984 voted for the Republican candidate, Reagan. Thus, the behavior of these people who place themselves in the middle of the ideological scale becomes of special interest and worthy of our analytical focus.

How can we account for the voting preferences of people in the center? In this regard, any factor which successfully differentiates the centrists who vote for the party or candidate of the left from centrists who vote for the party or candidate of the right can be helpful. It would be especially significant, however, if we could identify some factor which more significantly differentiates the vote of the centrists than it does the rest of the people. People who place themselves to the left or right of center are called *noncentrists* here. Since many of them lean only very slightly to the left or right, it would probably be a mistake to call them ideologues. What they have in common is that they have avoided putting themselves in the middle or center of the left–right scale, hence, the label noncentrist.

The first possibility considered here is that the centrists vote retrospectively. Since they are not motivated to vote on ideological grounds, they may be especially likely to be influenced by their assessment or judgment of how things have been going recently. More specifically, their vote might be especially likely to be prompted or affected by practical considerations (e.g., "the price of eggs") and their judgment about how the incumbent administration has been doing. If they have been doing poorly, the voters may decide to "throw the rascals out." If they appear to have been doing at least a satisfactory job of running the government, one might as well vote to let them keep their current positions (Fiorina, 1981; Key, 1966).

We have examined direct evidence pertaining to retrospective judgments and retrospective voting in both Sweden and the United States. It is apparent that the behavior of centrist voters in each recent U.S. election is prompted by retrospective judgments to a considerable degree. However, the retrospective voting coefficients are actually stronger for the noncentrists than for the centrists.

The results for Sweden are similar. In the 1985 survey, people were asked to make overall retrospective judgments, using an 11-point scale, of both the Social Democrats (who were in power in 1985 and had been since 1982) and the bourgeois parties (which had run the government during the years 1976–1982). Once again, there is evidence that the centrists vote retrospectively. However, the link between the vote and retrospective judgments was somewhat stronger for the noncentrists than for the centrists. The conclusion implied by these results is that part of the explanation for why people in the ideological center vote as they do is retrospective voting. There is evidence of retrospective voting among these centrists, but at the same time, retrospective judgments actually appear to be less potent among the centrists than among the noncentrists.

The second possibility examined is that perhaps there are certain specific issues which differentiate the vote of the centrists, even though they are homogeneous in placing themselves on the left–right scale. This possibility was considered by taking a series of specific attitude responses and seeing how well each could predict the vote of noncentrists and centrists. The corresponding correlations between issue–attitude and vote were almost invariably higher for the noncentrists than for the centrists in both Sweden and the United States. Overall, the results on issue voting corresponded closely to those for retrospective voting. That is, there is at least some mild evidence of issue voting among centrists in both Sweden and the United States, but it appears that there is less issue voting among the centrists than among the noncentrists.

Another possibility is that the voting decision of the nonideological voters is affected by abstract values not captured in the left–right dimension. In 1982 and 1985, Swedish respondents were asked to rate various future possible developments for their society (see chapter 4). These values were related in varying degrees to the vote of the centrists, but once again the corresponding correlations were substantially stronger among the noncentrists.

By now it may seem that whatever predicts the vote of noncentrists also predicts the vote of the centrists – only to a lesser degree. However, we shall now show that this is not always true. As implied at the beginning of this section, we feel we would be making considerable progress toward understanding the voting choices of the centrists if we could find some variable or set of variables which predicted the vote among the centrists more successfully than it did among the noncentrists. The final possibility considered here is that centrists who vote for the socialist bloc may really define the political context differently from the way it is implicitly defined by centrists who vote for the bourgeois bloc. Table 6.6 presents pertinent evidence on this, showing the average perception of the position of each of the five parties on the left–right scale, comparing socialist and bourgeois bloc voters, and making each comparison separately for noncentrists and centrists. In 11 of 15 comparisons the difference in perception between socialist and bourgeois bloc voters was stronger among the centrists than among

Table 6.6 *Average placement of the five parties in Sweden on the 0–10 left–right scale by centrist and noncentrist socialist and bourgeois bloc voters*

		Centrists			Noncentrists		
Party being placed		Socialist bloc voters average	Bourgeois bloc voters average	diff.	Socialist bloc voters average	Bourgeois bloc voters average	diff.
Communist	1985	1.5	0.9	+0.6	1.1	0.7	+0.4
	1982	1.4	0.6	+0.8	1.0	0.5	+0.5
	1979	1.4	0.9	+0.5	1.1	0.6	+0.5
Social	1985	3.8	2.6	+1.2	2.8	2.5	+0.3
Democratic	1982	3.9	2.5	+1.4	2.7	2.4	+0.3
	1979	4.0	2.7	+1.3	2.8	2.5	+0.3
Center	1985	6.0	5.6	+0.4	6.3	6.3	0.0
	1982	6.1	5.6	+0.5	6.5	6.5	0.0
	1979	6.3	5.5	+0.8	6.4	6.3	+0.1
Liberal	1985	6.3	5.7	+0.6	6.6	6.7	−0.1
	1982	6.1	5.4	+0.7	6.3	5.8	+0.5
	1979	6.0	5.5	+0.5	6.2	6.1	+0.1
Conservative	1985	8.8	8.6	+0.2	9.3	8.9	+0.4
	1982	8.8	8.7	+0.1	9.3	8.9	+0.4
	1979	8.7	8.3	+0.4	9.3	8.8	+0.5

Note: As defined in the text, centrists are people who placed themselves at position 5 on the 0–10 left–right scale. Noncentrists are people who placed themselves at some position other than 5 on the left–right scale.

noncentrists. Perceptions of the parties' positions on the left–right scale predict the bloc vote better among the centrists than among the noncentrists. This result is reinforced in regression analyses in which perceptions of the positions of the five parties on the left–right scale were the independent variables and bloc vote the dependent variable. This regression analysis was run separately for noncentrists and centrists in each of three years. Overall, the variance in the bloc vote that could be attributed to perception of the positions of the five parties was much higher for the centrists (average $R^2 = .24$) than for the noncentrists (average $R^2 = .11$). Thus, over twice as much variance in the bloc vote is explained by perception of the parties' positions on the left–right scale among the centrists, in comparison to the noncentrists.

Another fact is quite evident in table 6.6. That is the degree to which placement of the Social Democratic Party predicts the vote among the centrists ($r = .41$). This perception was by some margin the most significant factor in both the bivariate and regression analyses. Thus, at least for Sweden, we have isolated a factor which differentiates bloc voting more successfully among the centrists than among the noncentrists. If one is interested in predicting the vote of the people in the middle of the ideological dimension, it is helpful to know where they place the political parties on the left–right scale, and especially helpful to know how they perceive the position of the Social Democratic Party. In each year, centrists who vote for the socialist bloc perceive the Social Democratic Party as being considerably closer to the middle position than do the centrists who vote for a party in the bourgeois bloc. This certainly implies that how people see the political world may be important.

In the United States, the results tended to be in the same direction but were less pronounced. The largest differences occurred among the centrists in perceptions of the Democratic candidate in 1972 and the Democratic Party in 1980. Centrists who voted for the Democratic candidate tended, in those instances, to see George McGovern and the Democratic Party as much closer to the center than did centrists who voted for the Republican candidate. As in Sweden, a regression analysis was run separately in each year for centrists and noncentrists. Averaging across years, perception of the position of the parties and candidates explained slightly more of the vote among centrists (average $R^2 = .13$) than among noncentrists (average $R^2 = .09$). Even though the results were less definitive in the case of the United States, we can say with confidence that perception of the parties' and candidates' positions predicts the vote in the United States at least as well, if not better, among the centrists, in comparison to noncentrists.

In a sense, we have only scratched the surface when it comes to understanding and explaining the vote of the people who place themselves in the middle of the ideological dimension. One could, of course, ask the prior question of how they become centrists. It would also be desirable to differentiate between true centrists and those who put themselves there because they do not really know just where they belong on the left–right dimension. Many alternatives could be specified and tested besides those examined here. Nonetheless, we have considered some important possibilities: issue voting, retrospective voting, value differences, and differences in the way the political alternatives are perceived. Only the last of these possibilities led to results that are really interesting. It appeared that perceptions of the positions of the parties and candidates are more useful in predicting the vote of the centrists than in predicting the vote of the noncentrists. If people lack a clear ideology themselves, then perceptions may be especially important.

Proximity and attraction

We have sought to examine certain facets of the proximity factor in political psychology. We did this first by acknowledging and demonstrating a rather strong link between where people place themselves on the ideology dimension and how they vote. Although present in both countries, the tendency is more pronounced in Sweden than in the U.S. The factor of proximity was differentiated into a more objective dimension, called actual similarity, and a more subjective dimension, called perceived similarity. These dimensions have been used by prior researchers, but they have generally used one or the other. We used both, observing that they were more strongly related to each other and also to attraction in Sweden than in the U.S.

This led to our formulation of the contingently rational model of the relation between perceived similarity and attraction. That relation can be regarded as rational provided there is a substantial relationship between perceived and actual similarity. The results for Sweden more closely resembled the contingently rational model than did those for the U.S. Similarity and attraction were modeled across time for both the U.S. and Sweden. Actual similarity is more strongly linked to attraction in Sweden while for the United States, the more crucial link is between perceived similarity and attraction. Attraction was also shown to vary as a positive function of perceived similarity within candidate or party preference groups.

Finally, we examined the behavior of the people who place themselves in the middle of the ideological spectrum. Their behavior was rather distinctively linked to their perceptions of the positions of the political parties on the ideological dimension. In Sweden perceptions of the position of the Social Democratic Party were observed to be especially important when trying to predict the vote of the centrists who place themselves neither to the left nor the right on ideology.

7 The preference–expectation link and voting behavior

In a survey done by the League of Women Voters before the 1932 U.S. election, 93 percent of those preferring Franklin Roosevelt thought Roosevelt would win, whereas only 27 percent of those preferring Herbert Hoover thought Roosevelt would win (Hayes, 1936). This is a strong bivariate relationship ($r = +.63$), based on a very large sample ($N = 7,343$). However, the sample was not representative, and the study was done before polls were widely publicized and, of course, long before television provided a detailed account of the daily progress of a presidential campaign. Nonetheless, it serves as an initial indicator of a link between what people would like to occur in the future (preference) and what they think will occur in the future (expectation).

The classic study of the 1940 U.S. presidential election, *The people's choice*, found that in Erie County, Ohio, "there was a close relationship between vote intention and expectation of winner" (Lazarsfeld, Berelson, and Gaudet, 1944, p. 106). Here, by coincidence, the correlation was also $+.63$. Apparently, people are inclined to expect that their preferred candidate will win. Studies in the context of the 1976 and 1980 U.S. elections indicate that these early findings can be replicated in more recent years (Carroll, 1978; Brown, 1982).

Frenkel and Doob (1976) found that in Canada people tended to be optimistic about their preferred candidate's prospects, especially if asked immediately after they voted. In a study of citizens and politicians in Oregon, Lemert (1986) found evidence of wishful thinking in surveys done prior to referenda in 1982 and 1984. This "looking glass phenomenon," as Lemert called it, occurred among both groups, although it was somewhat stronger among citizens.

In spite of shortcomings, these varied studies point in the same general direction. It appears there is a significant and substantial relationship between preference and expectation. The question then becomes whether this is a causal relationship and, if so, of what form. There is no clearer statement of the problem of causal flow between preference and expectation than that of Lazarsfeld (1946). If preferences cause people to alter their expectations in an optimistic direction, this indicates *wishful thinking*. If expectations cause people to alter their preferences to coincide with their expectations, it is a *bandwagon effect*.

This problem can be pursued in several ways. Laboratory and field experiments have been conducted in which preference or expectation is manipulated to see if variations in the one can produce changes in the other. Manipulation of preference has been shown to affect expectation in a wishful thinking direction (Crandall, Solomon, and Kellaway, 1955; Irwin, 1953; Marks, 1951; Pruitt and Hoge, 1965). Almost any experiment, which demonstrates social influence as a consequence of informing subjects of the responses of others, could be regarded as an experimental analogue of a bandwagon effect (Asch, 1956; Hovland and Pritzker, 1957; Navazio, 1977). However, such experiments can only show how things *can* work in the real world (Henshel, 1980) – not how they *do* work. Although a laboratory experiment can add to the plausibility of an interpretation, the problem of the causal flow between preference and expectation will *not* be settled by a laboratory or field experiment.

To further elaborate our thinking, we shall now describe how we view the bandwagon and wishful thinking models. To help complete the picture and further guide our analysis, we reintroduce in this context as a third alternative, the rational democratic model.

Bandwagon model

The idea of a bandwagon effect came from efforts during the Great Depression to identify different forms of propaganda (Lee and Lee, 1939). The assumption seemed to be that if propaganda in its various forms were more thoroughly understood, and if this knowledge and understanding were widely disseminated, people would be less susceptible to being manipulated and mobilized even by skillful propagandists. In this context, a bandwagon effect was considered to be a form of social influence in which people rather mindlessly go along with the apparently prevalent view so as to avoid being different or isolated. Propaganda appeals designed to create a bandwagon effect concentrate on the message that many people in ever increasing numbers are doing a certain thing.

Subsequently, the idea was adapted in the early election studies to refer to the effect of expectation on preference, intention, and behavior (Berelson *et al.*, 1954; Lazarsfeld *et al.*, 1944). The spiral of silence is a recent theory, originating in Germany, about shifts in public opinion that can occur because of the need people have to avoid feeling isolated (Noelle-Neumann, 1974, 1984; Taylor, 1982).

In the bandwagon model, people are reliant or dependent on others for cues in the development of preferences and as guides to behavior. Humans are thus viewed as *heteronomous*, either incapable of making, or disinclined to make, rational decisions on their own. People perceive prevailing sentiments and trends and develop expectations as a consequence. Expectations then determine preferences because of a desire to avoid isolation and to be on the side of the majority or with a successful social movement. In this model, expectations play a dominant role, determining both preference and behavior.

This picture is obviously overdrawn and something of a caricature of what people are really like. Nonetheless, the question is whether this model successfully captures a significant human tendency and one for which there is no counterbalancing tendency (Ceci and Kain, 1982). If so, then expectations constitute a potential locus or entry point for people, such as politicians, who are interested in exerting social influence.

Wishful thinking model

In a pure wishful thinking model, preference exerts a dominant influence on various types of expectations. With regard to an election or referendum, people would expect a preferred outcome. Similarly, with regard to long-range determination, people would expect to see their policies enacted and followed as public policy. In this model, people are viewed as *autistic*, living in a dream world with their judgments and expectations *not* anchored or constrained by political reality.

The causal flow in the wishful thinking model can be understood in relation to theories of cognitive balance (Heider, 1958) or hedonic consistency (McGuire, 1981), in which people are motivated to alter their expectations to fit their desires. Such theories tend to view people more as rationalizers than as rational. Again, the picture drawn of what people are like is overstated. Empirically, the question becomes whether there is any correspondence between the model and reality, that is, whether there is a wishful thinking effect and how strong and ubiquitous it is.

Rational democratic model

Distinct from the bandwagon and wishful thinking models, we also specify a third alternative, the rational democratic model. In this model, preferences of citizens would determine their behavior in democratic processes. Voters would be well informed and not indulge in wishful thinking. People would be *autonomous* decision makers, although in arriving at their decisions they would take into account the views of other individuals and groups. As part of their being well informed, they would be aware of, and accurately perceive, the preferences of other people and the positions of reference groups, candidates, leaders, and parties.

Although these external factors would be considered, people would not be so gullible or suggestible as to sway whichever way the wind blows or to have their preferences and behavior be unduly influenced by their impression of the prevailing public sentiment. Thus, under the rational democratic model, even when there is sufficient variation in preferences and expectations, there would be no systematic relationship between preference and expectation. Regardless of the causal flow, a significant relationship between preference and expectation can indicate a departure from rationality. That is, neither wishful thinking nor a bandwagon effect is indicative of a rational process. In the rational democratic model, one would also not anticipate any direct effect of expectation on behavior. In a rational democratic situation, people's behavior would be guided by their values, preferences, and interests, and people would expect policy determination to be linked to the outcome of elections.

The three models that have been delineated here do not purport to closely simulate political reality. Rather, they should help to clarify the alternatives and guide the subsequent empirical analyses.

Preferences and expectations in United States elections, 1952–1984

Having stated various ways of modeling the relationships among preference, expectation, and behavior, we now begin an analysis of relevant data. We first consider evidence from the United States pertaining to the general question of whether preference and expectation are related and, if so, to what degree.

For each of nine U.S. presidential elections, the national election study, undertaken by the University of Michigan, included in the preelection survey the following questions about expectation and preference: (a) Who do you think will be elected President in November? and (b) How do you think you will vote for President in this election?

Table 7.1 shows that, as in the studies referred to previously, there was a significant relationship between preference and expectation. In each year, the relationship was in the same direction and was significant. By a ratio of 4:1, with relatively little overall variation across years, people tended to expect that their preferred candidate would win. In these studies, the bivariate correlation between preference and expectation varied only from a low of $+.42$ (1972 and 1984) to a high of $+.68$ (1980).

In table 7.1, Republicans appear to be slightly more optimistic than Democrats, but in all likelihood this is because the Republican candidate

Table 7.1 *Relation between preference and expectation in nine United States presidential elections, 1952–1984*

Year	Percentage who prefer and expect same candidate to win	Percentage of respondents intending to vote Democratic who expect Democrat to win	Percentage of respondents intending to vote Republican who expect Republican to win	Pearson correlation between preference and expectation	Preference and expectation correlation adjusted for unequal marginals	Percentage who do not know on expectation	Percentage of respondents voting for candidate expected to win	Pearson correlation between expectation and vote
1984	71	28.8	99.0	.42	.73	7	68	.34
1980	84	87.0	80.4	.68	.68	13	76	.53
1976	82	84.2	80.6	.65	.65	15	77	.53
1972	77	24.7	99.6	.42	.79	10	71	.29
1968	81	62.5	95.4	.63	.71	16	74	.50
1964	81	98.6	30.5	.45	.69	10	74	.32
1960	81	78.4	84.2	.63	.63	22	77	.54
1956	80	54.6	97.6	.60	.73	12	75	.47
1952	84	81.4	85.9	.67	.67	16	79	.57
Average	80	66.7	83.7	.57	.70	14	75	.45

Note: Column 1 gives the extent to which preference and expectation are the same for those who prefer and expect one of the two leading candidates to win. Columns 2 and 3 break this data down according to candidate preference. Columns 4 and 5 are indications of the strength of the preference–expectation relationship and give a simple and adjusted correlation. Column 6 gives the percentage who said "don't know" based on the number of "don't know" responses over the number of "don't knows" plus the number who predicted that one of the two major candidates would win. Column 7 gives the percentage of people who later voted for the candidate they had expected to win, and Column 8 expresses this bivariate relationship as a correlation coefficient.

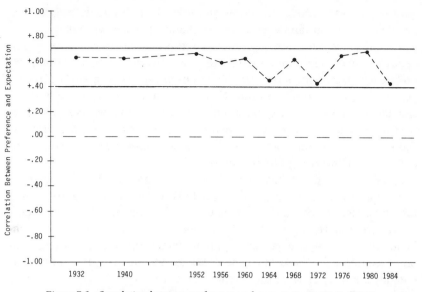

Figure 7.1. Correlation between preference and expectation in United States presidential elections, 1932–1984.

won six of the nine elections from 1952 to 1984: Figure 7.1 shows the relatively small band of variation in this relationship across the U.S. elections for which we have comparable coefficients.

If a bandwagon effect occurred, how could it be detected? First, among those with a preference and an expectation in the preelection survey, voting behavior should be affected by expectation when initial preference is controlled. Secondly, among those who lack a preference but have an expectation, voting behavior should be predictable from expectation. Thirdly, if both preference and expectation are measured at two (or more) points in time prior to the election, expectation at Time 1 should have an effect on preference at Time 2 when the stability of preference is controlled. The first two of these possibilities can be tested in each of the nine Michigan election studies.

The two right-hand columns in table 7.1 show that about three-quarters of the people in the nine surveys voted for the candidate they had previously indicated as their expected winner. The average correlation was $+.45$ between preelection expectation and voting behavior asked on the postelection survey. Thus, there is a rather consistent tendency for people to vote for their expected winner. This could, however, be an entirely spurious correlation. We must be alert to the danger of a *post hoc, ergo propter hoc* (after this, therefore because of this) fallacy.

Thus, for each of these nine U.S. elections, we did a regression analysis with self-reported vote as the dependent variable and candidate preference, party identification, and expectation as the independent variables. In each year, party identification continued to exert a direct effect on voting behavior when expectation and preference were controlled. Candidate preference exerted the strongest effect in each regression analysis. In each year except 1960, however, the effect of expectation on the vote was not significant when party identification and candidate preference were controlled. Similarly, the effect of expectation on the vote was also not significant when only preelection candidate preference was controlled, again with 1960 being the exception.

Thus, in this form of analysis, only in 1960 did a significant bandwagon effect appear. Specifically, it seems to have occurred among those who initially preferred Nixon. People who preferred Nixon but expected Kennedy to win were more likely to vote for Kennedy (21%) than were those who preferred Nixon and expected Nixon to win (5%). Among people who preferred Kennedy, those who expected Nixon to win were about as likely to vote for Kennedy as were those who expected Kennedy to win.

The results for 1960 should not obscure the fact that in the other eight elections a bandwagon effect did *not* occur. The results for 1980 are especially interesting in this regard. The strongest evidence for a bandwagon effect at the aggregate level would be if the preelection polls typically underestimated the margin of victory (Hennessy, 1975, pp. 118–119). In general, they do not, but in 1980 they did. Therefore, the 1980 results deserve an additional look. Our regression analysis for 1980 revealed no bandwagon effect. Of those preferring Reagan, 98 percent of those expecting Reagan to win subsequently voted for Reagan compared to 95 percent of those who expected Carter to win. Among those preferring Carter, 88 percent of those expecting Carter to win voted for Carter compared to 91 percent of those expecting Reagan to win. Neither of these differences was significant, i.e., no bandwagon effect.[1]

The second way of examining for a bandwagon effect is to identify people who have an expectation but lack a preference on the preelection survey.[2] Among those who said "don't know" on preference but who had an expectation, expectation did *not* predict behavior in a strong or reliable manner. In nine analyses, only in 1976 was expectation a significant predictor of behavior among the people who lacked a preference. In 1976, among those without a preference, 73 percent of those expecting Carter to win subsequently voted for Carter, whereas 43 percent of those without a preference but who expected Ford to win later voted for Carter (r = +.30, N = 148).

Thus, in 18 tests with the U.S. data, we observed only two minor instances of a possible bandwagon effect – among people who intended to

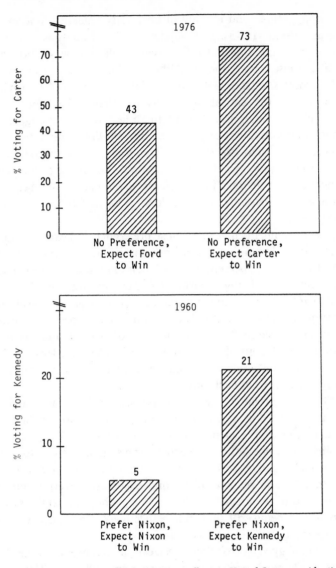

Figure 7.2. Two apparent bandwagon effects in United States presidential elections, 1960 and 1976.

vote for Nixon in 1960 and among those who lacked a preference in 1976. These two instances, in which it is plausible to infer that a bandwagon effect occurred, are shown in figure 7.2. Perhaps it is not the case that a bandwagon effect never occurs. But to find one, it takes some looking.

We have analyzed two panels in which preference and expectation are both measured in two preelection waves, the 1940 election study by

Lazarsfeld *et al.* (1944) and a study of university students done in 1980 (Granberg and Brent, 1983). In Lazarsfeld's (1946) analysis, it appeared that both wishful thinking and a bandwagon effect were occurring. We wish to add these observations. Although Lazarsfeld started with a reasonable sample size (N = 193), most of these people (149) provide no information about the causal flow, because they either change both preference and expectation from Time 1 to Time 2, or they change neither, which leaves an informative sample size of only 44. Preference among those 44 was more stable than expectation. Twenty percent of the respondents changed their expectation from Time 1 to Time 2 compared to 9 percent of the respondents who changed their preference. Similarly, Campbell (1963) reported the autocorrelations to be .82 and .60 for preference and expectation, respectively.

Among the respondents in 1940 whose preference and expectation were initially different and who changed one but not the other (thereby becoming consistent at Time 2), 70 percent changed their expectation to be consistent with their preference. Using a form of regression suggested by George Bohrnstedt (1969) for use with panel data, the effect of preference at Time 1 on expectation at Time 2, controlling for stability of expectation, was .27 (beta). The comparable coefficient for the effect of expectation at Time 1 on preference at Time 2, controlling for stability of preference, was .16. These regression coefficients are both significantly different from .00 but not significantly different from each other.

In addition to the relatively small sample size of the 1940 panel, each variable was measured as a dichotomy, thus providing no possibility for a minor shift in the degree of preference or expectation. Thus, the 1980 student panel data were gathered to expand the sample size and to increase the number of alternatives to seven in both the preference and expectation measures. In this data set, preference and expectation were significantly related in an optimistic direction at both Time 1 and Time 2, the synchronous correlations being .59 and .52, respectively. Preference was more stable than expectation, the autocorrelations being .87 and .56, respectively. The cross-lagged correlations between preference at Time 1 and expectation at Time 2 (.50) and between expectation at Time 1 and preference at Time 2 (.48) were not significantly different.[3]

In this study, the effect of expectation at Time 1 on preference at Time 2, controlling for the stability of preference, was not significantly different from .00. This does not support the presence of a bandwagon effect. The effect of preference at Time 1 on expectation at Time 2 (beta = .26), controlling for stability of expectation, was significantly different from both .00 and the other regression coefficient. Of the people who were inconsistent at Time 1 and who changed either preference or expectation, thus becoming consistent, 87 percent changed their expectation to coincide with their preference.

Overall, then, the panel data in which preference and expectation are measured in two preelection waves are not inconsistent with our other analyses. A bandwagon effect may occur, but it is generally weak, and it is hard to find truly compelling evidence that it has occurred. Preferences are consistently more stable than expectations, and people appear more likely to alter their expectations so as to coincide more closely with their preferences than the reverse.

If it is easy to observe a strong and reliable relationship between preference and expectation but difficult to find solid evidence of a bandwagon effect, does this imply by default that the bulk of the preference–expectation relationship is due to wishful thinking? Perhaps, but we should also be able to observe the effect of some intervening variables that would be consistent with that view. We might expect, for instance, that in some elections the anticipated outcome would be so unambiguous that wishful thinking would be minimal.

When a person states an expectation, this can be viewed as an observed behavior to be explained in terms of the individual's frame of reference. This frame of reference consists of internal and external factors operating at a given time, and it is from central psychological structuring that behavior follows. When the external stimulus situation is unstructured (ambiguous), internal factors such as needs or preferences increase in importance in the determination of behavior (Sherif and Sherif, 1969b). It follows that preferences can influence expectations to the extent that the actual outcome is in doubt.

For the nine elections, the percentage in each sample coded as "don't know" on the expectation question could be taken as an indication of the ambiguity of the outcome for that election. The noticeably low "don't know" percentages for 1964, 1972, and 1984 in table 7.1 correspond with the common knowledge that the outcome of the elections in those years was largely a foregone conclusion. If we consider 1964, 1972, and 1984 as low-ambiguity elections and the remaining six as high-ambiguity elections, it is clear that the tendency to predict a preferred outcome is stronger in the high-ambiguity years.

Another way of viewing this relationship is to recognize that the bivariate correlations in table 7.1 are affected by differences in the marginals. People preferring Barry Goldwater in 1964, George McGovern in 1972, and Walter Mondale in 1984 were not as likely to think their preferred candidate would win – a reality constraint, as it were. The correlations for the nine years become more nearly equal when we corrected for the effect of the marginals while preserving the relation between the rows and the columns (e.g.,

Deming, 1943; Mosteller, 1968; Myles, 1979). This implies that if the elections of 1964, 1972, and 1984 had been anticipated to be as close as those of other years, the relationship between preference and expectation would have been at least as strong as in those other years. Although these analyses provide support for the importance of *ambiguity*, they do not provide a basis for anticipating the *direction* of the effect (Sherif, Sherif, and Nebergall, 1965). That is, a minimal level of ambiguity may be necessary for wishful thinking to occur and a lack of ambiguity may diminish the effect, but the ambiguity factor does not tell us *why* people predict a preferred outcome. It may be that there is a human tendency toward wishful thinking and that this tendency is more likely to be manifest in some situations than in others.

When asked to prophesy an electoral outcome, respondents are, in a sense, attributing predispositions to the electorate as a whole. In doing so, most people may not realize *adequately* the extent to which their own "sample" is biased (Ross, 1977). People are not asked to state the basis of their expectation, but it is reasonable to suppose it is affected by reports in the mass media and personal contacts. Most people fail to recognize their own *ethnocentrism* and the extent to which their perceptions and judgments are influenced by the sociocultural web in which they are immersed (Segall, Campbell, and Herskovits, 1966; Sherif and Sherif, 1964).[4]

Kenneth Boulding (1970) suggested that one of the objectives for education should be "to develop a lively appreciation of the nature and necessity of sampling and a distrust of purely personal experiences ... One of the greatest ... problems arises from the tendency to generalize from [one's] own personal experience to ... society as a whole" (p. 44). If education makes one more aware of the selectivity in interaction patterns and the inadequacy of one's unrepresentative sample, then one might expect the tendency toward wishful thinking to be diminished as education increases. Across years, the preference–expectation link averaged .63 for those with less than a high school education, .59 for high school graduates, .50 for those with some college, and .46 for college graduates. In each of the nine elections, people with the least education showed a stronger tendency toward wishful thinking than people with the most education. The moderating effect of education could be due to a generally higher level of political information held by people with more education.

If the preference–expectation link is due to wishful thinking and is a form of motivated cognitive distortion, it should become evident when we compare people who are at different levels of involvement in politics. Already Lazarsfeld *et al.* (1944) reported that people with the highest level of interest yielded a correlation of .68 between preference and expectation compared to "only" .59 for those at lower levels of interest. In our analyses

Table 7.2 *Correlation between preference and expectation as a function of information and involvement*

Degree of involvement	Low	Low	High	High
Degree of political information	Low	High	Low	High
Year				
1984	.38	.37	.50	.36
1980	.62	.67	.73	.70
1976	.48	.40	.58	.55
1972	.38	.34	.45	.40
1968	.74	.40	.78	.61
Average r	.52	.44	.61	.52
Average N	104	122	153	422

Note: The coefficients in this table are correlations between preference and expectation. The categories of people were formed by selecting people using two criteria simultaneously: level of involvement as indicated by how much people said they cared or were concerned about the outcome of the election, and how informed people were about politics, based on the interviewer's ratings.

of nine elections the preference–expectation correlation averaged .61 for the very interested, .59 for those somewhat interested, and a still strong .54 for those with not much interest. The surprise here is the pervasiveness of the wishful thinking effect, which extends even to subsamples with low levels of political involvement.

As another indicator of involvement, strong partisans might be especially motivated to engage in wishful thinking. Across nine elections, strong partisans (average r = .60) evidenced a slightly stronger relationship between preference and expectation then did weak partisans (.52) or independents (.55). Although this difference is in the anticipated direction, once again the ubiquity of the relationship is actually more impressive.[5]

Thus, we have not found that the preference–expectation link is greatly weakened by a low level of political involvement. Another possibility is that involvement and information work in opposing directions and overall tend to offset each other. If so, people who are highly involved but poorly informed would show the strongest tendency toward wishful thinking.

To examine this possibility, we grouped people according to involvement and information. For involvement, we used the question about concern about the outcome. For information, we used the interviewer's ratings (on a 5-point scale) about how well informed the respondent seemed to be about political matters. We omitted those who scored a 3 on the scale and grouped the others as either well or poorly informed. Table 7.2 gives the preference–expectation correlation for each of four involvement-informed categories for each of five elections.

Although the link is again pervasive, in *each* year people who were *highly involved but poorly informed* showed the strongest tendency toward wishful thinking. Thus, people are motivated toward wishful thinking, but this is subject to a reality constraint that acts as a counterforce. The highly involved but poorly informed people are the ones who simultaneously have the strongest motivation and the weakest counterforce to wishful thinking, and so the tendency toward wishful thinking is strongest among them.

As indicated before, wishful thinking can be interpreted by reference to the human tendency toward cognitive or hedonic balance (Heider, 1958; McGuire, 1980). People who attribute their own preference to the majority of the people can be regarded as in a state of balance. However, this would only be true for people who hold a favorable attitude toward the electorate.

The national election studies do not contain a measure of people's attitudes toward the electorate as a whole, and it may not be unreasonable to assume that these attitudes are generally favorable. The 1980 student panel, however, included an item measuring attitudes toward the "U.S. electorate (U.S. voters)". People who rated the electorate favorably did show a stronger tendency toward wishful thinking ($r = +.65$ between preference and expectation) than did those who held a more unfavorable attitude toward the electorate ($r = +.42$). This difference is clearly supportive of a hedonic balance interpretation of wishful thinking, but the pervasiveness of the link remains somewhat puzzling. That is, why should preference and expectation be positively correlated, albeit at a lower level, among people with unfavorable attitudes toward the U.S. electorate?

The view that wishful thinking is a form of motivated cognitive distortion also implies that the strength of the preference–expectation relationship should vary directly with the strength of one's candidate preference. Combining across years, the preference–expectation correlation averaged $+.68$ for those with highly favorable attitudes toward their preferred candidate, $+.56$ for those rating their preferred candidate very favorably, $+.48$ for those with only mildly positive attitudes toward their preferred candidate, and $+.43$ for those with relatively unfavorable attitudes toward their preferred candidate. The ordering of these groups is consistent with the view that wishful thinking is a form of motivated cognitive distortion.

Finally, we compared the strength of the preference–expectation relationship at the state and national levels. In five of the U.S. election studies, people were asked which candidate was going to carry their own state – as well as which candidate was going to win the election at the national level. Across these five elections, the preference–expectation relationship averaged $+.42$ at the state level but a stronger $+.57$ at the national level. Perhaps voters are more informed about their own state than about the nation as a whole, and it could be that decreased ambiguity at the state level weakens the tendency toward wishful thinking. Another possibility, however, is that people may be more motivated to engage in wishful thinking at the level that really matters, i.e., the national level.

When preference and expectation are consistently related at a relatively strong level, when there are at least a few instances in which a bandwagon effect may have occurred, and when wishful thinking is shown to be a form of motivated cognitive distortion all comprise evidence against the applicability of the rational–democratic model in the U.S. context. At the same time, it was shown that higher education reduces wishful thinking and unambiguous elections impose a reality constraint limiting the autistic tendency toward wishful thinking.

The 1980 U.S. national election study contained an item that asked people's impression of poll results. In a rational democratic model, knowledge of poll results could be processed along with other information in deriving one's expectation of the electoral outcome. Second, people might derive their expectation about the national outcome from how things seem to be going in their state. People may tend to assume that "as my state goes, so goes the nation." For people living in a large state or a bellwether state, and given the decrease across years in interstate variance in voting, such an information-processing inference is not unreasonable.

In 1980, there was a significant, though not especially strong, relationship between perception of recent poll results and expectations ($r = +.34$). Of those who thought Reagan was ahead in the polls, 60 percent thought Reagan would win, compared to 24 percent of those who thought Carter was ahead in the polls.[6] However, when we did a regression analysis with perception of poll results, expectation at the state level, and candidate preference as independent variables, and expectation at the national level as the dependent variable, candidate preference clearly exerted the strongest effect. All three variables were significant, and combined to explain about 36 percent of the variance in expectation at the national level. Thus, in this analysis, expectations were based more on wishful thinking than on the relatively more rational sources.

Prophecy bends in Sweden

We now shift our attention back across the Atlantic and consider evidence from Sweden pertaining to the linkages among preference, expectation, and behavior. Thus far, this chapter has dealt only with U.S. data, but we are no less interested in making cross-national comparisons on this topic. As will become evident, the Swedish data are less extensive on this topic but also unique in certain important respects.

The analyses presented thus far rather firmly established certain generalizations. At least within the United States, preference and expectation are strongly related in an optimistic direction, wishful thinking is motivated cognitive distortion but can be constrained by an unambiguous context, preferences are more stable than expectations, and bandwagon effects are rare and difficult to demonstrate. There is the possibility that these U.S. findings, while containing a certain intrinsic interest, could be limited to that context and thus lacking in generalizability. The U.S. is thought to exemplify the philosophical tradition called "pragmatic optimism" (Biddle, 1979). In an optimistic achievement-oriented culture, it is understandable that people would tend to expect preferred outcomes. Insofar as the findings can be generalized to a context as different from the United States as Sweden, they would take on an increased interest and importance.

The Swedish data in which preference and expectation are measured are from studies done in connection with the parliamentary elections of 1968 and 1982 and the nuclear power referendum of 1980. Rather than take these studies up in chronological order, we consider them in order of the quality of the data for present purposes. That is, these three studies differ substantially in the potential they contain for analysis on this topic, and the bulk of our analyses focuses on the nuclear power referendum study. First, however, let us consider evidence from two parliamentary elections.

Preference and expectation in 1982 and 1968

A small mailed survey was done in the city of Göteborg, Sweden shortly before the parliamentary election of 1982 (Granberg, 1983). Included in this preelection survey were questions measuring party preference and expectation regarding the outcome of the election. Expectations were measured with four possibilities, ranging from the "Social Democrats get a majority of the vote and form the government" to alternatives in which the bourgeois parties get a majority of the vote and form the government. The two dimensions of preference and expectation were *not* independent in this context. If we collapse the parties into the two blocs and the possible electoral outcomes to two, all (N = 79) of the Social Democrats and Communists (socialist bloc) in this survey expected a socialist government after the election, compared to 65 percent of those preferring one of the three bourgeois parties (N = 71). This difference converts into a correlation of +.49, comfortably within the normal range for the U.S. (+.40 to +.70, figure 7.1). Thus, it appears that people in Sweden tend to expect a preferred outcome perhaps roughly to the same degree as in the U.S.

While people in Sweden tended to expect a preferred outcome, this tendency was obviously constrained by external reality, more specifically by published polls and newspaper accounts. While supporters of the bourgeois parties were much more likely than socialist party supporters to expect a bourgeois victory, it was also true that a majority of the bourgeois supporters expected a socialist victory. They were, in a sense, in a comparable position to supporters of Mondale, McGovern, and Goldwater in the United States in 1984, 1972, and 1964, respectively.

A more specific finding involves a comparison of the two socialist parties, the Communists and Social Democrats. Although both groups had the realistic expectation of a government dominated by the Social Democrats, the specific form varied in an interesting way. The Communists were much more likely to expect the Social Democrats to form a minority government than were the Social Democrats (81 to 35%).[7] Elsewhere in the same survey, people were asked to predict the percentage of the vote that would be obtained by each party, as well as the percentage which they would prefer to be obtained by each party.[8] Analyses of these data also supported the hypothesis that people would tend to "predict" a preferred outcome.

Our second source of Swedish data is the National Election Study undertaken in connection with the parliamentary election of 1968. In addition to the usual questions measuring party preference and voting intention, people in the preelection interview were asked this question measuring expectation: "We currently have a Social Democratic government. How likely does it seem to you that there will be a change in government after the election this year?" People were given four alternative answers to use: very likely, quite likely, not especially likely, or not at all likely. Since this study was national in scope, had a larger sample, and was a panel in which the same people were asked after the election how they had voted, it contains the potential for clarifying matters further.

The 1968 election victory by the socialists was anticipated in the preelection polls. A poll done in August, the month prior to the election, found support for the two socialist parties to be at about 51.5 percent, compared to 46.5 percent for the three bourgeois parties combined (Holmberg and Petersson, 1980). Nonetheless, there was at least some, and probably sufficient, ambiguity in the anticipated outcome. This is reflected in the overall results on the expectation question in table 7.3. Only 7 percent thought it was very likely that there would be a change in the government, i.e., a bourgeois government, as a consequence of the upcoming election, but 27 percent thought it was quite likely. On the other hand, 48 percent regarded it as not especially likely, and 18 percent chose the "not at all likely" alternative.

Results show once again a significant relationship or linkage between preference and expectation. Overall, the Social Democrats were least likely to expect a change in government, while the Conservatives were most likely.

Table 7.3 *Relationship between voting intention and expectation regarding the outcome of the 1968 Swedish election (upper portion) and between expectation and the vote (lower portion)*

| | | Preelection expectation | | | | | |
| | | "We currently have a Social Democratic government. How likely does it seem to you that there will be a change in government after the election this year?" | | | | | |
		Not at all likely	Not especially likely	Quite likely	Very likely	Total	N
	Communist	20	40	27	13	100	15
Pre-election	Social Democrat	28	55	14	3	100	619
voting	Center	9	45	37	9	100	166
intention	Liberal	5	43	40	12	100	167
	Conservative	3	30	49	18	100	118
	Overall	18	48	27	7	100	1313
	Communist	2	1	2	1		
Post-election	Social Democrat	83	61	33	27		
self-reported	Center	9	16	26	23		
vote	Liberal	5	14	20	26		
	Conservative	1	8	19	23		
	Total	100	100	100	100		

Note: The upper portion shows preelection expectation as a function of voting intention in row percentages. The lower portion shows voting behavior as a function of expectation in column percentages. The sixth row, giving the overall percentages on the expectation question, is based on an N (1313) which exceeds the sum of the Ns for rows 1–5 because some people gave an answer to the expectation question but did not intend to vote for one of the five parties shown here.

In fact, two thirds of the Conservative Party supporters stated they thought it was either very likely or quite likely that there would be a change in government, compared to only 17 percent of the Social Democrats.

If we dichotomize both variables, the correlation between bloc preference and expectation is +.37. This reflects a 36 percent difference as 82 percent of the socialist party supporters had a socialist expectation (that a change in government was either not at all likely or not especially likely), compared to 46 percent of the bourgeois party supporters. The strength of this tendency to expect a preferred outcome also varied with the degree of one's partisanship: +.48 among strong partisans, compared to +.28 for weak partisans, +.29 for people who only lean toward a party, and +.21 for those who intend to vote for one of the parties but do not identify with or lean toward a party. Thus, the tendency to expect a preferred outcome is once more replicated in Sweden, this time on a national representative sample.

However, the strength of the relationship appears slightly weaker than that in the U.S. surveys.

The lower portion of table 7.3 shows a relationship between expectation measured on the preelection survey and how people report having voted on the postelection survey. There a rather substantial tendency can be observed for people's vote to vary as a function of their expectation. Among those with the strongest bourgeois expectation, only 27 percent voted Social Democratic, while among those with the strongest socialist expectation, fully 83 percent voted for the Social Democratic slate. If we collapse these variables, 68 percent of those with socialist expectations voted for one of the socialist parties, compared to 34 percent of those with bourgeois expectations. This 34 percent difference converts to a correlation of +.33. This is in the same direction but again slightly lower than the average expectation–vote correlation for the U.S. surveys (+.45).

The results are by themselves compatible with a hypothesized bandwagon effect. They are, however, by no means sufficient to declare with confidence that a bandwagon effect occurred. As was indicated in the analyses of U.S. data, it is entirely possible that the expectation–behavior link observed here is altogether spurious. Stronger evidence would be required before we could be confident that a bandwagon effect had occurred.

First, rather compelling evidence of a bandwagon effect would be obtained if expectations were observed to be significantly related to behavior after one controls for initial preference. Initially, we focused on the people who intended to vote for the Social Democratic Party, because this is the largest homogeneous group (N = 590) in regard to intention. Among these Social Democratic intenders, voting behavior was unrelated to prior expectations concerning the outcome of the election. The same conclusion was drawn for those who expressed a preference for one of the three bourgeois parties.

For example, 91 percent of the Conservative Party intenders with bourgeois expectations (N = 74) subsequently voted for the Conservative Party, but an even larger percentage (94%, N = 36) of the Conservative intenders with socialist expectations voted for the Conservative Party. Similar results were obtained in analysis of expectation, intention, and behavior at the bloc level. Movement across bloc lines from intention to behavior was *not* moderated by expectations.

Second, people who lacked an intention when interviewed in the pre-election survey, but who had an expectation at that time and who subsequently voted for one of the parties were selected for a separate analysis. Given that they lack a preference, they could be especially susceptible to a bandwagon effect should there be one. When we consider these people, then, is their vote predictable on the basis of their expectation?

The answer for the 1968 Swedish data, as for eight of the nine U.S. elections considered, was no, not to a significant degree. When we single out the people (N = 173) who lacked an intention and dichotomize both their expectations and their votes, the latter two variables were not significantly correlated. Overall, a majority (59%) of those without a preference ended up voting for one of the bourgeois parties in 1968, but the magnitude of this tendency was not significantly affected by expectations concerning the outcome of the election.

The 1968 and 1982 parliamentary election studies indicate that a reliable relationship can be observed in Sweden between preference and expectation. This relationship may be slightly weaker than in the United States, and close analyses did not reveal support for the bandwagon hypothesis.[9] In interpreting this relationship, therefore, we would reassert a major alternative, wishful thinking. The evidence from the two Swedish studies considered thus far is compatible with the idea that people consciously, subconsciously, or unconsciously form and alter their expectations to correspond more closely with their preferences than could reasonably be anticipated to occur by chance.

Sweden's nuclear power referendum of 1980

Our third set of Swedish data is a panel study done in connection with Sweden's national referendum on nuclear power in 1980. The preelection interview in March 1980 contained two questions that measure expectations. The first (E_1) asked people to estimate the percentage of the vote that would be obtained by the antinuclear alternative, Line 3. The second (E_2) asked people how many nuclear plants they thought would be operating in Sweden in 25 years. The alternatives provided on this question and the period of time used correspond to the discussion during the campaign preceding the referendum. Advocates of Line 3 said no new nuclear plants should be brought into operation and the six then in use should be phased out of operation within, at most, ten years. Advocates of Lines 1 and 2, on the other hand, supported doubling the number of nuclear power plants in operation from the current six to 12. They did not favor building more than a total of 12, and when considering how long these nuclear plants should be kept in operation, the discussion centered on a period of about 25 years. However, supporters of Lines 1 and 2 did not commit themselves to an exact date or interval by which time using nuclear power to generate electricity in Sweden would definitely be a thing of the past (cf. Holmberg and Asp, 1984).

Thus, in this survey, we have both a measure of short-term expectations regarding the outcome of the referendum and a measure of long-range

Table 7.4 *Relationship between line preference in Sweden's nuclear power referendum and two measures of expectation (column percentages)*

		Line preference			
		Line 1 (%)	Line 2 (%)	Line 3 (%)	Overall (%)
Estimate of vote expected to be obtained by Line 3	50% or more	6	9	31	17
	43–49%	10	12	21	15
	36–42%	40	32	35	35
	31–35%	21	21	6	15
	30% or less	23	26	7	18
	Total	100	100	100	100
Number of nuclear power plants expected to be in use in Sweden in 25 years	More than 12	32	15	14	18
	12	35	35	19	29
	7–11	19	22	12	18
	1–6	10	17	26	19
	None	4	11	29	16
	Total	100	100	100	100

Note: The right-hand columns give the univariate distribution of responses to the expectation questions, excluding people who said "don't know," or who gave some other uncodable answer. The Ns for these right-hand columns are 1218 and 1332 for the upper and lower portions, respectively.

expectations concerning the outcome of policy determination. This unique combination of questions regarding expectations, together with measures of preferences and behavior, permit some further exploration of our three models.

First, let us take a look at the results of the referendum study to see whether there is a relationship between preference and expectations in this context. Using voting intention as the measure of preference, the results are in the direction consistent with our prior analyses, as can be seen in table 7.4. Thirty-one percent of the people who chose Line 3 expected Line 3 to get a majority of the vote, compared to only 6 percent of the people who favored Line 1. The magnitude of this relationship was presumably constrained by knowledge of public opinion polls. The average estimate of the vote that would be obtained by Line 3 was 40.4, very close to what would be projected from preelection polls and to the actual outcome (Holmberg and Petersson, 1980).

With regard to what the situation would be in 25 years, 55 percent of the supporters of antinuclear Line 3 expected that there would be six or fewer nuclear plants in operation then, compared to only 28 percent of the supporters of Line 2 and 14 percent of the supporters of Line 1. Thus, both with regard to the outcome of the referendum *and* to long-range public policy, we observe a tendency for people to expect a preferred outcome. The preference–expectation correlations in these analyses (+.35 and +.33 for preference–referendum outcome expectation and preference–long-range policy expectation, respectively) are in the same direction but slightly weaker than the corresponding correlations in the United States. Taken at face value, the correlations here and from the 1968 and 1982 parliamentary studies would imply that wishful thinking occurs in both countries but to a slightly lesser degree in Sweden than in the United States. However, the measurements are sufficiently different to limit the confidence that should be placed in that generalization.

Given that we have the unique combination of questions measuring expectation regarding the outcome of the referendum *and* expectation regarding the long-range policy outcome, it is of considerable interest to know whether, and the extent to which, these two expectations are positively related. The rational democratic model would call for them to be closely and positively related. In fact, these two expectations are not independent. People who expected the antinuclear Line 3 to get a majority were more than twice as likely (65 to 24%) to expect six or fewer nuclear plants to be operating in 25 years than people who expected Line 3 to get 30 percent of the vote or less. Toward the other end, people who had a low expectancy for Line 3, expecting it to get 30 percent or less in the referendum, were twice as likely (53 to 26%) to expect that 12 or more nuclear plants would be operating in 25 years than people who expected Line 3 to get a majority.

On the other hand, it is also true that two expectations were not closely related (r = +.23). That the overall relationship between E_1 and E_2, the two measures of expectation, was not stronger *could* be interpreted as evidence of skepticism among the citizens as to the impact of the referendum on the eventual policy outcome.[10] Of those expecting Line 3 to get a majority, only 37 percent actually expected that there would be no nuclear power plants operating in Sweden 25 years hence. (Recall that Line 3 called for phasing out *all* nuclear power plants within 10 years!) Thus, when 63 percent of those who expected Line 3 to get a majority expected that nonetheless there would still be some electricity generated from nuclear power in 25 years, those people especially may have been expressing skepticism regarding the efficacy of the referendum. Similarly, among all the people answering the question pertaining to long-range expectations (E_2), 18 percent expected that there would be more than 12 nuclear power plants operating in Sweden in 25 years. Given that *none* of the three alternatives called for more than 12 reactors to be built, these people may have been implicitly conveying a somewhat cynical view regarding the referendum.[11]

It can be shown that both preference and expectation about the outcome

Table 7.5 *Percentage of people expecting no nuclear plants to be operating in Sweden in 25 years as a function of line preference and expectation regarding the outcome of the referendum*

		Expectation of Line 3's vote		Effect of expectation regarding outcome of referendum on policy expectation
		49% or less	50% or more	
	Line 1	2	8	6
Line Preference	Line 2	9	18	9
	Line 3	19	47	28
Effect of line preference on policy expectation	Line 1 vs. Line 3	17	39	

Note: The effects are measured as percentage differences.

of the referendum had an effect on long range expectations. Table 7.5 permits us to observe, in percentage terms, the effect of E_1 on E_2, holding line preference constant, and also for the effect of line preference on E_2, holding E_1 constant. The link between E_1 and E_2 appears to have occurred most strongly among Line 3 supporters. Table 7.5 also shows a rather substantial effect of line preference on E_2 when E_1 is controlled. The two variables of line preference and E_1 combine to produce substantial variation in E_2. Specifically, of those who preferred Line 3 and expected Line 3 to get a majority, 47 percent expected no nuclear plants to be operating in 25 years, compared to only 2 percent of those who preferred Line 1 and expected Line 3 to get *less* than a majority.

Modeling preference, expectations, and voting behavior

Before examining the implications of the three models presented previously, it seemed desirable to have a measure of preference regarding nuclear power that was relatively independent of the referendum itself. Therefore, we developed a nuclear power attitude index out of three highly interrelated items (average $r = +.80$).[12] In the regression analyses that follow, self-reported vote (V) in the referendum is used together with the measures of expectation (E_1 and E_2) and the preference index (P).[13]

The nuclear power referendum data enable analyses not possible with the U.S. election studies. Thus, our regression analyses proceed somewhat differently. Here rather than comparing the wishful thinking model against the bandwagon model, each of these models is compared with the rational democratic model. As indicated previously, the rational democratic and wishful thinking models generate opposing predictions concerning the relations among preference and expectations. These models are shown in

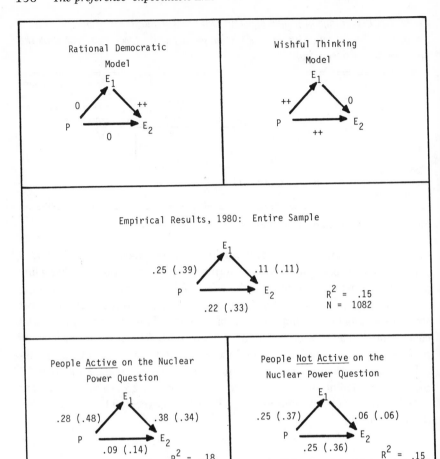

Figure 7.3. Modeling preference and expectation – the rational democratic model and the wishful thinking model.
Note. The results show the relationship between preference regarding nuclear power (P), expectation regarding the outcome of the referendum (E_1), and long range expectation regarding the use of nuclear power in Sweden in 25 years (E_2). The upper portion gives the theoretical models, the middle gives the results for the 1980 survey, and the lower portion gives the results separately for active and nonactive people. The coefficients in parentheses are standardized regression coefficients, while the other coefficients in the figure are unstandardized regression coefficients.

the upper portion of figure 7.3 as contrasting versions of the dynamics among P, E_1, and E_2. The rational democratic model anticipates a strong relationship (indicated by + +) between E_1 and E_2 but no relationship (indicated by O) between P and E_1 and between P and E_2. By contrast, the wishful thinking model anticipates a strong relationship between P and E_1 and between P and E_2 but no real relationship between E_1 and E_2.

The center of figure 7.3 summarizes a regression analyses in which P and E_1 were independent variables and E_2 the dependent variable. The results indicate a substantial tendency toward wishful thinking, and it appears that overall, the results may more closely resemble the wishful thinking model.

However, we repeated this analysis separately for active and nonactive people (lower portion of figure 7.3). The question used to divide the sample into active and nonactive asked whether the person had taken a position and tried to influence others to vote for a particular alternative in the referendum. By this criterion, 15 percent were designated as active and 85 percent as not active. As shown in the lower portion of figure 7.3, the results for the active people more closely resemble the rational democratic model, while those for the nonactive people more closely resemble the wishful thinking model. At least this is true if one focuses on the direct effects of P and E_1 on E_2. At the same time, the relationship between P and E_1 is stronger for the active than the nonactive people. This relationship reflects an apparently greater tendency toward wishful thinking on the part of the active people in relation to the outcome of the referendum. This could be a consequence of a heightened desire to see one's preferred alternative succeed which, in turn, could be due to the greater commitment with which active people approached the referendum (Kiesler, 1971). That is, if the relationship between P and E_1 is an instance of wishful thinking, as seems probable, it is understandable that it would occur more strongly among people who are more actively committed since they care more about the outcome. This parallels the result from the U.S. in which the preference–expectation relationship was somewhat stronger among people with a higher level of involvement.

We now return to the question of whether expectation regarding the outcome of the referendum can have an influence on voting behavior (V), after the influence of nuclear power attitude or preference (P) is controlled. The bandwagon model predicts that there would be a strong relationship between E_1 and P and a strong relationship between E_1 and V, after the effect of P on V is controlled. By contrast, the rational democratic model predicts a strong effect of P on V but no relationship between P and E_1 or between E_1 and V. These models are shown in the upper portion of figure 7.4.

The central part of figure 7.4 summarizes regression analyses in which P and E_1 were the independent variables and V the dependent variable. The most impressive aspect was the very robust relationship between P and V and thus, the very high percentage of variance explained. The strong link between P and V, together with the lack of a relationship of any substantive

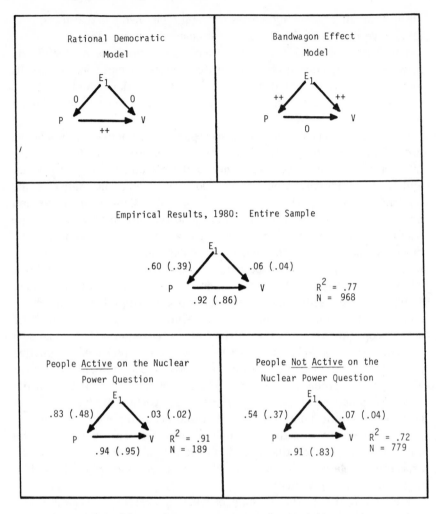

Figure 7.4. Modeling preference, expectation, and voting behavior – the rational democratic model and the bandwagon model.
Note. The results show the relationship between preference regarding nuclear power (P), expectation regarding the outcome of the referendum (E_1), and voting behavior (V) in the referendum. The upper portion gives two theoretical models, the middle gives the results for the 1980 survey, and the lower portion gives the results separately for active and nonactive people. The coefficients in parentheses are standardized regression coefficients, while the other coefficients in the figure are unstandardized regression coefficients.

significance between E_1 and V, bears a close resemblance to the rational democratic model. The relationship between E_1 and V was reduced from .39 to .04 when the influence of P was controlled.

Dividing the sample once again into active and nonactive people, the results for the active people resembled the rational democratic model in important ways. Among active people, the effect of P on V was especially robust, the percentage of variance in V that was explained was very high (91%), and the effect of E_1 on V was not significant.

However, the strong link between P and E_1 appearing for both active and nonactive people is not consistent with the purely rational democratic model. This relationship is a significant departure from the rational democratic model and could be due to either wishful thinking or a bandwagon effect. Since expectation regarding the outcome of the referendum was measured only once in this study, we cannot offer a definitive conclusion in that regard.

The regression analysis in figure 7.4 contains some evidence compatible with the occurrence of a bandwagon effect. Although small, E_1 continued to exert a statistically significant effect on V when the effect of P on V was controlled, considering the sample as a whole. That could be combined with an apparent indirect effect of E_1 on V through P to imply a bandwagon effect of at least a marginal significance. We do not favor that interpretation, for reasons explained below, but the results in figure 7.4 prompted us to look into it somewhat further.

First, as in other election studies, we identified those who lacked a voting intention on the preelection survey, but who nonetheless voted in the referendum. The bandwagon model implies that the vote of these people would be predictable on the basis of their expectation, but it was not ($r = +.10, N = 75$). Among these undecided people who later voted, it was actually those with medium (realistic) expectations for Line 3, rather than those who had higher expectations for Line 3's success, who were most likely to vote for Line 3 – albeit by a small margin. Similarly, people who intended to vote for Lines 1 or 2 and had high expectations for Line 3 were not more likely to switch and vote for Line 3 than people who intended to vote for Lines 1 or 2 and had lower expectations for Line 3.[14] Within each intention category, the correlation between expectation and voting was not significant. These analyses make it doubtful that a bandwagon effect occurred in the nuclear power referendum.

A more realistic model

As mentioned before, the models presented in this chapter were heuristic devices to help us examine various possibilities. We never anticipated that the empirical data would conform precisely with one of the models and not at all with the other two. Overall, our judgment is that the data are most supportive of the rational democratic model, somewhat supportive of the wishful thinking model, and least supportive of the bandwagon model. In

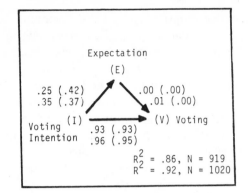

Figure 7.5. A realistic model of the relations among intention, expectation, and voting in Sweden.
Note. In each case, the upper number is based on an analysis of data from the 1980 nuclear power referendum study and the lower number is based on the 1968 parliamentary election study. Numbers in parentheses are standardized regression coefficients, while the other coefficients are unstandardized regression coefficients.

fact, in the Swedish context, no evidence of a bandwagon effect was observed which could not be eliminated by controlling for voting intention or more plausibly attributed to wishful thinking.

Thus, a more realistic model of how things really work, in terms of the dynamics of the relations among preference, expectation, and behavior, would include aspects of both the rational democratic and the wishful thinking models. Such a model, using voting intention (I) as a surrogate for preference, is shown as figure 7.5. This figure incorporates comparable empirical results from the 1968 Swedish parliamentary election study and the 1980 nuclear power referendum study. In the model, the effect of I on V is taken to represent the rational democratic process and is, of course, very substantial in both studies. The wishful thinking model is represented by the effect of I on E and is also significant in both studies. Finally, the erstwhile bandwagon effect is represented by the effect of E on V and is not significant when the effect of I on V is controlled. This serves as a good example where a significant bivariate relationship (.41 and .36 for the E to V relation for 1980 and 1968 studies, respectively) is reduced to nonsignificance when a theoretically relevant third variable is controlled.

Interpreting the linkages

Our results suggest that the findings of a relationship between preference and expectation does, indeed, generalize to both sides of the Atlantic to political contexts as different as the U.S. and Sweden. The relationship was observed to occur in the context of several U.S. elections, Sweden's referendum on nuclear power as well as in two Swedish parliamentary elections. This implies that the relationship may have a rather substantial generalizability and may even represent a fundamental human tendency.

The analyses of U.S. and Swedish data were used to conduct numerous tests for the hypothesized bandwagon effect. There were two instances (of 18) in the U.S. and none in Sweden in which it is plausible to think that a bandwagon effect probably occurred. Many people assume that a bandwagon effect is real and that it has a high probability of occurring and exerting a significant impact on the electoral outcome. Our analyses suggest, on the contrary, that bandwagon effects are rare and difficult to find. As implied in our earlier discussion of the three models, the anticipation of a bandwagon effect may say something about an underlying conception of human nature – a conception which, given our results, may deserve to be reexamined.

The concept of a bandwagon effect and the belief in its frequent occurrence is based on a perspective that overestimates the tendency of people to sway with the wind. In psychological terms, the fundamental question is how suggestible and subject to social influence people are, given no more than information about how other people have behaved or are likely to behave. The laboratory analogue to the bandwagon effect is the situation in which people observe or become informed about the responses of others and then alter their behavior to conform with the majority to avoid being isolated or different (Asch, 1956; Hovland and Pritzker, 1957; Navazio, 1977). A close reading of experimental studies like these prompts the conclusion that, while a significant degree of social influence is demonstrated, by no means were the subjects blind conformists. In the classic Asch experiment, the behavior of the experimental subjects actually more closely approximated a standard of autonomy or self-reliance than it did a standard of heteronomy. Moreover, our reading of prior analyses of survey data and our own analyses yield the conclusion that it is difficult to find solid or conclusive evidence of a bandwagon effect (Granberg, 1984; Holmberg and Petersson, 1980). In the case of the evidence of Lazarsfeld *et al.* (1944, chart 32, p. 108), the time lag is too long and perhaps inappropriate and the effect too weak for the alleged effect to be credible. If a bandwagon effect occurs in U.S. elections, it may be more likely in a primary election than in the general election. Preferences are more labile in primary elections, and the actual differences among the candidates on the issues or ideology may be rather small. While plausible, one recent effort to demonstrate a bandwagon effect in U.S. primary election campaigns used two-stage regression analyses of cross-sectional data (Bartels, 1985). It is not easy to see how anyone can make a strong case for a bandwagon effect without panel data.

Generally speaking, it is probably not the case that a bandwagon effect never occurs. Even if a weak one occurs, in a close election it could make a difference. On the other hand, a bandwagon effect may be less likely to occur in a close election. People whose preferred candidate appears to be only a few points behind in the polls (say 48 versus 52 percent) would hardly have cause to feel isolated. Here is a major difference from the Asch situation which focused on how people dealt with confederates who were making unanimously wrong judgments. One of Asch's (1956) manipulations showed that people were more likely to stand up for the truth as they saw it if there was at least one person who saw things their way.

Overall, it seems more plausible to suppose that a bandwagon effect might occur in a campaign focused on personalities vying for office than in an issue-oriented campaign like Sweden's referendum on nuclear power. On the other hand, Sweden's referendum on nuclear power was preceded by an intense campaign in which political parties and social movement organizations were highly involved in trying to mobilize support.

Future research could develop panel data in which party or candidate preference and expectation are measured at appropriate time intervals prior to and during the campaign and ultimately related to behavior. Such research may enable generalizations concerning the circumstances under which a bandwagon effect occurs. However, that will not be easy, given the problem of timing and the fact that even when a bandwagon effect occurs, it is probably a rather subtle effect.

Given that the preference–expectation link is reasonably strong, reliable, and pervasive, and given that this link generally cannot be attributed to a bandwagon effect, this takes us back to the major alternative, wishful thinking. People in both the U.S. and Sweden have shown a tendency toward wishful thinking, although in political matters this tendency may be slightly stronger in the U.S. than in Sweden. In a purely rational democratic model, there would be no room for wishful thinking, which, after all, is essentially irrational in nature. This is what Paul Samuelson (1970, p. 8) meant when he wrote that "Wishful thinking is bad thinking and leads to little wish fulfillment."

While we cannot argue that wishful thinking is rational, optimism may be in some sense functional. If a person beginning a political campaign were to realistically think through and accurately anticipate all the problems, obstacles, and difficulties that would be encountered along the way, the project might not seem worth the effort.

Perhaps the great innovators, leaders, and explorers in human history have had a certain tendency toward wishful thinking – without being self-absorbed or out of touch with reality. It may require a vision and a minimal level of optimism to suppose one can do something that has never been done before. It is in this sense that we suggest that wishful thinking or optimism may be functional and even have some evolutionary significance. A certain degree of optimism has beneficial consequences in that it enhances striving and a willingness to venture into new areas of endeavor, and this may enhance achievement and success in adaptation. If people were completely aware in advance of all the difficulties they would encounter by embarking on a particular path, they might be more likely to do nothing.

8 From intention to behavior in election campaigns

We have seen several areas in which the interests and problems of political scientists coincide, or at least overlap considerably, with those of social psychologists. When we turn to the relationship between intention and behavior, we face another situation. Each area has a real interest in understanding the relationship between what people say they will do and what they subsequently do.

For political scientists, the problem is usually embedded in an interest in the general topic of voter volatility. Volatility refers here to instability in party or candidate preference. This can be treated at the individual or the aggregate level. For instance, what is the degree of fluctuation in the aggregated vote for, or attitudes toward, a particular party or politician across time?

Within social psychology, the most sustained treatment of the intention–behavior relationship is the work of Martin Fishbein (1963, 1980). Together with Icek Ajzen, Fishbein has developed a "theory of reasoned action" which focuses on intentions, their antecedents, and behavior (Ajzen and Fishbein, 1980; Fishbein and Ajzen, 1975; Liska, 1984). This theory has its origins in a series of studies, beginning with the classic article by Richard LaPiere (1934), which showed a disjuncture, or at the very most a weak relationship, between attitudes and behavior (Hill, 1981; Schuman and Johnson, 1976). Given the devotion of social psychologists to the study of attitudes, this line of research has been, to put it mildly, rather disconcerting.

Along with many others, Fishbein and Ajzen sought a way out of this predicament. Their solution, which is to say their theory, was that insofar as social psychologists are interested in predicting behavior, they would do well to focus on behavioral intentions rather than attitudes. Behavioral intentions, it was claimed, would bear a close relationship to behavior. In fact, in their theory, behavioral intentions are regarded as equal or similar to behavior.

The antecedents to behavioral intentions were identified as consisting of attitudinal and normative components. The attitude, however, was phrased as an attitude toward an act (rather than toward an object) and the act should be carefully specified. The attitude toward an act was a function of two elements, perceived consequences of doing the act, and an evaluation of those consequences. The normative component consisted of the perceived preferences of other people, considered in conjunction with the person's motivation to do what these people prefer. The relative importance of the attitudinal and normative components was regarded as an *ad hoc* empirical question and would depend upon the situation. Their theory can be seen as a cognitive, information-processing approach to the attitude–behavior problem.

Fishbein and Ajzen's theory suggests that the intention to perform a certain act is prompted by attitudinal and normative considerations, and that behavior follows directly from behavioral intentions. They make no provision in their theory for any factor, other than intentions, to have a direct effect on behavior.

Fishbein and Ajzen acknowledge that the actual degree to which intention and behavior are related will vary considerably, depending on the circumstances. If the intention and behavior are measured at the same level of specificity, if the time between the two is small, if the base rate in the sample is split about evenly for both intention and behavior, if the behavior in question is under the voluntaristic control of the person, and if the individual has the ability and resources to do it, then the intention–behavior relationship is expected to be very strong.

In writing about volitional control, Fishbein and Ajzen (1975) acknowledge that habit could exert an effect so that some people end up doing what they have done in the past rather than their intended behavior. Notice, however, how they exclude the behavior of interest here, voting behavior, from such a caveat.

> Another possible breakdown in the intention-behavior relation may be due to a person's *habits*. Although a person may intend to do one thing, by "force of habit" he may do something else. Before leaving home, a person may intend to try a new route to his office, but later he finds himself driving along the same route he takes every day. In fact, many well-learned skills (e.g., playing the piano, driving a car) are performed almost automatically without much conscious effort. *Most behaviors* of interest to social scientists, however, do not involve such automatic sequences of motor responses. Instead, investigators attempt to predict a person's decisions, participation in various activities, purchasing behavior, *voting for political candidates*, and interactions with other people ... these kinds of behavior are under volitional control and thus can be predicted from the person's intentions. (Fishbein and Ajzen, 1975, p. 371, emphasis added)

When their model was applied to voting behavior in England and the United States, Fishbein *et al.*, (1980) stated that factors other than intentions can have only an indirect effect on behavior. Based on what has been published previously, we fully expected to observe a strong relationship between voting intention and voting behavior (Kelley and Mirer, 1974; Lazarsfeld *et al.*, 1944). However, we also expected that other factors could have a direct effect on behavior, even when the effect of intention is controlled or held constant. What might these other factors be? First, we expected that a person's self-identity, in this context an identification of oneself with a political party (Biddle *et al.*, 1985), and one's prior behavior could modify the intention–behavior relationship. People who intend to behave in a way that is implied by their self-identity may be more likely to do it than people who intend to do something not implied by their self-identity. Also, other things being equal, people who intend to do something they have done before may be more likely to do it than people who intend to do something different from what they have done before – even when we are considering a volitional behavior such as voting. Second, involvement in the matter under consideration might be expected to strengthen the intention–behavior relationship.

Most of the research by Fishbein and Ajzen, and that stimulated by their approach, has focused on the attitudinal and normative antecedents of behavioral intentions and has presumed that the relationship between intention and behavior would be strong. Our focus is on the question of once an intention is formed, what happens along the road from intention to behavior. The old proverb that "the road to hell is paved with good intentions" strongly implies that people, for one reason or another, do not always get done that which they intend to do.[1]

These are not idle matters. At a practical level, the reputation of public opinion polling organizations in many countries depends in large measure on their being able to forecast accurately the outcome of elections. The accuracy of such forecasts based on preelection polls depends upon the intention–behavior relationship being very strong *or* on a symmetrical distribution of people whose behavior departs from intention.[2] For people involved in practical politics, it is useful to know what the people are like who are most prone to change during a campaign in one direction or the other.

It is also of considerable relevance to normative democratic theory to know the characteristics of people who change their party selection across elections or who change from intention to behavior within an election campaign. The paradox that the adaptability of a democratic system depends on the volatility of its less admirable citizens who are politically apathetic and poorly informed emerged from the early election studies done in the U.S. (Lazarsfeld *et al.*, 1944; Berelson *et al.*, 1954). Knowing that apathetic, less knowledgeable citizens are more changeable may have led political parties, candidates, and political consultants to gear political campaigns at a rather low level of sophistication.

As with the other problems we have analyzed, we did not presume that things would necessarily work similarly in political systems as different as Sweden and the United States. Thus, the intention–behavior relationship becomes another context in which we can examine how the political system matters.

Analyzing volatility at the individual level is usually done by comparing stability in individual preference or behavior across years, and within election campaigns. The best estimates of either form of individual volatility use panel data. Across years or across election volatility can be defined as the percentage of individuals who report voting for different parties or candidates at Time 1 and Time 2. This can also be assessed, but with less confidence, by using cross-sectional data and asking people how they voted in the prior election and how they voted in the current election. However, people cannot always remember accurately how they voted some years previously, and they may not always be inclined to tell the truth – even when they know it. These facts create some methodological problems in assessing volatility.

The ideal method of measuring within campaign volatility would be to measure people's preferences or voting intentions when the campaign begins, then again at various points during the campaign, and then finally have a measure of how the same individuals actually voted in the election. The results we report in this chapter touch briefly on across-election volatility but focus mainly on within-campaign volatility from intentions to behavior. The data include nine U.S. and six Swedish election studies in which people were asked during the campaign how they voted in the prior election and how they intended to vote in the coming election, and then, within a panel design, after the election how they had voted in the current election. These data enable us to make a number of comparisons between Sweden and the United States pertaining to questions about intention–behavior volatility.

The basic intention–behavior relationship

We begin our analysis by examining the overall percentage of people for whom intention and behavior were different in nine U.S. and six Swedish election studies (figure 8.1). The results for Sweden are shown in two ways: first, considering any change across party lines from intention to behavior, and secondly, movement across bloc lines within the main five-party system. These results are based only on those people who had an intention when interviewed in the preelection survey and who indicated in the

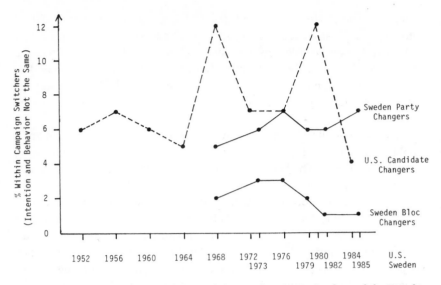

Figure 8.1. Percentage of intention–behavior changing in Sweden and the United States.

postelection survey that they had voted for one of the parties in the election. Thus, people who either had no intention or who did not vote are excluded. Overall, it appears that in Sweden about 94 percent vote for the party they had previously indicated as their intention. The percentage of party changers from intention to behavior showed little variation across the six elections in figure 8.1. The smallest percentage of intention–behavior changers in the Swedish studies was 5 percent (1968), and the largest was 7 percent (1976 and 1985). The percentage of people who vote for a party within the bloc of the party they indicated as their intention is even higher, averaging 98 percent across years. In the two most recent elections, only 1 percent of the people crossed bloc lines, that is voted for a party in the bloc other than the one containing their intended party. Thus, the expectation that there would be a strong relationship between intention and behavior was certainly fulfilled in the case of Sweden.

The comparable analyses for U.S. elections, also in figure 8.1, indicate that in six of the nine elections, the percentage of people for whom intention and behavior were the same was 93, 94, or 95. Two interesting exceptions, in which that percentage dropped to 88, occurred in 1968 and 1980, the years in which there was a significant third-party or independent candidate (George Wallace in 1968, John Anderson in 1980).[3] In 1984, the percentage for whom intention and behavior were different dropped to an all-time low (for the years for which we have comparable data) of 4 percent.

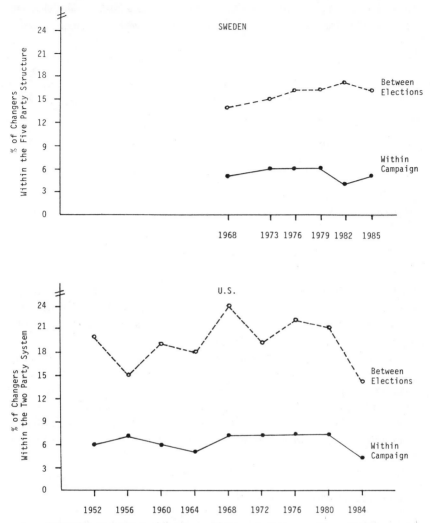

Figure 8.2. Percentage of changers within an election campaign and between elections in Sweden and the United States.

Most of the analyses that follow focus on those who intended to vote for one of the five largest parties in Sweden or for the Democratic or Republican nominee for President in the United States, since these "actors" have constituted a continuing core structure within the two political systems during this period. The estimates of across-election changers in figure 8.2, limited to the five parties in Sweden and the two parties in the U.S., are based on two questions: asking people in the preelection survey to recall how they had voted in the prior election and asking in the postelection

Table 8.1 *Percentage of intention–behavior changers as a function of gender, age, and education, based on results combined across six Swedish and nine United States national election studies*

		Sweden	Sweden	U.S.
		Percentage bloc changers	Percentage five-party changers	Percentage two-candidate changers
Gender	Men	2	5	6
	Women	2	5	6
Age	61 or over	2	5	5
	31–60	2	5	6
	30 or under	2	5	7
Education	High	1	4	5
	Medium	2	6	7
	Low	2	5	7

Note: The Ns in this table are about 5350 for Sweden and 10 025 for the U.S.

survey how they voted in the current election. The percentage of people who changed, by this measure, averaged 16 percent for Sweden and 19 percent for the United States.[4] In both countries, across-election changing exceeds within campaign changing by a ratio of about 3:1.

We also considered the relationship between party preference, measured before an election, and how people reported voting when asked after the election. The percentage for whom preelection preference and vote were not the same averaged 9 percent for Sweden (considering again only the five main parties) and 17 percent in the United States. Thus, in both countries, intention predicts voting behavior better than party preference which in turn predicts voting behavior better than prior behavior.[5]

A brief look at demographics

In order to check that subsequent analyses would not be greatly complicated by demographic differences, for each of nine U.S. and six Swedish election studies we examined whether intention–behavior volatility varied as a function of three demographic variables, gender, age, and education. The results in table 8.1 show no variation as a function of gender and very little variation as a function of age and education.

It is widely believed that young people are more politically volatile, and a more complex analysis could sustain that thesis. However, in the intention–behavior relationship among people who had an intention, such an effect does not appear at all in the Swedish data and at the very most, in a very muted form in the U.S. In both the U.S. and Sweden, those with the highest amount of education were least likely to behave in a way that departed from their intentions, but the differences among the education groups are very small and probably trivial.

The time dimension

It is customary to think that time cannot cause anything. Time does, however, allow other things to happen. In regard to the intention–behavior problem, time could be important inasmuch as the more time that has elapsed between when intention and behavior are measured, the more likely it is that something will have happened so that by the time the behavior is to occur, the person's intention will have changed. Thus, one generally might expect a weakening of the intention–behavior linkage as the time between measuring the two increases.[6]

For each Swedish and each U.S. study, we divided the preelection samples roughly in half, with those who were interviewed early and late comprising two subsamples. The Swedish campaign is shorter than the U.S. campaign, and this is reflected in when the studies are done. The preelection interviews in Sweden cover a period of about four weeks and those in the United States cover about eight weeks. Thus, comparing the intention–behavior relationship across the two nations, the last half of the U.S. samples may be roughly comparable to the entire Swedish preelection samples in the average amount of time between when intention and behavior are measured.

In the U.S., across elections the percentage of intention–behavior changers was about 7 percent for those interviewed early, compared to 5 percent for those interviewed later in the campaign. This is a small difference, albeit in the expected direction. In Sweden combining across elections, the percentage of people who intended to vote for one of the five main parties but later voted for another of those five parties, was 5 percent for both those interviewed early and those interviewed late in the campaign. Thus, within Sweden, when people were interviewed during the election campaign had no discernible effect on the strength of the intention–behavior linkage.[7] Within the U.S., it appears to have had no more than a slight effect.

It is likely that more dramatic evidence of the importance of the time dimension would be observed if the interval between the measures of intention and behavior had been greater. For instance, in February 1980, 60 percent of the people in a U.S. survey indicated an intention to vote for Jimmy Carter, while only 31 percent intended to vote for Reagan. The election result that November, in which Reagan obtained 51 percent of the vote to Carter's 41 percent, strongly implies that many people changed their minds sometime between February and November. Thus, if we had the percentage of individuals in a February–November panel for whom intention and behavior are not the same, the figure would have to be much higher than any of the percentages in figure 8.1. At the same time, it is some comfort to know that within the maximum of a two-month interval in these election studies, the strength of the intention–behavior relation is not affected much by exactly when the preelection interview was done.

Politically relevant intervening variables

Thus far, we have seen that the intention–behavior relationship is very strong in both Sweden and the United States, and that the relationship is largely independent of gender, education, age, and when the interview was made. Now we turn to some politically relevant variables, and here we find that there are several factors which appear to have a significant moderating effect on the strength of the intention–behavior link. That is, they intervene on the road from intention to behavior.

Table 8.2 shows a breakdown of the intention–behavior relationship in Sweden as a function of which party the person intended to vote for in the coming election. There are some noteworthy differences. Combining across years, it appears that the Social Democrats are most successful in retaining people who intend to vote for their party (97%). The Conservative (93%), Center (92%), and Communist parties (92%) were somewhat less successful, and the Liberals (87%) were least successful in obtaining the votes of people who intended to vote for their respective party. These differences are probably real, but an adequate explanation would have to consider in some detail the political and historical circumstances of recent Swedish elections, a task beyond our scope. Briefly, the relatively high numbers for the Social Democratic Party in table 8.2 are related to the strength of party affiliation and attachment to that party that is felt by many Social Democratic supporters. By comparison, supporters of the bourgeois parties move across party lines within the bourgeois bloc with somewhat more ease, *relatively* speaking. While Liberals have been the least successful over the years in obtaining the votes of people who intended to vote for that party, notice that in 1985, a year in which this party was on the ascendance and experienced a considerable increase in support, the percentage was higher than in any previous year.

When the comparable analysis is done for the two U.S. parties, it appears that across years, Republican candidates have been slightly more likely to obtain the votes of people who intend to vote for them than Democratic candidates. However, the difference is trivial overall (94 to 93%), and there are two elections, 1960 and 1976, in which the Democratic candidate was more successful in this regard. Also, the winning candidate did not

Table 8.2 *Subsequent vote of people intending to vote for one of the five largest parties in Sweden*

Voting intention		Percentage voting for							
		Communist	Social Democrat	Center	Liberal	Conservative	Other	Total	N
Communist	1985	93	2	0	0	0	5	100	44
	1982	94	3	3	0	0	0	100	33
	1979	94	3	0	3	0	0	100	37
	1976	84	13	3	0	0	0	100	31
	1973	91	9	0	0	0	0	100	34
	1968	91	9	0	0	0	0	100	11
Social	1985	2	97	0	1	0	0	100	423
Democrat	1982	2	97	0	0	1	0	100	481
	1979	1	97	0	1	1	0	100	455
	1976	1	96	2	1	0	0	100	466
	1973	1	96	3	0	0	0	100	403
	1968	1	98	1	0	0	0	100	596
Center	1985	0	1	87	4	2	6	100	95
	1982	0	0	95	0	4	1	100	117
	1979	0	3	90	2	4	1	100	154
	1976	1	4	90	2	2	1	100	173
	1973	0	3	94	0	3	0	100	186
	1968	0	2	94	2	2	0	100	159
Liberal	1985	0	4	3	92	1	0	100	76
	1982	0	4	4	83	7	2	100	46
	1979	1	5	2	84	8	0	100	101
	1976	0	0	5	89	6	0	100	98
	1973	0	4	4	87	5	0	100	74
	1968	0	2	7	87	3	1	100	155
Conservative	1985	0	1	1	7	91	0	100	209
	1982	0	1	1	2	95	1	100	214
	1979	0	0	1	4	95	0	100	170
	1976	0	2	2	2	94	0	100	124
	1973	0	1	2	1	96	0	100	108
	1968	0	2	3	3	91	1	100	112

invariably hold on to his intended voters better than the losing candidate. In 1964 and 1968, the losing candidates actually did better in that regard. Across years, Ronald Reagan in 1980 was most successful in obtaining the votes of people who intended to vote for him (97%), while among the nominees of the two large parties, Jimmy Carter in 1980 and Adlai Stevenson in 1956 were least successful (89%). Once again, there would be no way of accounting for such variations between candidates and elections without considering the particular details of each election campaign.

Table 8.3 summarizes the results for some politically relevant variables which were regarded as possible intervening variables in the intention–behavior relationship. The results are combined across years because, first,

Table 8.3 *Percentage of intention–behavior changers as a function of five politically relevant intervening variables in Sweden and the United States*

	Percentage intention–behavior changers		Sweden	U.S.
	Sweden	U.S.	N	N
Degree of partisanship				
Strong identifiers	2	4	2119	3817
Not strong identifiers	5	8	1540	3753
Lean toward a party	9	7	1282	1792
No party preference	11	8	223	681
Prior vote and intention				
Same	4	4	4311	5901
Different	18	16	531	1202
Current party preference and intention				
Same	4	4	5062	7941
Different	28	17	131	1420
Plan to vote				
Yes	5	6	5263	9807
No	24	17	95	246
Ideological extremity				
Relatively extreme	4	3	1583	1226
Near the center	6	6	2246	1250
At the center	5	8	1441	1170

there are no interesting variations in specific years and, second, because for some categories the number of cases is not adequate in some years – yet quite adequate when combined across years.

Strength of party identification operates as expected in Sweden. Those who strongly identify themselves with a party are most likely to have the same intention and behavior (98%), followed by those who identify with a party but not strongly (95%), those who lean toward a party but do not identify with it (91%), and those with no party preference (89%). Thus, the last of these categories is more than five times as likely to have a different intention and behavior as the first. The results for the United States are similar to those of Sweden only through the first two categories. Intention and behavior are more likely to be the same for strong party identifiers (96%), but the other three categories (92% for not strong identifiers, 93% for leaners, and 92% for no party preference people) hardly differ at all from each other.

In both countries, people who intend to vote for the party they recall voting for in the prior election are much more likely to vote in line with their intention (96% in both Sweden and the U.S.) than are people who intend to vote for a party different from the one they recall voting for in the prior election (82% for Sweden, 84% for the U.S.). Similar results were obtained when we considered the compatibility between party preference and voting intention. Some people in both countries intend to vote for a party or a party's nominee which does not coincide with their current party preference. In the U.S. context, voting for a candidate of a party other than the party a person identifies with has been called cross-over voting (Lazarsfeld *et al.*, 1944). Here we can show that people who intend to cross-over and vote for a party other than their preferred party are less likely to behave in line with their intention (i.e., they are less likely to actually do it) than are people whose intention and party preference coincide. Specifically, people who intend to vote for a candidate of a nonpreferred party in the United States show considerable slack in the intention–behavior relation (17%), especially in comparison to those for whom intention and party preference coincide (4%). For Sweden, the difference is in the same direction but even more pronounced. Those for whom preferred party and intended vote coincide are very likely (96%) to vote in line with their intentions, much more so than the comparable figure for the few people whose preferred party and intention are different (72%).

Incidentally, the results for the 1980 Swedish referendum on nuclear power are quite similar. Overall, in that context 94 percent had the same intention and behavior. However, for those who intended to vote for an alternative other than that endorsed by their preferred party, 13 percent were intention–behavior changers. This compares to only 3 percent intention–behavior changers among those who intended to vote for the alternative endorsed by their preferred party. In this referendum context, the concept of cross-over voting may be more relevant than in the regular parliamentary elections.

The results on these intervening variables are wholly consistent from election to election in each country. Therefore, we can have considerable confidence in the following propositions. Even on a volitional behavior such as voting, *people who intend to behave in a way implied by their self-concepts are more likely to actually do what they intend than are people who intend to behave in a way other than that implied by their self-identity. Also, people who intend to do what they have done before are more likely to actually do it than people who intend to do something new or different.*

Next, we wanted to see whether the effect of these two important intervening variables could be observed simultaneously. Thus, for each person for whom the information was available in six Swedish and eight U.S. surveys[8] regarding recalled prior behavior, current party preference, voting intention, and voting behavior, an analysis was made of whether intention and behavior were the same. The results are summarized as two effect tables in table 8.4. It appears that the two intervening variables exert

Table 8.4 *Percentage of within-campaign intention–behavior changing as a function of the compatibility of prior voting behavior, current party preference, and intention*

Sweden		Party preference and intention		Effect of
		Same	Different	party preference
Prior vote	Same	3	14	11
and intention	Different	15	37	22
	Effect of			
	prior vote	12	23	

United States		Party preference and intention		Effect of
		Same	Different	party preference
Prior vote	Same	3	11	8
and intention	Different	11	22	11
	Effect of			
	prior vote	8	11	

Note: Entries are the percentages of people for whom intended vote and self-reported vote are not the same. Thus, for instance, in the upper table, of those who intended to vote for a party that was the same as they voted for previously but different from their current party preference, 14 percent had an intention and a behavior which were not the same. The Swedish data are based on the combined results of six elections and the U.S. data on the combined results of eight elections. For Sweden, the Ns for the upper left, upper right, lower left, and lower right cells are 4184, 43, 413, and 73. For the U.S., the corresponding Ns are 5092, 476, 560, and 506.

an independent effect in both countries. There also may be an interaction effect, especially in Sweden, such that when neither prior behavior nor self-identity is the same as intention, the intention–behavior linkage loosens rather considerably. If self-identity and prior behavior both point in the same direction as intention, intention and behavior are *very* likely to be the same (97% in both countries). If both prior behavior and self-identity are different from intention, the odds that intention and behavior will be the same are substantially reduced (78 and 63% in the U.S. and Sweden, respectively).

Notice that we are not saying that those for whom prior behavior and self-identity are different from intention do not behave in line with their intentions. In fact, a majority of them do in both countries. It is rather a matter of probability in that they are significantly less likely to do so. When one but not the other of these intervening variables reinforces voting intention, the resultant intention–behavior relationship is intermediate in strength.

The implication of these findings is clear. Prior behavior and a person's self-identity not only affect intentions but also exert a direct effect on behavior when intentions are held constant. Results such as this require a modification of the Fishbein–Ajzen model to include relevant aspects of the person's self-identity and relevant prior behavior as having a direct effect on behavior, even when the effect of intentions on behavior is taken into account.[9]

It was also expected that ideological extremity might intervene in the intention–behavior relationship. In the U.S. elections, results were about as expected (table 8.3) across the four studies for which data on self-designated ideology were available. People in the middle of the ideological spectrum were most likely to be intention–behavior changers (8%), followed by those who leaned slightly to the left or right (6%), and finally, those who were farther to the left or right of center (3%). The results for Sweden on this matter were more irregular. Combining across elections, people who leaned slightly to the left or right of center were most likely to have a different intention and behavior (6%), followed by the centrists (5%), and those farther to the left or right were least likely (4%). This result can be understood with reference to the variety of alternatives available to Swedish voters. Regardless of where people are on the ideological spectrum, they can find another party other than their currently preferred one without traveling too far in ideological distance. On the other hand, in the United States people at or near the ideological extremes have really "no place to go" if they become dissatisfied with the party that is in the closest proximity to their own ideological position. The results for Sweden come closer to what was expected if we use across-bloc changing rather than across-party changing. Among those at or near the ideological extremes, only 1 percent intended to vote for a different bloc from the one they voted for, compared to 2 percent of those to the left or right but near the center, and 3 percent for the centrists. Of course, even the latter group showed an amazingly low level of bloc intention–behavior changing.

Strength and firmness of intention

We also have evidence that the strength and firmness of the intention makes a difference. In each study, if people said they did not intend to vote, they were nonetheless asked for which party or candidate they would vote if they were to vote. Such answers get a bit hypothetical, and they are not unlike asking a person who just denied an intention to buy a car in the coming year, well, if you were to buy a car what kind do you think you would buy? It is not clear that answers to such follow-up questions should be regarded as intentions.[10] Perhaps they should be called inclinations to indicate their more conditional status. In fact, some of these people who say they do not plan to vote, but have an erstwhile intention or inclination, do actually vote. Can their behavior on election day be predicted by knowing their stated hypothetical intention? The answer seems to be yes in both countries, but to a lesser degree than for those who plan to vote. As shown in table 8.3, of those who plan to vote, intention and behavior were different for only 6 percent in the United States and 5 percent in Sweden, while the comparable percentages for those who do not plan to vote were 17 for the U.S. and 24 for Sweden.

Along a similar line, in the U.S. studies between 1952 and 1976, some people were coded as intending to vote for a candidate but with qualifications. Most people stated an intention without qualifying it, and they may be said to have a more firm intention. This difference is reflected in the strength of the intention–behavior relationship. Of those with a firm intention, 95 percent had the same intention and behavior, compared to only 79 percent of those with a more qualified, less strong intention.

The preceding findings suggest that perhaps both the direction and intensity of the intention should be measured. Some of the intervening variables may have operated less strongly if the intensity as well as the direction of the intention had been measured. We cannot assess this possibility directly within the available data sets. However, a check was made to see whether the attitude pattern made a difference. Of those who intended to vote and later voted for one of the two main candidates in the United States, some held positive attitudes toward both candidates (+ +), some held neutral attitudes (00) toward both, and some were negative toward both (− −). In addition, some people were positive toward one and neutral toward the other (+ 0), some were positive toward one and negative toward the other (+ −), and some were neutral toward one and negative toward the other (0 −).

Combining across four U.S. elections (1972–1984), the + − people were least likely to be intention–behavior changers (3%, N = 2517). Among the other groups which held different attitudes toward the candidates, the corresponding figures were 7 percent (N = 739) for the + 0 people and 9 percent (N = 81) for the 0 − people. Our hunch that people who held basically the same attitude toward the two candidates would show more intention–behavior change was sustained but with a rather interesting pattern. The + + people were the least volatile of these groups (10%, N = 1295), the − − people the most volatile (23%, N = 48), and the 00 people intermediate (17%, N = 52). The fact that the double negatives were most likely to change calls to mind a finding of Sheth and Newman (1981), who reported from their community survey done in Illinois in 1980 that many of the intention–behavior switchers were voting against someone rather than for someone. It may be that the intention–behavior link is most tenuous for people who are experiencing an avoidance–avoidance (− −) conflict.

When we attempted the same type of analysis for Sweden using data from three elections and focusing on the two largest parties, we could get enough people in only three of the six possible categories. For those three categories, the results are essentially the same as for the United States. The + − people were least likely to be intention–behavior changers (3%, N = 1481), followed by the +0 people (5%, N = 207), and the + + people (9%, N = 220).

The implication is that attitude and the attitude pattern a person holds can affect the strength of the intention–behavior link. Since the election studies generally do not have a measure of the intensity of the intention, we cannot confront that matter directly with empirical data. However, it seems reasonable to presume that the link between intention and behavior would tighten as the intensity of the intention increases. We could no more than speculate as to whether some of the apparently rather strong intervening variables we have identified would continue to play a role if the intensity of the intention were to be measured. It seems plausible to hypothesize that they would.

Interest and knowledge

We now turn to some intriguing empirical materials that have a bearing on normative democratic theory. Previously, reference was made to the paradox which emerged from early U.S. election studies (Berelson *et al.*, 1954). If a political system is to be adaptive or protean, some citizens within it must be prone to change their preferences across time. Yet the early U.S. election studies found that the switchers were neither very interested nor very knowledgeable about politics. From the vantage point of classical democratic theory regarding what a citizen in a democracy would be like, these are not the people whom one would want to change during an election campaign. Ideally, is it not the people who are interested in politics and who know what is happening that should be changing? If it is the people who are least interested and least knowledgeable who are shifting the most from intention to behavior, as may be the case in U.S. elections, is this not a situation in which parties and candidates will be tempted to make simplistic or demagogic appeals to the lowest common denominator?

Given prior research on involvement and volatility, it might be expected that there would be a simple linear relationship such that the strength of the intention–behavior relationship increases as involvement increases. As a matter of fact, it appears to work that way for the United States but not for Sweden. Figure 8.3 summarizes the effect of interest on the intention–behavior relationship combining across nine U.S. and six Swedish elections.[11]

The results for interest as an intervening variable in the U.S. are clear cut and consistent. In each of nine elections, those who said they were "very

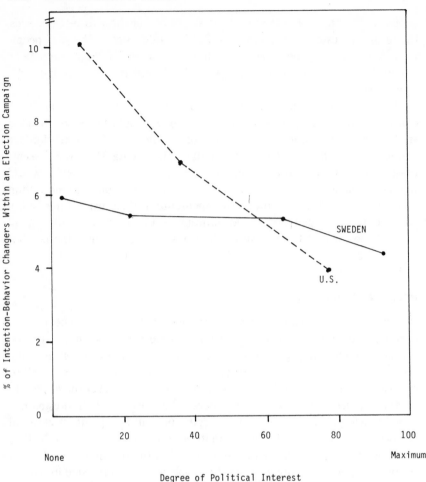

Figure 8.3. Percentage of intention–behavior changers in Sweden and the United States as a function of political interest, based on data combined across six Swedish and nine United States national election studies.

much interested" in the political campaign were least likely to change from intention to behavior (average across years = 4%), followed by those who were "somewhat interested" (7%), and those who were "not much interested" (10%). Because the groups were ordered the same way in each election and because the numbers of people on whom the preceding percentages are based are very large (4283, 4121, and 1597 for high, medium, and low interest, respectively), one can have considerable confidence that the effect shown for the U.S. is highly reliable.

On the other hand, the effect of interest as an intervening variable in the intention–behavior relationship for Sweden is weak and not consistent across years. In 1985, for instance, of those who said they were very much interested in politics, 94 percent had the same intention and behavior, compared to 94 percent of those with quite a lot of interest in politics, 96 percent for those not especially interested, and 96 percent for those not at all interested in politics. Combining across six elections, the percentage whose intention and behavior were different varied within a very narrow range for the four interest groups, as can be seen in figure 8.3. Taking the results for the two countries together, what we observe is a system-by-problem interaction, i.e., another instance in which the findings look noticeably different within the two political systems. The results for Sweden indicate that there is nothing inevitable or inexorable about the inverse relationship between involvement and volatility that has long been thought to exist in the U.S. (Berelson *et al.*, 1954; Lazarsfeld *et al.*, 1944).[12]

When we considered knowledge rather than interest as an intervening variable in the intention–behavior link, the results are similar. The 1985 Swedish study and the 1960 U.S. study contain several indicators of how well informed people are. The U.S. questions asked for knowledge about the two presidential candidates, while the Swedish survey had five issue questions and four questions dealing with the party affiliation of high-ranking members. When the items were combined to form a scale, the resulting knowledge indexes had reliability coefficients of .79 for the United States and .77 for Sweden (Cronbach's alpha).

Our concern here is whether knowledge appears to intervene in the intention–behavior relationship. That is, does the propensity to change from intention to behavior vary as a function of one's level of political knowledge? As with interest, the answer seems to vary as a function of the political system. In Sweden, as shown in figure 8.4, there is virtually no relationship between level of knowledge and propensity to change from intention to behavior. The percentage of changers varies only between 4 and 7 percent for the five knowledge levels, with the highest level of intention–behavior changing occurring among the highest and the moderately low levels of knowledge. So the finding for Sweden is a flat function with only minor deviations. In Sweden, the least knowledgeable citizens are clearly *not* the most volatile.

The results for the United States, also in figure 8.4, are similar but with one major exception. The people in the U.S. with the least knowledge were unusually likely to be intention–behavior changers (20%). The level of intention–behavior changing was low with little variation among the next three levels of knowledge (5%, 6%, 5%), and those with the most knowledge were the least likely to change from intention to behavior (3%). These results can also be seen as a system-by-problem interaction effect in

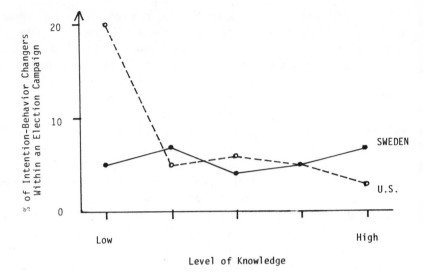

Figure 8.4. Percentage of intention–behavior changers in Sweden and the United States as a function of political knowledge, based on data from the 1985 Swedish and the 1960 United States national election studies.

which the relationship between level of knowledge and intention–behavior volatility is noticeably different for Sweden and the U.S.

Because the measures of knowledge were quite different and taken at different times in Sweden and the U.S., we also considered an alternative measure of political knowledge that has been used in five more recent U.S. election studies (1968–1984). After the interview, the interviewer is asked to rate the respondent's "general level of information about politics and public affairs" using a 5-point rating scale.[13]

We compared the percentage of intention–behavior changers among people who were rated above average, average, and below average by this subjective measure of political knowledge. In each study, those rated above average in knowledge were less likely to be intention–behavior changers than those rated below average in political knowledge. Combining across the five elections, of those rated below average in knowledge, 11 percent (N = 943) were intention–behavior changers, compared to 6 percent (N = 2041) of those who were rated average, and 4 percent (N = 2550) of those rated above average in political knowledge. Thus, by another measure of political knowledge, we see that in the United States, those with little political knowledge are more likely to change from intention to behavior than people with more knowledge. Yet, there is no reason to think it works that way in Sweden.

That the results for interest and knowledge would show similar results is

Table 8.5 *Intention–behavior changing in three election studies and position on an interest–knowledge index*

			Percentage of intention–behavior changers	Percentage of sample	Difference
Sweden	Interest–	High	37	27	+10
1985	knowledge	Medium	35	44	−9
	index	Low	28	29	−1
			100	100	
U.S.	Interest–	High	7	24	−17
1984	knowledge	Medium	61	54	+7
	index	Low	32	22	+10
			100	100	
U.S.	Interest–	High	19	30	−11
1960	knowledge	Medium	32	42	−10
	index	Low	49	28	+21
			100	100	

Note: The left-hand column gives the percentage of the intention–behavior changers who are at a given level on the interest–knowledge index. The second column gives the percentage of the sample who are at each level of the interest–knowledge index. The third column gives the difference between the two percentages.

not surprising in that these two intervening variables are not independent. In each survey, interest and knowledge are positively correlated, +.44 in Sweden in 1985 between political interest and the knowledge index, +.47 in the U.S. in 1960 between interest in the campaign and the knowledge index, and +.44 in the U.S. in 1984 between interest in the campaign and interviewer rated knowledge. Therefore, we wanted to see what happens when interest and knowledge are given equal weight and combined into an index. This was done for each of these three surveys, and then the distribution was divided as nearly as possible into a 30–40–30 split on the interest–information index.

The results in table 8.5 reinforce earlier findings. Within the U.S. those low in interest and knowledge are overrepresented among the intention–behavior switchers, while in Sweden those high in interest and knowledge are overrepresented among the intention–behavior switchers.

An interest–partisan typology

An alternative approach in the search for intervening variables in the intention–behavior relationship focuses on the intersection of interest and partisanship. Some years ago, Allen Barton (1955), in a methodological discussion of property space, suggested a typology considering political interest and party identification simultaneously. Those who identified with a party and had considerable interest in politics were called *partisans*. People with higher interest but who did not identify with a party were called *independents*. Those who identified with a party but lacked interest in politics were called *habituals*, and finally nonidentifiers who lacked interest were called *apathetics*. While such labels may be descriptive, whether what they imply is accurate (e.g., whether the "habituals" really are habitual voters) is an empirical question. This typology seemed to be potentially useful for our purposes, even though it is not clear that Barton went beyond creating the typology.

A similar typology was devised and used by Olof Petersson (1977) in his analysis of the 1976 Swedish election. He described four types: *partiaktiva* (interested partisans), *fribrytare* (interested nonpartisans), *vaneröstare* (uninterested partisans), and *passiva* (uninterested nonpartisans), and showed how differentiating people in this way could be useful in political analysis. For instance, the four categories differed noticeably in how well their vote could be predicted from class and ideology, how much political trust they had, and how likely they were to split their vote at the local and national levels. Most suggestive for our purposes, Petersson showed the four types differed significantly in across-election volatility and in when they decided how they were going to vote in the current election. Curiously, the interested nonpartisans (*fribrytare*) were the most volatile across elections and also the most likely to report having decided how to vote relatively late during the election campaign (Petersson, 1977; Esaiasson, 1985b).

Tables 8.6 and 8.7 show the trend in the percentage of these four types across time in Sweden and the United States, respectively. Within Sweden, things are quite stable between 1968 and 1985 with perhaps a slight increase in the proportion of interested nonpartisans and uninterested nonpartisans. In the United States, there is a rather sudden increase in the percentage of apathetics between 1968 and 1972. The percentage of interested partisans seems to have dropped across years, especially if one compares 1964 and 1984 (Wattenberg, 1986; 1987).

The same tables show how the percentage of intention–behavior changers varies across the four types. In Sweden, the uninterested partisans are *least* likely to change from intention to behavior, followed closely by interested partisans. Interested nonpartisans and uninterested nonpartisans were considerably more likely to be intention–behavior changers and did not differ significantly from each other. The lower portion of table 8.6 repeats the analysis but with regard to intention–behavior changing across

Table 8.6 *Four types of voters in Sweden and the percentage of each type who are intention–behavior changers*

Political interest		High Yes "Partiaktiva" (%)	Low Yes "Vaneröstare" (%)	High No "Fribrytare" (%)	Low No "Passiva" (%)	Sum (%)	N
Partisan		Sweden					
	1985	34	21	18	27	100	1164
	1982	36	24	16	24	100	1334
	1979	37	23	19	21	100	1175
	1976	35	24	18	23	100	1301
	1973	34	23	17	26	100	1116
	1968	37	27	14	22	100	1270
Five-party	1985	5	2	8	7		
changers	1982	4	1	7	11		
intention–	1979	4	4	10	8		
behavior	1976	3	5	15	12		
	1973	3	5	10	10		
	1968	2	3	11	10		
	Combined	4	3	10	10		
Bloc	1985	1	0	2	3		
changers	1982	1	1	2	1		
intention–	1979	1	2	4	3		
behavior	1976	1	3	3	8		
	1973	1	3	6	4		
	1968	1	1	3	4		
	Combined	1	2	3	4		
	N	2346	1510	691	806		

blocs rather than across parties. There is not much variance to explain there, but it appears that partisans are less likely to change across bloc lines from intention to behavior than are nonpartisans.

The results for the U.S. in table 8.7 present a rather different picture. The apathetic or passive uninterested nonpartisans are the most likely to be intention–behavior changers followed by the uninterested partisans, the interested nonpartisans, and the interested partisans. Thus, with regard to intention–behavior changing, different patterns emerge in Sweden and the United States. In Sweden, partisanship is the key, and interest is not important in determining the probability of intention–behavior changing. In the United States, on the other hand, interest appears to exert the stronger effect.[14]

Table 8.8 examines what percentage of the changers are of each type and how that compares with the percentage of that type in the population.

Table 8.7 *Four types of voters in the United States and the percentage of each type who are intention–behavior changers*

Interest in campaign		United States					
		High	Low	High	Low		
		Yes	Yes	No	No		
Partisan		"Partisans" (%)	"Habituals" (%)	"Independents" (%)	"Apathetics" (%)	Sum (%)	N
	1984	21	43	8	28	100	2229
	1980	20	43	10	27	100	1546
	1976	27	36	10	27	100	2862
	1972	22	42	9	27	100	2696
	1968	27	42	12	19	100	1544
	1964	32	44	7	17	100	1553
	1960	30	45	8	17	100	1902
	1956	24	49	6	21	100	1748
	1952	28	46	9	17	100	1762
Two-party	1984	1	6	3	6		
changers	1980	3	9	1	13		
intention–	1976	4	8	7	10		
behavior	1972	6	8	7	8		
	1968	5	8	5	9		
	1964	4	6	6	5		
	1960	4	7	4	14		
	1956	2	9	10	9		
	1952	3	7	3	10		
	Combined	4	7	5	9		
	N	3332	4196	942	1520		

Among intention–behavior changers, the uninterested partisans are clearly underrepresented in Sweden but overrepresented in the United States. On the other hand, the interested nonpartisans are overrepresented among the intention–behavior changers in Sweden but underrepresented in the United States. Thus, the label given by Barton (1955) to the uninterested partisans, "habituals," seems to fit the behavior of uninterested partisans in Sweden quite well, but the comparable group in the U.S. less well.

To summarize the two previous sections, it has long been recognized in normative democratic theory that people who are willing and ready to change between and within election campaigns provide flexibility and adaptability to a political system. Ideally, however, one would want people in this "floating bloc" to be interested, attentive, and informed as to what is going on in politics and specifically regarding the nature of the alternatives in electoral politics. It does not take us far beyond the data we have presented to suggest that the changers in Sweden more closely approximate that ideal or standard than do their counterparts in the United States.

Table 8.8 *Comparison of the percentage of intention–behavior changers in each of four types of voters with the percentage of those types of voters in Sweden and the United States*

	Sweden			United States		
	Percentage of intention–behavior changers	Overall percentage	Difference	Percentage of intention–behavior changers	Overall percentage	Difference
Interested partisans	30	44	−14	20	33	−13
Uninterested partisans	17	28	−11	50	42	+8
Interested nonpartisans	25	13	+12	8	10	−2
Uninterested nonpartisans	28	15	+13	22	15	+7
	100	100		100	100	
N	282	5353		617	9990	

Intentions beyond the mainstream

Our analysis so far has focused almost entirely on people who intend to vote for one of the five parties represented in the Swedish Parliament or for the presidential nominee of one of the two large parties in the United States. What about the other people who intend to vote outside or beyond this mainstream? Combining across years, we located 156 people in the Swedish studies who intended to vote for some party other than the five main ones and who also later reported their vote. Of these people, 118 (76%) behaved as implied by their previously stated intention. Thus, it appears that people who intend to vote for a party outside the mainstream are less likely to vote in line with their intention than people who intend to vote for a mainstream party.[15]

Within Sweden, there are two parties, the Christian Democratic and Environmental parties, which have received about 2 percent each of the vote in recent elections. By 1985, neither had come really close to the 4 percent minimum required for representation in the parliament. Nonetheless each had enough support to show up in reasonably adequate numbers in the election studies, especially if one combines across years. Across years, 87 percent of those who intended to vote for the Christian Democratic Party later reported doing so (N = 99). So it appears that the Christian Democratic Party was about as successful in obtaining the votes of people who intended to vote for it as the least successful of the five main parties, the Liberal Party.

The Environmental Party came on the scene somewhat later, and thus shows up in somewhat smaller numbers in the combined surveys. Thus far, the Environmental Party has received only 70 percent of the votes of people who intended to vote for it (N = 33). In 1986 and 1987 (after the Chernobyl disaster), the public opinion polls often reported support for the Environmental Party to be well above 4 percent. This would seem to enhance their prospects for the 1988 election. The Communist Party, which has remained just barely above the 4 percent threshold over several elections, has been relatively well able to retain the vote of people who intended to vote for it (table 8.2). Moreover, the Communist Party has been the beneficiary of tactical voting by some people who really prefer the Social Democratic Party but who do not see it as in their interest that the Communists be excluded from the parliament (Holmberg, 1984).[16]

Since World War II, several third-party and independent candidates for the presidency in the U.S. have been sufficiently strong to attract attention by the mass media and to register significant minorities in public opinion polls, as well as actual votes on election day. One might mention in particular the candidacies of Henry Wallace and Strom Thurmond in 1948, George Wallace in 1968, and John Anderson, Ed Clark, and Barry Commoner in 1980. Although none came close to actually winning the presidency, in a democratic system with a different set of rules (e.g., proportional representation in a parliament), the forces represented and mobilized by these candidates would have been more successful in securing a voice in government.

If we trace George Wallace in 1968 and John Anderson in 1980 in the polls, Anderson appears to have peaked sooner (June), and experienced a larger fall-off in support than Wallace, who peaked later (September). However, both candidates lost considerable support between September and the election in November. Anderson's support was approximately cut in half during this time, while Wallace appears to have lost about a third of his erstwhile supporters.

Thus, when we turn to the election study panels of these years, we expect to find a relatively high level of intention–behavior changing among the Wallace and Anderson intenders. Among the 120 people who intended to vote for Wallace, 85 (75%) later reported having voted for Wallace. This is substantially lower than the corresponding percentage for people who intended to vote for one of the two major party candidates, Hubert Humphrey (91%) and Richard Nixon (also 91%). Among the Wallace intenders who abandoned Wallace, the majority voted for Nixon rather than Humphrey (by a ratio of 63:37).

Similar results were obtained in 1980. Among the 86 people in the 1980 election study who intended to vote for Anderson, only 51 (59%) later reported doing so. This is substantially lower than the corresponding percentages for the two major party candidates, Jimmy Carter (86%) and Ronald Reagan (96%). Again, the Republican candidate was the major beneficiary among the Anderson intenders who departed from their intentions. Coincidentally, by the same ratio as in 1968, Anderson intenders who changed from intention to behavior favored Reagan over Carter in their vote by a margin of 63 to 37 percent.

So a major problem for third-party and independent candidates for the U.S. presidency is not only to attract support but also to retain the support they have succeeded in attracting. The usual reaction to this fall-off problem is rather facile – "Well, people don't want to throw away their votes." As we shall see, such an explanation may contain, at the most, part of the picture of why there is this fall-off in support for the "other" candidates (Smallwood, 1983).

Because Wallace's support was higher in September and October and more concentrated demographically than Anderson's, the 1968 results offer more potential for internal analysis than those of 1980. If the "not wanting to throw one's vote away" explanation were valid, people's expectations regarding the outcome of the election should make a difference – that is, expectation should intervene in the intention–behavior relationship. In 1980, of those who were interviewed in the election study, only a few indicated that they expected Anderson to win. However, in 1968 a substantial minority (32%) of the Wallace intenders said they expected Wallace to win. Were these people who expected Wallace to win more likely to stick with him in their votes than other Wallace intenders who expected Humphrey or Nixon to win? We can detect no more than a slight trend in that direction. Among Wallace intenders who expected Wallace to win, 73 percent (N = 30) later voted for him, compared to 67 percent (N = 78) of the Wallace intenders who expected Humphrey or Nixon to win. This difference is so small that it could easily be nothing more than a random fluctuation, even though it is in the "right" direction.

In the preelection polls, it was evident that Wallace was drawing relatively more support from young white men with little formal education living in the southern region of the U.S. Berelson *et al.* (1954, p. 283) theorized that "Intentions supported by one's social surroundings are more predictably carried out than are intentions lacking such support."[17] For reasons having to do with the magnitude of the difference and the nature of the demographic categories, the regional difference seems the most suitable for a test of the Berelson *et al.* proposition. Among Wallace intenders living in the "Deep South" where he had more support overall, 81 percent (N = 52) later voted for Wallace, compared to 63 percent (N = 68) of the Wallace intenders living elsewhere in the U.S. The only other intervening variable differentiating the behavior of the Wallace intenders was political interest. Among the Wallace intenders who expressed a great deal of interest in the political campaign, 83 percent (N = 58) later voted for Wallace, compared to 60 percent (N = 62) of the Wallace intenders with lower interest.

In 1980, there was a trend for middle-class Anderson intenders to be more likely to vote for Anderson than working-class Anderson intenders (66 to 42%). Also, younger Anderson intenders may have been somewhat more likely to vote for Anderson than older Anderson intenders.

The most intriguing finding regarding Anderson intenders and their subsequent behavior pertains to their attitudes toward the three main candidates measured before the election. When intention is held constant in 1980, could subsequent behavior be related to attitudes held when intentions were measured? Anderson intenders who subsequently voted for Anderson had, on the preelection survey, rated Anderson more positively (+ 3.1) than Anderson intenders who later voted for Carter (+ 1.8) or Reagan (+ 2.9).[18] Moreover, among Anderson intenders who departed from their intention, it was predictable which way they would turn. That is, Anderson intenders who later voted for Reagan had previously indicated that they liked Reagan (+ 0.3) more than Carter (− 1.2). Similarly, Anderson intenders who later voted for Carter had indicated liking Carter (+ 0.1) more than Reagan (− 2.2). These results are theoretically important in that they indicate that attitudes can be used to predict behavior even among people who have the same intention (Bentler and Speckart, 1979; Zuckerman and Reis, 1978). As additional support for the idea that attitudes can exert a direct effect on behavior even when intention is held constant, people who intended and later voted for Carter were both more favorable to Carter and more unfavorable toward Reagan in preelection attitudes than people who intended to vote for Carter but later switched to Reagan.[19]

Finally, in thinking about the relatively high intention–behavior volatility among people who intend to vote *outside* the mainstream, recall what was shown to intervene in the intention–behavior relationship among people whose intention was *within* the mainstream. Most of these people intended to vote as they had before and in a way implied by their party preference, and the intention–behavior link among these people was especially strong. The intention–behavior relationship was shown to weaken very considerably for people whose intention was different from their prior behavior or whose intention was different from their party preference. If neither prior behavior nor self-identity reinforced intention, the intention–behavior linkage weakened very considerably. In fact, the intention–behavior relationship for these people may have been about as strong as that of the Wallace and Anderson intenders. Thus, when we consider the relatively high fall-off in support from intention to behavior for the Wallace and Anderson intenders, it is important to recall what they lack, in comparison to most other voters. Namely, Wallace and Anderson intenders were intending to do something new which they had not done before and also something that was not implied by the party preference facet of their self-identity. On these grounds alone one would expect them to show a relatively high rate of intention–behavior defection.

On the road from intention to behavior

The social psychologist is interested in the theoretical issue of what happens along the way from intention to behavior. In the context of what we are studying, the answer of the political scientist is that an election campaign takes place in which some people change their minds while others hold fast to their original intention. Still others may vacillate during the campaign but end up behaving as would be implied by initial intention. We have seen that overall the intention–behavior relationship is very strong in both Sweden and the United States and does not vary much as a function of gender, age, education, or when during the campaign the intention was measured.

Several political scientists have used vote intention as a surrogate measure for the vote. However, we have shown that certain politically relevant variables, especially political interest and information in the U.S., partisanship in Sweden, vote in the prior election, and whether party preference reinforces or contradicts the voting intention are significant intervening variables. Also, people who have social support for their intention may be more likely to do what they intend to do. Finally, in both Sweden and the U.S., people who intend to vote for a party or candidate outside the mainstream are less likely to do so than people who intend to vote for an alternative within the mainstream.

By some margin the most intriguing finding in this chapter has to do with the characteristics of the intention–behavior changers in Sweden and the United States. The findings for the United States constitute an extensive replication of the early analysis pertaining to the Berelson–Lazarsfeld paradox. That is, the flexibility and adaptability of the U.S. system depends upon citizens who do not fit the classical conception of the ideal citizen in a democracy. In the United States, intention–behavior changers tend disproportionately to be those who know little and lack an interest in politics. Sweden, with its strong party system, presents a very different picture. Within Sweden, there is a category of people who identify with a party but lack an interest in politics (*vaneröstare*), and they show low volatility between elections and within election campaigns. The intention–behavior changers in Sweden are *not* likely to be especially low in either political interest or political knowledge. One of the groups with the highest proportion of intention–behavior changers in Sweden is the interested non-partisans (*fribrytare*).

9 Prior behavior, recalled behavior, and the prediction of subsequent voting behavior

Is voting behavior better understood by reference to what people have done in the past or by how they currently reconstruct their past actions? The fallibility of human memory provides an opportunity to address this matter. Within social psychology, the general theoretical orientations of behaviorism and field theory generate different perspectives on this problem.

Behaviorism as a school of thought in psychology is well known for its focus on describing, predicting, and controlling behavior (Skinner, 1973). These topics are pursued to the exclusion of phenomena of interest to other investigators (e.g., experience, motivation, personality, perception, and memory). A fundamental tenet of behaviorism has been that in order to predict how a person will behave in a certain situation, observe how the person has behaved in similar situations in the past. Humans, like other animals, are seen as being in large measure creatures of habit, their behavior being shaped and modified by varying environmental contingencies.

As an example of predicting subsequent behavior on the basis of prior behavior, one of the best predictors of how members of the U.S. House Judiciary Committee voted regarding the impeachment of Richard Nixon in 1974 was a "Presidential Support Score" ($r = .86$), based on the degree to which each Representative had voted in line with the preferences of Nixon in 1973 (Granberg, 1980). Thus, even in the relatively novel situation of considering removal of a President from office through impeachment, prior behavior was a strong predictor. Most social psychologists would assume that the attitudes of the Representatives toward Nixon would affect their voting in both 1973 and 1974. To the strict behaviorist, however, the concept of attitude is neither necessary nor useful and, in fact, is regarded as nonscientific or prescientific. The behaviorist might say that Representatives had developed a habit of supporting (or opposing) Nixon and this habit had a strong, almost dominating influence on their subsequent behavior.

Field theory, by contrast, claims to be *ahistorical* in its approach to analyzing behavior. According to field theory, a person's behavior is a function of the individual's life space, that is, features of the person and the environment which can exert a force at a given point in time (Lewin, 1943).

The past, including past behavior, can have an impact on subsequent behavior only insofar as it is represented in the person's current life space.[1] Thus, from this vantage point, it is not important to know how an individual has behaved in the past. Rather, it is important to know the construction or reconstruction the person currently places upon events that have occurred previously.

To examine these alternative perspectives empirically, it is necessary to create or find a situation in which a person's current memory or construction of the past departs from the person's prior behavior in some significant way. For many decisions, prior behavior and recalled behavior coincide. Although they may be distinguishable analytically and operationally, they often cannot be separated empirically. If one decides to buy a home in the suburbs rather than a condominium in the center of a city, one will be reminded daily of the decision. So unless one is out of touch with reality, prior and recalled behavior would be the same in that situation. However, in the case of voting in elections, the situation is quite different.

Prior and recalled voting behavior can vary mainly because of the inconsequentiality or lack of genuine efficacy of an individual's vote. That Margaret Thatcher is Prime Minister of Britain, for example, *by itself* tells the individual British citizen next to nothing about his or her vote in the prior election, inasmuch as her election was determined indirectly by the aggregated votes of the British electorate for Members of Parliament. This inconsequentiality increases, of course, as the size of the electorate increases. In a large electorate, the probability of a person's vote making a difference in the outcome is minuscule. Anthony Downs (1957) has even argued that strictly speaking it is almost never rational for the individual in a large electorate to spend the time and energy it takes to cast an informed vote.[2]

Overall, it may be relatively easy for citizens to forget how they voted, especially for people who are subject to cross-pressures, low in political involvement, or volatile in their voting pattern.[3] Also, people may not like to admit, to themselves or to others, that they have changed parties.

Voting and recalled voting thus comprise a situation in which past behavior and recalled behavior might diverge. Our research questions in this chapter, therefore, are twofold. First, we want to examine the level of inconsistency in recalling prior voting behavior and to identify factors associated with this inconsistency. Secondly, for those for whom prior behavior and recalled behavior are not the same, comparisons are made to see whether prior behavior or current recollection of past behavior more effectively predicts subsequent behavior. Behaviorism implies that memory is not relevant and there should be a direct effect of prior behavior on subsequent behavior. Field theory, on the other hand, implies only an indirect effect of prior behavior on subsequent behavior, as mediated through recalled behavior.

Studying recalled voting behavior

In studying recalled voting behavior, cross-sectional data are of some interest but difficult to use. It is well known, for instance, that following his assassination in 1963, many more people in representative samples of U.S. adults claimed to have voted for John Kennedy for President than his actual share of the 1960 vote. In the General Social Surveys done by the National Opinion Research Center of the University of Chicago in March of 1982 and 1983, the number of people claiming to have voted for Jimmy Carter outnumbered those claiming they voted for Ronald Reagan in 1980. This is rather intriguing, given that Reagan actually outpolled Carter by 10 percent (51 to 41) in 1980. This finding most likely bears some relation to the rather dire economic circumstances of the U.S. recession during Reagan's first term as President, although it could also conceivably be due to a sampling or other methodological problem.

Although it may be worthwhile to relate the recalled voting behavior of a population to crucial events such as war, depression, assassination, or impeachment in cross-sectional analyses (Mueller, 1973), ambiguities are endemic in such analyses. Panel data, focusing on the individual as the unit of analysis, clearly permit a more incisive analysis. It is common in panel studies to ask people to recall or reconstruct how they voted in previous elections. When responses to this and similar questions have been analyzed in panel data by political and social scientists, their focus has often centered on the question of the validity of the recall responses (Clausen, 1968; Katz, Niemi, and Newman, 1980; Niemi, Katz, and Newman, 1980; Smith, 1984; Traugott and Katosh, 1979; Traugott and Tucker, 1984). For instance, can we validly measure how people voted in 1980 by asking them in 1984 how they voted in 1980? This led to the associated question of how people who recall their vote inaccurately or inconsistently differ from those whose recall is accurate or consistent (Himmelweit, Biberian, and Stockdale, 1978; Waldahl and Aardal, 1982; van der Eijk and Niemöller, 1979, 1983; Weir, 1975).

With regard to validity, one can raise the question, what is it that we are really trying to measure? Political scientists generally have assumed that if we ask people in 1985 how they voted in 1982, we are trying to measure how they voted in 1982. A social psychologist working from a field theory perspective might say that we *could* be trying to measure how the individual currently recalls voting, or reconstructs the voting act, three years after the fact.

Six panel studies

Each of the six panel studies used here began with a sample drawn to be representative of adults in that society.[4] Four panel studies of Swedish voters (1976–1979, 1979–1982, 1980–1982, 1982–1985) and two panel studies of the U.S. electorate (1956–1960 and 1972–1976) provide the data for our analysis. The 1980–1982 Swedish panel deals with voting and recalled voting in the nuclear power referendum, while the other three Swedish panels deal with voting and recalled voting in regular parliamentary elections. The two U.S. panels deal with voting and recalled voting in presidential elections. In our analyses, *prior behavior* is measured by asking people shortly after an election (1956, 1972, 1976, 1979, 1980, 1982) how they voted in that election. *Recalled behavior* is measured by asking people some years later (1960, 1976, 1979, 1982, 1985) how they voted in the previous election. *Subsequent behavior* is measured by asking people shortly after the next election (1960, 1976, 1979, 1982, 1985) how they voted in that election.

We realize that this interpretation is not beyond question. If people's reported vote is different from how they recall voting when asked some years later, all that is certain is that they could *not* be reporting their vote correctly both times, given that the two behaviors are mutually exclusive. Also, people who report their vote consistently could be incorrect both times. However, there are theoretical and empirical reasons for assuming that people are generally more accurate in reporting their behavior when the behavior has occurred very recently. Therefore, people who have worked on this problem have generally assumed that if people report their vote inconsistently, it is most likely the later answer that is incorrect (Waldahl and Aardal, 1982; Weir, 1975).

Consistency in reporting candidate and party voting

An indication of the overall results for these panels is given in Table 9.1. In the 1956–1960 U.S. panel, 90 percent of the people recalled their prior vote accurately (i.e., gave the same response) four years later. However, people who voted for Dwight Eisenhower in 1956 were more likely to recall, in 1960, voting for Eisenhower (93%) than Adlai Stevenson voters were to recall voting for Stevenson (84%). This difference reflects the tendency that has been called a "drift toward the winner" (Weir, 1975).

A comparable drift did not occur in the 1972–1976 U.S. panel in which,

Table 9.1 *Percentage reporting their vote inconsistently and therefore inaccurately in six panel studies*

	Presidential elections		Parliamentary election			Nuclear power referendum
	U.S. 1956–60	U.S. 1972–76	Sweden 1976–79	Sweden 1979–82	Sweden 1982–85	Sweden 1980–82
All	10	7	8	8	8	17
Sex						
Men	9	5	7	7	8	17
Women	12	9	9	10	9	18
Age						
61+	7	7	7	5	8	19
31–60	10	7	8	10	9	17
18–30	19	9	10	8	7	15
Education						
High	7	5	9	8	8	14
Medium	14	10	7	10	10	18
Low	9	10	9	6	7	19
Political interest						
High	8	6	6	3	9	11
Medium	12	9	5	7	7	14
Low	14	6	11	9	10	23
Strength of partisanship						
Strong	6	8	3	2	3	11
Not strong	15	8	7	7	8	18
Leaners	9	6	15	14	13	22
None	14	4	9	16	16	31
Crossover voter						
Yes	23	19	29	25	37	28
No	8	4	5	6	5	13
Volatile voter						
Yes	26	17	33	32	31	25
No	7	4	2	3	3	13

Note: This table is based on questions asking people twice which party, candidate, or line they voted for, first shortly after the election and then again two to four years later. Each percentage in the table is the percentage of people in a given category who gave a different answer to the two questions. Since the two behaviors are mutually exclusive, two inconsistent answers could not both be correct as to how they voted. The percentage who gave the same answer both times would be 100 minus the percentage in this table. This would be the percentage who reported their behavior consistently, although we cannot say for certain that they did so accurately. Only people who said they voted and later recalled voting for one of the two main candidates in the U.S., for one of the five main parties in Sweden, or for one of the three alternatives in the referendum are included in the calculations in this table.

overall, 93 percent of the voters accurately recalled in 1976 their vote from four years previously. Those who voted for George McGovern were about as likely in 1976 to recall having voted for McGovern in 1972 (92%) as Richard Nixon voters were to recall voting for Nixon (93%). Nixon's political demise in 1974 may have prevented a drift toward the winner, if that is indeed the normal tendency.

With a multiparty system, one might suppose that the accuracy level in recall would be lower in Sweden than in the United States. For one thing, the chance level of giving the same answer on two occasions is much less when there are five alternatives (20%) than when there are only two alternatives (50%). Moreover, as the Norwegian researchers, Ragnar Waldahl and Bernt Aardal, put it, "The possibilities of remembering wrongly or mixing up parties [in a multiparty context] is naturally greater than when there are only two" (1982, p. 104). In their analyses of three Norwegian panel studies, an average of about 15 percent reported their vote inconsistently. This percentage is even higher, about 28 percent, in three panels from the Netherlands (van der Eijk and Niemöller, 1979). This is presumably due, in part, to the large number of political parties in the Dutch political system. Himmelweit, Biberian, and Stockdale (1978) reported that an average of about 25 percent in four British panel studies recalled their previous vote inaccurately.

However, the expectation that error in recall might be higher in Sweden's multiparty system than in the two-party U.S. system was not sustained. Overall, 92 percent of the Swedish voters recalled their prior vote in the parliamentary elections correctly. This high level is quite likely due to the strength and stability of party loyalty and identification in Sweden (Holmberg, 1981, 1984). Furthermore, when we consider the alignment of the five parties in Sweden's *Riksdag* into the socialist bloc and the bourgeois bloc, the percentage with accurate recall is even higher. Using this dichotomy, nearly all of the Swedish voters recalled correctly the bloc they had voted for three years previously (97%, 97%, and 98% in the first, second, and third panels, respectively).

The overall accuracy of 92 percent in the three Swedish panels was actually quite different for the specific parties. Combining data from the three panels, 97 percent of the Social Democratic voters recalled their vote correctly, compared to 91 percent for Center Party voters, 89 percent for the Conservatives, 87 percent for the Communists, and 80 percent for the Liberal Party. These differences reflect many factors at work including different levels of commitment to a particular party, volatility in voting within the bourgeois bloc, and the ups and downs in electoral support.

For instance, only 73 percent of those who voted for the Liberal Party in 1979 recalled doing so in 1982. This is associated with the decline of the Liberal Party during this three-year interval. Thus, in addition to "drifting away" from the Liberal Party in their vote, people also were disproportionately inclined to forget or deny their past votes for the Liberal Party. On the other hand, in 1985, 88 percent of those who had voted for the Liberal

Party three years earlier recalled doing so. This 15 percent difference in recall is associated with the almost unprecedented resurgence of the Liberal Party between 1982 and 1985 (Holmberg and Gilljam, 1987). Similarly, it has been shown that a substantial proportion of Communist voters in 1982 were tactical voters who really preferred the Social Democratic Party (Holmberg, 1984). Therefore, it is not surprising that only 79 percent of the Communist voters in 1982 accurately recalled their vote three years later.[5]

The results for the nuclear power referendum panel, shown in the right-hand column of table 9.1, present a rather different picture. Despite the time interval being slightly less, and the number of alternatives being only three instead of five, this 1980–1982 panel yielded 17 percent reporting their referendum vote inconsistently. This is about twice the level of inaccuracy in recall of parliamentary voting. Those who voted for the antinuclear alternative, Line 3, were more likely to later recall their vote accurately (92%) than were those who voted for the more pronuclear alternatives, Line 1 (77%) and Line 2 (76%).

Beyond specific candidate, party, or line preferences, we wish to identify factors associated with errors in recall, i.e., reporting one's vote inconsistently. Table 9.1 gives a breakdown of the tendency to report one's vote inaccurately as a function of sex, age, education, political interest, strength of partisanship, cross-over voting, and volatility in voting behavior. In each of the panels, men were more likely than women to report their vote consistently, but the difference was trivial. The effect of age was neither consistently linear nor large. With the exception of the nuclear power referendum, older people were at least as likely as younger people to report their vote consistently. In the U.S. panels, there was a slight tendency for people with more education to report their vote more accurately, but this was not true for the three Swedish parliamentary election panels.

There may be a tendency to report one's vote more accurately as political interest increases, but in the 1972–1976 U.S. panel, this effect was not there, and in the 1982–1985 Swedish panel, the medium interest voters were most accurate. Results for strength of party identification were similar. That is, strong identifiers were generally more likely to report their vote consistently, especially in the Swedish panels. In the U.S., however, this intervening variable produced irregular results.

By some margin, the variables in table 9.1 most strongly linked with inaccuracy in reporting one's vote were cross-over voting and political volatility. People whose vote coincides with their party identification are much more likely to later recall their vote accurately than people who cross-over and vote for an alternative other than that associated with their preferred party. Similarly, if prior behavior and subsequent behavior are the same, then prior behavior and recalled behavior are much more likely to be the same. Thus, *accuracy in recall is facilitated by consistency between self-identity and behavior and by consistency in behavior.*

The trend in regard to volatility was similar in both countries and reinforces previous reports (e.g., van der Eijk and Niemöller, 1979; Waldahl and Aardal, 1982). Yet, this trend appears somewhat more pronounced in Sweden than in the United States. In both countries volatile voters were much more likely to be inaccurate in recalling their prior voting behavior. However, in the United States volatile voters were only about four times as likely as stable voters to have inaccurate recall, while in Sweden volatile voters were more than ten times as likely to show inaccurate recall as stable voters. Although we have no direct evidence, this difference could be due to a normative factor. It is quite possible that the pressure to avoid admitting a change may be somewhat greater in Sweden. That is, people in the United States may feel more free to switch from one election to the next and may also be more willing to acknowledge that they have switched in this manner. Attachment to a party probably means more to people in Sweden than attachment to a party and its nominees in the United States.

We can also consider accuracy in recalling one's bloc vote in Sweden as a function of bloc volatility. Among people who voted for a different bloc than they had three years previously, 31 percent recalled their prior bloc vote incorrectly, compared to only 1 percent among those who voted for the same bloc in both elections. Clearly, volatility in voting is a key to understanding accuracy in recalling one's prior voting behavior.

.The strong anchoring effect of party preference is evident in the Swedish data. This feature of the Swedish political system may account *simultaneously* for why accuracy in recalling one's vote is as high in the Swedish parliamentary panels as in the U.S. presidential panels, in spite of the greater number of alternatives in Sweden, and why the accuracy is higher in Sweden than in other multiparty systems such as the Netherlands and Norway. This view is reinforced by the referendum data, in which the link between party preference and voting was weaker and the accuracy of recall in voting was also lower.

Our search for variables that could be related to accuracy in recalling one's voting behavior did not yield anything better than volatility in voting. Although it is not a better predictor of inaccuracy in recall than volatility, we want to at least mention another variable that is linked to inaccuracy because it is analytically distinct from volatility. The variable is *differential candidate evaluation*, indicated by the absolute difference between a person's affective ratings of the two candidates. The evidence from the 1972–1976 U.S. panel indicates that the differential candidate evaluation scores were considerably higher for people who recalled their vote accurately than for those recalling incorrectly. To use a marketing analogy, the more different

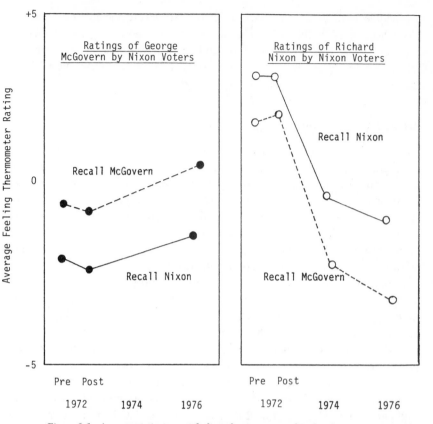

Figure 9.1. Average ratings on a feeling thermometer of Richard Nixon and George McGovern, 1972–1976, by people who reported voting for Nixon in 1972 but recalled having voted for McGovern when asked in 1976 (dotted lines), and by people who reported voting for Nixon in 1972 and recalled having voted for Nixon when asked in 1976 (solid lines). People were not asked to rate McGovern in 1974. As in prior chapters, the feeling thermometer scores are transformed from 0–100 to a −5 to +5 scale.

the brands seemed initially to the consumer, the more memorable the selection.

Finally, it might be assumed that people who recall their vote inaccurately would evaluate the candidates differently from people who recall their vote accurately, even though their initial behavior was identical. But at what point would such differences exist or emerge? Figure 9.1 shows that, in the case of Nixon voters, the differences were there all along.

Nixon voters who later recalled voting for Nixon rated Nixon significantly more favorably and McGovern significantly less favorably than Nixon voters who later recalled voting for McGovern in each of seven comparisons going from the preelection survey of 1972 through 1976. Notice that by 1976, the people who voted for Nixon but recalled voting for McGovern rated McGovern considerably higher than Nixon on the feeling thermometer. However, those who voted for Nixon and recalled having done so continued to rate Nixon higher than McGovern, even in 1976, two years after Nixon had resigned from the presidency in disgrace.

Reporting and recalling whether one voted

So far, we have focused on the candidate, party, or alternative in the referendum people chose and whether they later recall that selection in a consistent manner. This has also been the primary focus of others who have addressed the matter of accuracy in recalling one's voting behavior. However, the question could be shifted back to whether the person reported voting or not. Then, some years later, people are asked whether they voted in the prior election. Again, if they answer inconsistently, we know they cannot have been correct both times inasmuch as the two alternatives (voting and not voting in a given election) are mutually exclusive.[6]

In Sweden, about 98 percent give the same answer both times, compared to 90 percent in the United States. Thus, on this measure of recall accuracy, Swedish citizens are somewhat more accurate than U.S. citizens. This is almost certainly a function of the difference in voter turnout between the two systems. In both countries, people who say yes, they voted, when asked at Time 1 are much more likely to give the same answer at Time 2 than people who say no at Time 1. In the United States, 97 percent of those who said yes at Time 1 say at Time 2 that yes, they voted at Time 1. However, of those who say no at Time 1, nearly half (48%) say yes at Time 2. The comparable percentages for the Swedish panels were 99 and 33. That is, Swedish respondents who state at Time 1 that they did not vote are less likely to later claim that they had voted at Time 1 than are U.S. respondents (33 to 47%).[7] On the other hand, Swedish respondents who state at Time 1 that they did vote are slightly more likely later to give the same answer than U.S. respondents (99 to 97%).

Predicting subsequent voting behavior

When it comes to predicting subsequent behavior on the basis of prior behavior and recalled behavior, we analyzed the data in various ways. Figure 9.2 shows regression models summarizing the results for five panels.[8] Prior behavior and recalled behavior were the independent variables and subsequent behavior the dependent variable. It was presumed that prior behavior would impact on recalled behavior, but the questions were whether prior or recalled behavior would have the stronger effect on

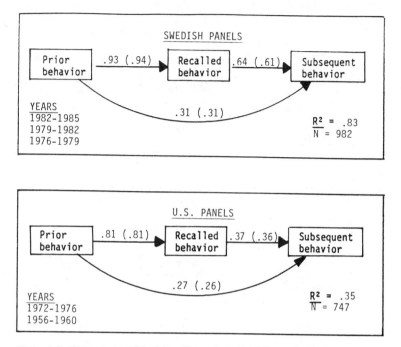

Figure 9.2. Regression model of the effects of recalled behavior and prior behavior on subsequent voting behavior in Sweden and the United States.
Note. The results for Sweden are based on an average of the results for three panels and those for the United States on an average of two panels. Coefficients in parentheses are standardized regression coefficients, while the other coefficients, other than R^2, are unstandardized regression coefficients.

subsequent behavior, and whether prior behavior would continue to exert a significant effect on subsequent behavior when the effect of recalled behavior was controlled.

The results should be interpreted cautiously because of the strong relationship between the independent variables in each panel, especially in Sweden. Nonetheless, in each panel, the regression coefficient for the effect of recalled behavior on subsequent behavior was stronger than that for the effect of prior behavior on subsequent behavior. Thus, if one were to choose, knowing which candidate or party the person currently recalls voting for provides a stronger predictor of subsequent voting choice than does knowing which party or candidate the person actually did vote for in a prior election.

Yet, it was also true that in each panel, prior behavior continued to exert a direct effect on subsequent behavior when the effect of recalled behavior on subsequent behavior was controlled. A reasonable interpretation would be that the results were mixed, offering some support for both

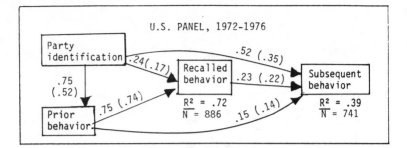

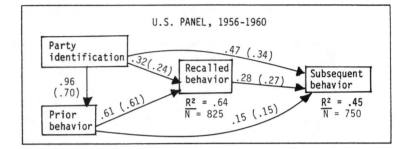

Figure 9.3. Regression model of the effects of party identification, prior behavior, and recalled behavior on subsequent behavior in two United States panel studies. Coefficients in the figure, in parentheses, are standardized regression coefficients. The other coefficients, other than R^2, are unstandardized regression coefficients. *Note.* Party identification is measured in the preelection surveys of 1956 and 1972. Prior behavior is measured on the postelection surveys in 1956 and 1972. Recalled behavior is measured on the preelection surveys of 1960 and 1976, and subsequent behavior on the postelection surveys of 1960 and 1976.

models but somewhat more for the field theoretical perspective than for behaviorism.

In figure 9.2, a much smaller percentage of the variation in subsequent voting behavior in the U.S. panels was explained than in the Swedish panels. Also, in the United States, party identification is analytically distinct from voting behavior and panel studies suggest that the former is actually somewhat more stable that the latter. It is well established that party identification is a major determinant and strong predictor of voting behavior in the United States. For these reasons, we repeated the regression analyses for the U.S. panels with party identification, measured at Time 1, as the third independent variable.

The results are shown in figure 9.3. Party identification had an effect on recalled behavior, though not so strong as the effect of prior behavior on recalled behavior. This means that people's recollection of how they voted is influenced by their party identification. Cross-over voters, that is, people

Table 9.2 *Subsequent voting as a function of prior behavior and recalled behavior, based on the combined results of two United States panels, 1956–1960 and 1972–1976*

		Percentage voting at Time 3		
		Recalled behavior, Time 2		Effect of recalled behavior
		Voted	Did not vote	
Prior behavior, Time 1	Voted	94	74	+20
	Did not vote	66	38	+28
	Effect of prior behavior	+28	+26	
		Percentage voting Democratic at Time 3		
		Recalled behavior, Time 2		Effect of recalled behavior
		Recall voting Democratic	Recall voting Republican	
Prior behavior, Time 1	Voted Democratic	87	69	+18
	Voted Republican	77	23	+54
	Effect of prior behavior	+10	+46	

Note: The entries within the two effects tables are percentages voting (upper) or voting Democratic (lower) at Time 3 as a function of prior behavior at Time 1 and recall at Time 2 of behavior at Time 1. Prior and subsequent behavior are based on self-report. The Ns within the upper table are 1683, 53, 149 and 156 for the upper left, upper right, lower left, and lower right percentages, respectively. The corresponding Ns for the lower table are 462, 65, 69, and 898. This table is based on a combination of results from the 1956–1960 and 1972–1976 U.S. panel studies.

voting for a candidate of a party other than the party they identify with, were shown in table 9.1 to recall their vote less accurately than people who are not cross-over voters (Weir, 1975).

Figure 9.3 also shows that party identification at Time 1 had a significant effect on subsequent voting behavior at Time 2, even when the effects of prior behavior and recalled behavior are controlled. In fact, the effect of party identification was the strongest predictor of subsequent voting behavior in these regression analyses involving three independent variables. Both prior behavior and recalled behavior exerted significant effects on subsequent behavior after party identification was controlled, but of these two, the coefficient for recalled behavior was stronger than that for prior behavior. This can be interpreted as additional support for the view that our results tend to favor field theory over behaviorism. Although the coefficients are not identical for the two panels, the relative magnitude and ordering of the coefficients are similar. This would seem to argue for the generalizability of our findings.

Because of the strong relationship between prior voting behavior and recalled behavior, our central problem should also be addressed by simply

Table 9.3 *Prior behavior, recalled behavior, and subsequent voter turnout in Sweden*

		Percentage voting at Time 3		
		Recalled behavior, Time 2		Effect of Recalled
		Voted	Did not vote	behavior
Prior behavior,	Voted	98	76	+22
Time 1	Did not vote	78	55	+23
	Effect of prior behavior	+20	+21	

Note: The entries within this effects table are the percentages voting at Time 3 as a function of prior behavior at Time 1 and recall at Time 2 of behavior at Time 1. Prior behavior at Time 1 and subsequent behavior at Time 3 are based on the vote measure as validated by Sweden's Central Statistical Bureau. The Ns within the table are 5115, 58, 150, and 172 for the upper left, upper right, lower left, and lower right percentages, respectively. The analyses are based on a combination of five preelection surveys, 1973–1985.

examining percentages rather than relying only on regression analyses. Table 9.2 shows the relevant U.S. results in percentage terms. In the upper portion of table 9.2, whether the person reported voting subsequently is the dependent variable. In that effects table, the behavior of the people in the upper right and lower left are of the greatest interest in that for them prior reported behavior and recalled behavior are in conflict. Of those 202 people, 55 percent behaved as implied by their recalled rather than their prior behavior. As the effect column and row indicate, it appears that both prior and recalled behavior have an effect in that analysis.

The lower portion of table 9.2 presents the comparable analysis of candidate selection. Not surprisingly, those who voted Democratic and recalled voting Democratic in the prior election are the most likely to vote Democratic in the subsequent election. Of the 134 people with conflicting prior and recalled behaviors, 54 percent voted in a manner consistent with their recalled behavior. The effects shown in percentage terms indicate that both prior and recalled behavior appear to have an effect on subsequent behavior when the other independent variable is held constant. However, the effect of recalled behavior appears slightly stronger.

The analysis of the Swedish data proceeded similarly, but here we take advantage of a special feature of the Swedish election studies. For each of five election studies, people have been asked before the election whether they voted in the prior election. This is used as the measure of recalled behavior. For each respondent, the official records were used to determine whether the person actually voted in the prior and current elections. Thus, the analysis in table 9.3 relied on one subjective recall question and two objective indicators of actual behavior. Perhaps the most direct reading of table 9.3 is that people who voted and recalled voting were most likely to

Table 9.4 *Percentage voting in a manner consistent with recalled behavior rather than prior behavior among those in three Swedish panels whose prior and recalled party voted for were different*

| Panel | Recall question asked on | | Overall | N |
	Preelection interview	Postelection interview		
1982–1985	56	68	62	58
1979–1982	48	69	61	62
1976–1979	73	74	74	61
Combined	59	70	66	181

Note: The three left-hand columns give percentages of people who later voted for same party as they recall voting for previously among people whose prior and recalled vote were not the same. The percentage of these people who voted for the same party as their prior vote would be 100 minus the percentage in this table. The right-hand column gives the number of people in each row.

vote subsequently (98%), those who did not vote and recalled not voting were least likely to vote later (55%), and those whose prior and recalled vote conflicted were intermediate. People who were false negatives in regard to the prior election (voted but recalled not voting) were only slightly more likely to vote subsequently than the false positives, who did not vote but recalled voting (78 to 76%).

Altogether, there were 208 people, combining across five election studies, for whom prior and recalled voting were in conflict with regard to turnout. Of these, 63 percent went with their recalled behavior rather than their prior behavior in their subsequent behavior. However, when the results are expressed in percentage differences as the effect of one while holding the other constant, both prior and recalled behavior appear to exert an effect, and the strength of the two effects is very similar.

When we turn to party choice in the three Swedish panels, we found a total of 181 people who voted for one of the five main parties, later recalled voting for another of these five parties, and later voted in a way that was consistent with either their prior or recalled behavior. As shown in table 9.4, 66 percent of these people went with their recalled rather than their prior behavior. The design of the Swedish surveys is that about half of the people are given a lengthy interview, containing the recall question, before the election and the other half is interviewed after the election. Table 9.4 shows the results may be affected somewhat by when the recall question is asked. For the people whose prior and recalled behavior are not the same, the likelihood of recalled behavior and subsequent behavior being the same is slightly higher for those asked the recall question after rather than before the election (70 to 59%).

To sum up then, the regression and percentage analyses seem to point toward roughly the same conclusions. The subsequent behavior of people whose prior behavior and recalled behavior are inconsistent is intermediate between those for whom prior behavior and recalled behavior is consistent. In support of field theory, there may be a trend in the data for recalled behavior to be a slightly better predictor of subsequent behavior than is prior behavior. However, this trend is not especially pronounced, and by no means dominant. Moreover, in support of behaviorism, it was demonstrated repeatedly that prior behavior not only exerts an indirect effect on subsequent behavior through recalled behavior, but it also exerts a direct effect on subsequent behavior even when the effect of recalled behavior is controlled. Thus, our conclusion is that the results are mixed and do not offer unequivocal or strong support for either behaviorism or field theory. The results tend to favor the perspective of field theory, though not by a large or decisive margin.

Recalling prior behavior and subsequent behavior

The finding that volatility and cross-over voting are directly correlated with inaccuracy in recalling one's past vote, while consistent with other reports, is not entirely obvious or self-evident. One might suppose, for instance, that if people have a stable party preference but that for some reason in a particular election, the person deviates from a well-trod path, this would be especially memorable. Apparently not. Consistency between self-identity and behavior and consistency in behavior across time appears to facilitate accuracy in recalling that behavior. Voters generally may be reluctant to acknowledge that they have changed their minds.

On the matter of whether prior behavior or recalled behavior is a better predictor of subsequent behavior our results, although mixed, tended to provide somewhat more support for field theory than for behaviorism. When prior behavior and recalled behavior do not coincide, the latter appears to provide a slightly better prediction of subsequent behavior. That this same finding was observed in five panels, including three from Sweden and two from the U.S. – political systems which differ both in form and content in many significant respects – offers some assurance of the generalizability of the findings. One might have hoped that the results would provide unequivocal support for one model or the other, but the real world of politics was not so accommodating. In this context at least, there is some support for both models, and indeed, a mixed model is perhaps the most appropriate.

How might a behaviorist view our results? First, because of the strong correlation between prior behavior and recalled behavior, the increment in predictive accuracy that one gets by using recalled behavior, rather than prior behavior, to predict subsequent behavior is not large – on the order of perhaps 5 percent explained variance. The counterargument, however, is that there is almost *no* increment at all in predictive accuracy by using both recalled and prior behavior to predict subsequent behavior over using only recalled behavior.

Overall, the rather sizeable consistency in individual behavior across elections in both countries could be interpreted as essentially supportive of the behaviorist approach. Behaviorists could also call attention to the concept of habit strength, as reflected in consistency in behavior. That people who vote for the same party are more likely to recall their prior behavior accurately than people who change is certainly relevant to the concept of habit strength. On the other hand, behaviorists might be puzzled by the facts that in the United States, party identification, a facet of self-identity, is more stable than voting behavior and that this aspect of self-identity is a better predictor of subsequent behavior than is prior behavior.

In closing, we are not so naive as to suppose that there can be any single critical test between these two very general theoretical approaches in psychology. Also, it could not have been known in advance whether our results would strongly support one theory or the other or present a more clouded picture. Nonetheless, it can be said that we did identify one situation for which the two theories seemed to have different and competing implications. In the actual event, the data provided mixed results, but the findings from each of the five panels tended to support field theory more than behaviorism, though admittedly not by a large margin.

10 Political systems, cognitive–affective processes, and voting behavior

Our success in demonstrating that "The political system matters" should be judged primarily on the basis of the differences we have identified between how things work in Sweden and the United States. In reviewing the results of our empirical analyses, however, it is equally important to mention the similarities. These similarities are important in that they may point toward some rather pervasive human tendencies, given the substantial differences between the political contexts of Sweden and the U.S. Without contradictory evidence, when an effect occurs in roughly the same way in both Sweden and the United States, it is not unreasonable to assume that similar findings could be obtained in other western democracies. When a social psychological process appears to work differently in Sweden and the United States, this implies a contextual effect and less generalizability. In such instances, a thorough explanation could only be achieved by understanding the specific relevant circumstances under which the observations were made.

Voters in Sweden and the United States compared

In both Sweden and the United States, there is a tendency for people to be in subjective ideological agreement with their preferred political actor and subjective ideological disagreement with a nonpreferred political actor. This tendency, however, is considerably stronger in Sweden, owing to the greater range and clarity of alternatives presented to the electorate. In both countries, most of the subjective agreement that is observed can be attributed to what we consider to be rational democratic processes. Although both subjective agreement and the division of voting groups by ideology were stronger in Sweden, the *relative* contribution of rational democratic processes to subjective agreement may be roughly the same in both countries.

Perceptual consensus regarding the positions of the parties and candidates is observed beyond the chance level in both nations, but the level of perceptual consensus is much higher in Sweden. This is true with regard to both an abstract ideological dimension and more concrete political issues. This system-generated difference lends itself to a straightforward interpretation. The degree to which an electorate displays perceptual consensus is a direct function of the clarity, i.e., lack of ambiguity, of the political alternatives confronted by the electorate.

In both countries, people tend to show a similar degree of perceptual distortion when estimating the positions of parties and candidates. Assimilation occurs when the position of a preferred political actor (party or candidate) is perceived to be closer to one's own position than it actually is, and contrast occurs when the distance between oneself and a nonpreferred political actor is exaggerated. These irrational tendencies occur in both nations, and make a minor contribution to the overall level of subjective agreement and disagreement. It appears that assimilation of a preferred actor is somewhat stronger than contrast of a nonpreferred actor. At the same time, we observed some rather definite limits to these perceptual distortions. In Sweden, they occur within a rather constricted range. That is, when people in Sweden are on the same general side of an issue or ideological dimension as their preferred party, there will be a direct relationship between self-placement and placement of the preferred party. However, this does not necessarily extend to those situations in which the citizen is opposed to the general position of a preferred party. In the United States, on the other hand, the tendency to assimilate the position of a preferred candidate is more pervasive and extends across the centrist position to people who are objectively at odds with the candidate's position.

Associated with this difference in the level of perceptual consensus, ideology was also shown to be more closely linked to specific issues and more stable across time in Sweden than in the United States. This is because of Sweden's strong and stable party system. Issues come and go and party leaders rise and fall, but the general ideological positioning of the parties has remained stable since the Swedish party system was formed some 70 years ago. Most issues in Sweden are linked to the dominant left–right ideological dimension, and leaders are generally assumed to be closely representative of the party. As a consequence of the strong anchoring cues provided by the parties and their left–right positions, considerably more constraint among attitudes was observed in Sweden than in the U.S. There is no comparable dimension in the United States. Attitudes among American people showed some degree of constraint, albeit at a milder level.[1]

Education exerts an intervening effect in both the United States and Sweden in the relationship between ideology and voting behavior. However, this intervening effect of education is much more pronounced in the United States, such that ideology and voting are rather strongly related among the most highly educated people but almost unrelated among the least educated. In Sweden, where there is no more than a slight trend in the same direction, ideology is still very strongly related to voting among the least educated citizens.

Both in Sweden and in the United States, people show more variance in attitudinal ratings of a nonpreferred political actor than in ratings of a preferred actor. In the case of the latter, the ratings tend to be generally positive with relatively little variation, while in the case of the former, ratings tend to be a heterogeneous mixture of positive, neutral, and negative ratings. That this tendency occurs in both Sweden and the United States implies considerable generality, but we do not necessarily assume it would be that way in every political system. Also, in ratings of the two largest parties or of their leaders or nominees, expressions of positive affect toward both are much more common than are expressions of negative affect toward both. This positivity effect was rather pronounced in Sweden as well as in the United States.

However, there were some noteworthy differences in the patterns of attitudes that correspond closely with the differences between the political systems. In Sweden, attitudes toward the different parties were more stable, more strongly correlated with each other, and more closely associated with voting behavior than were attitudes toward the leaders of those parties. In the United States the reverse was true. That is, in the United States attitudes toward individual candidates were more stable, more closely related to each other, and more closely associated with voting behavior than were attitudes toward the parties. Also, attitudes toward a party and that party's leader in Sweden showed more constraint than attitudes toward a party and that party's nominee in the United States. Regardless of whether we are considering self-placement on an ideology scale, attitudes on contemporary political issues, or attitudes toward parties, party leaders and nominees of the parties, responses to these affective types of measurement show more constraint and stability in Sweden than in the United States. These differences occurring at the social psychological level of analysis directly parallel known differences between the two political systems.

In Sweden, people tend to hold somewhat more positive attitudes toward party leaders than toward the political parties. By itself, this would be supportive of the person positivity hypothesis (Sears, 1983). However, in the United States, people tend to express more positive affect toward the political parties than toward the individual candidates nominated by those parties. Taking the two findings together, we proposed as an alternative, the principal actor hypothesis, in which people are expected to express less positive feelings toward the principal actors in a political system, namely the parties in Sweden and the individual candidates in the United States.

Evidence was presented showing that proximity voting occurs in both nations. The hypothesis that similarity leads to attraction, whether one focuses on actual similarity or perceived similarity, was consistently sustained. At the same time, the linkages among actual similarity, perceived similarity, and attraction to a party or candidate were significantly stronger in Sweden than in the U.S. Even within voting groups, attraction varied as a positive function of perceived similarity in both countries. In the U.S., however, attraction to a candidate did not vary systematically as a function of the actual similarity within a voting group whereas in Sweden it did. Overall, the evidence from Sweden on proximity voting was interpreted as more closely resembling a contingently rational model than the comparable evidence from the United States.

In both countries, preference and expectation are related to a significant extent. Especially when an election is ambiguous as to the anticipated outcome, people tend to expect a preferred outcome. Our analysis showed that it is more plausible to suppose that this is due to wishful thinking than to a bandwagon effect. There were a few instances in the United States, however, in which the results were compatible with a bandwagon hypothesis. The strength of the wishful thinking and bandwagon effects should also be considered in comparison to effects implied by a rational democratic model. In our view, the rational democratic model implied that there should be a strong relationship between what people prefer and how people choose and between the expectation regarding the outcome of an election and the anticipation people have regarding future public policy. Our analyses showed these effects to be substantial.

The level of accuracy in recalling one's presidential vote in the United States was about the same as the accuracy in recalling one's parliamentary vote in Sweden – in spite of the chance level of accurate recall being higher for the United States, with only two alternatives, than for Sweden with five alternatives (50% to 20%). In Sweden, however, recalling one's vote in a referendum, in which there was a substantial portion of cross-over voting, was done with less accuracy than recalling one's vote in a parliamentary election. In both nations, accuracy in recalling one's prior vote was facilitated when the prior behavior was implied by one's self-identity (not crossing-over) and when one's behavior was consistent across elections. Subsequent behavior appears to be predicted more successfully by recalled behavior than by prior behavior, but the margin of difference is quite narrow. This finding has theoretical implications, providing more support for field theory, with its emphasis on the impact of how people currently reconstruct the past, than for behaviorism, which emphasizes how people have actually behaved in the past.

In both Sweden and the U.S., intention measured during the preelection campaign period was very strongly linked with voting behavior. Switching parties or candidates from intention to behavior was more common among people whose intention was not implied by their self-identities and was not consistent with what they had done before. While these facets of the problem looked very similar in Sweden and the United States, some very fascinating and normatively significant differences were observed when we examined other characteristics of the intention–behavior changers. In the United States, the switchers tend disproportionately to be those who are apathetic and who are poorly informed. If candidates and campaign managers sense this, it obviously can have an effect on how a political campaign is geared and at what level of sophistication it is aimed. These findings, however, which are well known and linked to what has recently been called the "paradox of mass politics" (Neuman, 1986), are not replicated in the analysis of Swedish data. That is, in Sweden it is not necessarily the apathetic and ignorant citizens who are most susceptible to being influenced to change their party selection during a political campaign. If campaigns are geared at a higher level in Sweden and aimed more at the involved and knowledgeable nonpartisans, this could be part of the reason why.

Rationality observed in different political systems

The above summarizes the major findings of our analyses of empirical data in the Swedish and U.S. election studies. We also want to stand back somewhat and consider what the findings mean in a more general sense. Our research can be viewed in a larger context as part of "the dialectic in the social and behavioral sciences concerning whether humans are predominantly rational beings or predominantly rationalizers" (Granberg, Nanneman, and Kasmer, 1988). This question is tacitly addressed in many forums. The dominant theories of social psychology in the 1960s and the 1970s, especially Festinger's (1957) theory of cognitive dissonance and Heider's (1958) theory of cognitive balance, seemed to emphasize the rationalizing tendencies of people. For instance, it is argued that people behave a certain way and then actively alter their cognitions because inconsistency between attitude and behavior causes psychological discomfort. People distort their perceptions of other people's views so as to achieve or maintain a state of cognitive consistency. As Eiser (1986) has pointed out, since then the pendulum seems to have swung in the "cognitive revolution" to an emphasis on humans as rational information processers seeking to make accurate attributions regarding the attitudes and the causes of other people's behavior.

In our view, an adequate synthesis will take a situational or contextual rather than an extreme or one-sided view (McGuire, 1983). The goal should be to identify those circumstances which make the tendency to be rational or to rationalize predominate at a given time. For instance, in a hazy political system which focuses on the personal qualities of candidates, and in which most citizens are no more than moderately involved and informed, people may find something they like or dislike about a candidate. This may often be no more than a "gut-level" unarticulated feeling (Zajonc, 1980), but their subsequent perceptions may be influenced by their affective feelings about the candidates interacting with their own issue attitudes. On the other hand, it is relatively easy to observe signs of rational selection in a system in which the parties have well-known reputations and positions on a coherent ideological dimension that encompasses most contemporary issues.

Ideology or ideology by proxy?

Citizens in Sweden appear to approach more closely the rational democratic model than do people in the United States in terms of the social psychological processes we have observed. We regard this as an objective observation backed by a series of demonstrable differences between people in the two systems. It is in no way intended to cast aspersions on the American voters. It is, after all, not realistic to expect that voter groups be more divided along lines of ideology and issues than the alternatives confronting them in an election. V. O. Key's (1966) concept of an echo chamber has a direct application here. The echo chamber metaphor implies that there ought to be a relation between how *distinct* the alternatives are and the degree to which voter groups are *polarized*. The assumption is that voter groups echo, in a slightly muted form, the alternatives with which they are presented in elections. If the voter groups are not divided on an issue or on ideology, this is often traceable back to a lack of distinctiveness among the alternatives. The appropriateness of Key's metaphor is borne out by our analysis. The complicated nature of the U.S. political system makes it difficult for citizens to appear rational, and the U.S. system may be regarded in that sense as dysfunctional at the mass level.

However, it could be the case that the U.S. system has more rationality at the elite level while Sweden has more rationality at the level of the masses. In a multi-party parliamentary system, one could have considerable rationality at the level of the individual citizen, but this could break down when the parties form a governing coalition. Hence, there could in the final analysis be little relationship between people's preferences and voting and what sort of government and public policy they ultimately get. This matter has not been addressed directly in our research, and we must concede it is a possibility. At the same time, a coalition government in Sweden involving parties that are not ideologically adjacent or similar, e.g., between the Social

Democratic and Conservative parties, is most unlikely. When such coalitions occur, it is most likely in a country which does not have as strong or unidimensional an ideological system as that of Sweden.

The possibility of system-generated differences like those we have observed was anticipated by Converse (1975) and by Niemi and Westholm (1984). They suggested that people could appear to think and act as the Swedish voters do without really having an in-depth understanding of why they have the beliefs they have or why they act the way they do. Thus, in this view, Swedish citizens would have only the appearance or the "trappings" of a coherent ideological view without there being much substance to it. Although we have not addressed this "ideology by proxy" explanation in the prior chapters, we tend to reject it. Our view on this is informed by, among other things, the responses of Swedish voters to open-ended questions in which they are asked what they like and dislike about each party. These data have been analyzed in depth elsewhere (Holmberg, 1984), and they do not imply that citizens have only a superficial understanding of the parties, of contemporary issues, and of how these issues relate to broader ideological considerations and political conflict. On the contrary, these studies show that most Swedish voters have ideological convictions, understanding the meaning of the left-right dimension, and are quite capable of relating this dimension to the parties.

Of course, ideological views on the voter level are formed not in a vacuum but rather in relation to cues from the parties. The Swedish parties are important and effective in the opinion-formation process, and that is a central thrust in our argument. The strong party system in Sweden is one of the decisive factors in explaining why voters in Sweden show more ideological constraint and issue voting than voters in the United States. Evidently, the Swedish political parties are more effective in influencing the formation of voter attitudes than are American parties or candidates. This fact cannot be dismissed by theories of "ideology by proxy". Nor indeed can it be dismissed by any other explanation which treats the role of political parties in the opinion-formation process as suspect, as if it were somehow less autonomous than such other factors as mass media, friends, or personal experiences. Our view is that opinion formation in relation to positions espoused by political parties and candidates is an integral and legitimate process in a democratic system.

Notes

1 Social psychological processes in political context

1 The Müller–Lyer illusion is the visual tendency to see a line as shorter if it has "arrows" forming acute angles at each end than if it has "feathers" at each end forming obtuse angles.
2 People who have lived in Sweden three years but who are not Swedish citizens have the right to vote in local elections. It is of interest that of a large number and variety of countries, people in Sweden from the U.S. have the lowest turnout among people eligible to vote in the local elections. Apparently, it is a part of the American culture they bring with them.
3 The Michigan series also includes cross-sectional postelection surveys pertaining to the congressional elections in the years when there is no presidential election, a 1958 survey of members of Congress, a 1980 election year panel spanning a longer time (January–November), and a series of cross-sectional tracking polls during the primary election period in 1984. These data files are not used in our analyses.
4 In addition to what has already been described, there are also data in the Swedish election studies archive which we shall not use. In 1957, there was a survey done in regard to the referendum held that year pertaining to pension plans. In 1968–1969, members of the Swedish Parliament were interviewed in a study which paralleled the election study of that year (Holmberg, 1974; Särlvik, 1969). Also in the 1960s, a special panel was studied which spanned three parliamentary elections. The only parliamentary election since 1956 for which there was no election study was the special or extra election in 1958.

2 Subjective ideology

An earlier version of this chapter was published in *Research in Political Sociology*, 1986, 2, 107–143.
1 The questions from the 1968 Swedish survey analyzed in this section were repeated in the 1973 and the 1976 Swedish election studies. The data from the latter two surveys are not reported here to avoid redundancy. The corresponding results for 1976 have been published previously (Granberg, 1985a; Petersson, 1977) and are essentially the same as those for 1968 reported here.
2 Levitin and Miller (1979) used an alternative composite measure of ideology which includes self-placement on the 7-point scale, ratings of liberals and conservatives on the feeling thermometer, and feelings of closeness to liberals and conservatives. Such a scale, however, could not be used in the present

comparative analysis, as there are no measures in the Swedish surveys comparable to feelings of closeness and ratings of ideological groups on a feeling thermometer.

3 These differences are elaborated later in Chapter 5. However, we have also explored whether our results would be changed much if we focused on perceptual estimates of the parties in the United States or the party leaders in Sweden. The reader can be assured that the results and conclusions reported in this chapter would not be altered in any significant way by such a change (cf. Granberg, 1987).

4 This difference is due to a combination of question wording and an actual difference between the countries (cf. Inglehart & Klingemann, 1976). Respondents in the U.S. were given the option "... or haven't you thought much about it?", which increases missing data and was not used in the Swedish surveys. In the General Social Surveys of people in the U.S. by the NORC of the University of Chicago, people are not given this option when asked to place themselves on the 1–7 ideology scale, and the percentage of missing data is accordingly much lower (less than 10%) than on the University of Michigan CPS surveys. The NORC surveys could not be used for present purposes, however, since people in those surveys were not asked to make the placement judgments of the parties or candidates on the ideology scale. When one compares the distributions obtained in the NORC and CPS surveys, it appears that the CPS surveys contained a slightly higher percentage of people who place themselves to the right of center. That could be due to the difference in question wording, but it also could be due to other "house" effects. In any event, an important point is that there are large differences between the U.S. and Swedish election studies in amount of missing data. There are good reasons to believe that the large differences between the U.S. and Sweden reported in this chapter would have been even larger if the percentages of missing data for the two countries were more equal (Robinson, 1984).

5 The analyses of Inglehart and Klingemann (1976) show that these descriptive statistics cannot be taken for granted. They found several countries in which the distribution of self-designated ideology was skewed, multimodal, irregular, or departed from normality. There was even one country (Ireland) in which the modal response was actually the extreme right position.

6 This is distinct from evaluative consensus, that is, the extent to which there is agreement within a society or between groups on values or attitudes.

7 The standard deviation is obviously an indicator of agreement or consensus, but its magnitude is affected by the N and by the number of categories employed. Thus, the standard deviations for the larger Swedish samples making placement judgments in 11 categories would not be directly comparable to the smaller U.S. samples making placement judgments in 7 categories. Also, there is the problem of interpreting the meaning of a standard deviation which departs from zero. If everyone agreed where on a scale a particular party or candidate was located, and this was reflected in the placement judgments, the standard deviation would be zero and would correctly reflect a condition of complete perceptual consensus. But how would a condition of complete dissensus be detected? Our consensus coefficient varies from .00 to 1.00 and is relatively independent of the number of categories used and the number of people making the placement judgments. The

random distribution of judgments is assumed to be rectangular. This hypothetical dissensus standard is not the distribution that would yield the maximum
standard deviation. The latter would be obtained if half of the people placed the
party at one end of the scale and the other half placed it in the category at the
opposite end of the scale. That possibility did not seem realistic as a baseline for
inferring consensus in the present context.

8 It is our strong impression that this difference between Sweden and the United
States is *not* due to the use of an 11-point scale rather than a 7-point scale. We
compared our results to those of a 1982 survey done by SIFO, an opinion polling
organization in Sweden. In the SIFO survey, about 1000 people in Sweden were
asked to place themselves and the five political parties on a 7-point left–right
scale (Zetterberg, 1982). Consensus coefficients were calculated for the five
political parties in Sweden for that survey. The result was an average consensus
coefficient of .55, remarkably similar to the .54 we found for 1982 (Granberg,
1987). It should also be emphasized that the calculations for the coefficients are
based only on those people who actually made the requested estimates within
the prescribed range. Recall that the percentage of missing data is much higher
for the U.S. in these comparisons. In Sweden in 1985, about 95 percent placed
themselves and the five parties represented in the parliament somewhere on the
0–10 scale. It is also of interest to note that when Swedish respondents were
asked in 1985 to place two small parties (not represented in the Parliament) on
the same scale, the percentage of missing data went up considerably. About
88 percent placed the Christian Democratic Party (which was allied that year
with the Center Party and, thus, provided a readily available cue) on the left–
right scale, and about 78 percent placed the Green Party on the left–right scale.
The position of the latter party, whose leaders and members have tended to reject
the left–right dimension as antiquated and obsolete, on the left–right dimension
may have been rather ambiguous and consequently we see a relatively high
percentage of missing data.

9 The autocorrelations for the U.S. panel between 1972 and 1974 (.60,
N = 1042) and between 1974 and 1976 (.63, N = 1019) were slightly higher.
We have given the comparison in the text which seems most relevant, moving
from one presidential election year to another and from one parliamentary
election year to the next. It should be noted that the interval is three years for
Sweden and four years for the U.S. (cf. Niemi & Westholm, 1984). In 1980, we
also have an autocorrelation (.69, N = 773) for people in the U.S. placing
themselves on the liberal–conservative scale on both pre- and postelection
surveys. The average time between those two measures would be about six
weeks.

10 In 1979 people in the Swedish survey were asked directly which party they liked
least. The two measures of least-liked party were highly correlated (r = .89)
with 87 percent of the respondents having the same least-liked party by these
two measures. In this chapter, we use the like–dislike measure to infer the least-
liked party in all three Swedish surveys in order that the results will be more
comparable across years. It may be pointed out, however, that the results are
basically the same regardless of which measure of the least-liked party is used (cf.
Granberg & Holmberg, 1986a).

11 That people at position 4 differed significantly from those at positions 0, 1, 2, and

3, and that people at position 6 differed significantly from those at positions 8, 9, and 10 in placement of the nonpreferred party does constitute a slight departure from the subjective placement model.

12 The percentages placing themselves and their preferred party or candidate at exactly the same position are not comparable with these data in that the U.S. studies use a 1–7 scale and the Swedish studies a 0–10 scale. Elsewhere, an analysis has been reported using Swedish and U.S. data both with 1–7 scales. Among Swedish respondents, 49 percent placed themselves and their preferred party at the same point on the 1–7 left–right scale, and 48 percent placed themselves and their preferred party's leader at the same left–right position. The comparable percentages for the U.S. were 32 for self and preferred party and 30 for self and preferred candidate (Granberg, 1987). In addition, we examined the relationship in Sweden between self-placement and placement on the ideological scale of the party that the person indicated was liked second best after their preferred party. For most Swedish respondents, the party liked second best is within the same bloc as the party liked best. It appears that the Swedish respondents showed about as much or slightly more subjective agreement with the party they liked second best (.59 in 1979, .56 in 1982, and .61 in 1985) than people in the U.S. showed with their most preferred candidate (.50 in 1976, .47 in 1980, and .58 in 1984).

13 Judd, Kenny, and Krosnick (1983) criticized the use of this type of correlation to infer assimilation and contrast, because, among other problems, the correlation could be due, in part, to correlated error in measuring self-placement and placement of the parties. However, if that were a problem, the correlation between own and attributed position would be positive and significantly different from zero for the sample as a whole. Generally, this was not the case. The correlations between self-placement and placement of party, with no control for party preference, tended to be very close to zero. Moreover, the correlations for the sample as a whole which departed the most from zero were negative.

14 These correlations are slightly lower than those shown in figure 2.3 for 1968. This is presumably due to a methodological difference. In 1968, people were asked to place only their preferred party, while in 1979, 1982, and 1985, they were asked to place the five main parties. The magnitude of these correlations is constrained by the amount of variation in self-placement and the amount of variation in the perceptions within each party preference group. Obviously, such a correlation would be precluded if all the people in a party preference group placed themselves or the party at the same position on the ideology scale. But, in fact, the amount of variance for both variables was sufficient within each party preference group to allow assimilation and contrast to occur in this situation.

15 It is still an open question as to how the degree to which displacement effects occur is affected by the number of units on the scale. With 11 units, the respondent has more room to shift the parties than with 7 units, and this may explain why the average assimilation correlations were higher on the 11-point scale than on the 7-point scale. If the number of units is increased much beyond 11, however, the effect could be diminished due to an increase in random or unexplained variance.

3 Partisan political issues

An earlier version of this chapter was published in *Western Political Quarterly*, 1986, 39, 1, 7–28.

1 The concepts of assimilation and contrast are drawn from social judgment theory (Sherif & Hovland, 1961). In political science, these dual processes have also been called projection and negative projection drawing presumably from psychoanalytic theory and the general category of defense mechanisms (Page & Brody, 1972; Conover & Feldman, 1982).

2 This type of scale was first used in 1968 in relation to the Vietnam and urban unrest issues and was devised by Richard Brody, Benjamin Page, and Sidney Verba in studies done at Stanford University. The scales were later included in the University of Michigan's Survey Research Center's post-election survey of 1968 (Granberg & Seidel, 1976).

3 For instance, in placing Eugene McCarthy on the Vietnam scale in 1968, we know he was a dove, therefore, to the left of center (4.0), and also that he did not advocate the extreme left position (1.0) calling for an immediate and unconditional withdrawal of U.S. troops from Vietnam. But whether he was at position 2 or 3, or somewhere in between, was a subjective judgment.

4 Irrational in this context indicates systematically distorting, and thus to a certain extent being out of touch with reality to fulfill a psychological need. There is another sense in which assimilation (or contrast) could be regarded as rational or at least understandable. The person's perception of candidate A's position on a particular issue may simply reflect the person's best guess, knowing A's position on a number of other issues. The person, lacking information about A on this particular issue, may simply assume that A is closer to (or farther away from) the person's own position than is actually the case. Generally, however, when people make inferences on the basis of affect (e.g. I like candidate O, therefore O and I agree about issue X), this must be regarded as basically irrational.

5 In addition to the similarities, we also recognize certain procedural differences. People in Sweden were asked a preliminary question whether they had noticed a difference among the parties' positions on nuclear power. Those who said no were not asked to attribute positions to the parties, but a large majority (89%) of the respondents indicated that they had noticed a difference. That type of filter question was not used on the wage-earner fund question. The U.S. tax-cut questions were preceded by asking whether people had an opinion on this matter. Those who said they had no opinion or said they had not thought much about it were not asked the attitude and perception questions. This procedure, designed to reduce "nonattitudes," undoubtedly decreases the response rate (Robinson & Fleishman, 1984). The "easy out" alternative was less explicit on the abortion issue, but there too, if people said they did not know what their own position was, they were not asked the perception questions. In tables 3.1 and 3.2, we attempt to standardize these data somewhat by giving the percentage of people with an attitude who give their perceptions. Also, it is likely that the abortion and tax-cut issues were not as salient in 1980 in the U.S. as the nuclear power question was in 1979 or the wage-earner fund issue was in 1982 in Sweden.

6 While technically it would have been possible to shut down the nuclear power plants at once, as in alternative 1 in table 3.1, it was not considered a politically viable or realistic possibility. At the time, Sweden had six nuclear power plants operating and was getting about 5 percent of its energy supply and about 30 percent of its electricity from these power plants.

7 This is not to say that the positions of Carter and the Democratic Party on abortion were identical. However, most fundamentally, both accepted the Supreme Court decisions of 1973 which, in effect, legalized abortion on a national basis, essentially what is advocated in alternative 4. Carter's position was to avoid the use of federal money to fund abortions, while the Democratic Party favored the use of federal money to pay for the abortions of indigent women through the Medicaid program. However, note that the alternatives in table 3.2 say nothing about the funding of abortion, but rather deal only with the legal status of abortion (Granberg & Burlison, 1983; Legge, 1983). It may seem that Carter's position was ambiguous, being personally opposed to abortion but not favoring a Constitutional amendment against it. But, in the final analysis, Carter's position was to accept the prochoice status quo as it existed in 1980.

8 This is consistent with prior research which indicates that in order to observe a substantively significant effect on political perception, it is necessary to take into account simultaneously the interactive effect of the person's candidate or party preference and the person's own attitude rather than merely the person's candidate or party preference (Carlson & Habel, 1969; Granberg & Brent, 1974; Kinder, 1978; Sherrod, 1972).

9 These chance level agreement estimates would pertain if the attitudes and perceptions were distributed about equally among the alternatives. Chance level agreement is somewhat different when the distribution of the marginals is unequal or skewed.

10 The degree of issue voting in the 1980 election has been reported by Granberg and Burlison (1983) to average .21 (eta) across 12 issues with the highest coefficient (.39) being on the issue of the government providing social services. This matter is addressed further in chapter 4.

11 We also examined whether rated importance of an issue would vary as a function of whether the person held an attitude that conformed or deviated from the preferred party's or candidate's position. A discrepancy or conflict could be resolved by diminishing the importance of the issue. The results on this were not always supportive, but one consistency did emerge. In those cases in which the preferred party or candidate was advocating a change in the status quo (the Center Party wanting to phase out nuclear power, the Social Democrats wanting to establish wage-earner funds, and Reagan wanting to reduce taxes and make abortion illegal), people agreeing with their preferred party or candidate did rate the issue as more important than people disagreeing. There was also a relationship between attitude position and ascribed importance on three of the issues. Overall, people who opposed nuclear power, opposed the wage-earner funds, and supported the tax cut rated the issue as more important than people taking the opposing view.

12 The strong assimilation by Conservative Party voters of the Conservative Party on the wage-earner funds would seem to contradict the latter principle. The

position of the Conservative Party, unequivocally opposing wage-earner funds, was well known. But nearly all of the Conservative Party voters took an attitudinal position on this issue which was on the same side of the issue (3 or 4) as that of their preferred party. There were simply too few Conservatives on the side of the issue opposite that of their preferred party to provide an additional test of our hypothesis. Among Conservative voters who themselves took position 4, 99 percent thought the Conservative Party's position to be 4, compared to 72 percent of the Conservative voters who themselves took position 3. This difference reflects an assimilation tendency on the part of the Conservative Party voters who placed themselves at position 3.

13 The correlations for the entire sample (Granberg & Holmberg, 1986b) are not compatible with an interpretation based on correlated error in measurement (Judd *et al.*, 1983). If the correlations between a person's own attitude and perception of a party were biased in a positive direction, such correlations considered for the sample as a whole should deviate significantly from .00 in the positive direction. But the average of these 10 correlations for Sweden was −.01. Thus, the idea that assimilation of a preferred party only appears stronger than contrast of a nonpreferred party due to a methodological artifact (correlated error in measurement) is implausible. It is more plausible that this asymmetry in political perception is a valid result.

14 The actual turnout in the referendum was 75.6 percent of the eligible voters. The vote went 18.9 percent for Line 1, 39.1 percent for Line 2, 38.7 percent for Line 3, and 3.3 percent cast a blank ballot.

15 The overall figure of 71 percent, who reported having voted for the option supported by the party they had identified with or preferred on the preelection survey, showed some significant variation across parties. The Center Party was most successful (91%) in getting its supporters to vote for its option in the referendum, followed in order by the Communist Party (85%), the Social Democrats (70%), the Conservatives (67%), and the Liberals (39%).

4 Mass attitude systems

1 In 1980, the correlation between the military spending and relations with Russia items was only .12 but increased to .34 in 1984.

2 The first of these two asked people to respond, using one of five levels of approval or disapproval, to the proposal of decreasing social subsidy programs. The other provided a statement, "Social reform in this country has gone so far that in the future the government should decrease rather than increase subsidies and support for citizens," and asked people to agree or disagree, using four alternatives.

3 In Sweden, the measure of political knowledge consisted of five true–false items that pertained to current economic matters and four questions asking people to name the party to which each of four people belong. This may help to explain why level of political knowledge intervened much more strongly on the public–private economy questions than on the social welfare or environmental items.

4 We also checked to see whether this eta would change much if people voting for John Anderson in 1980 were included as a third category. It did not. Across 15 specific issues in 1980, the eta, with voting group as the independent variable

and attitude position as the dependent variable, averaged .26 regardless of whether two or three voting groups were used. This average, of course, masks some interesting variations on specific issues. There were some issues on which Anderson voters were similar to Carter voters, others on which they were more similar to Reagan voters, and still others on which Reagan and Carter voters were similar to each other but different from Anderson voters.

5   Variations within the U.S. and Sweden as a function of political activity, as shown in figures 4.3 and 4.4, should be compared cautiously. First, we have no data on members of the U.S. Congress in the 1980s that would be comparable to that of the Swedish parliamentarians. Second, the three levels of political activity are derived in different ways in the two countries, and the cutting points produce categories of different sizes. Thus, for instance, the highest level of activity among the Swedish electorate, active party members, included only 6 percent of the electorate, while the highest level of activity in the U.S., those who had done two or more of the six political actions, was less selective, including 17 percent of the population.

6   Unfortunately, the U.S. election studies do not contain a complete set of comparable questions. In 1958, people were asked two of the questions. Of those with an opinion, 55 percent favored the individualistic over the delegate role, and 70 percent favored the individualistic over the party role. A question which would have posed a conflict between the party and delegate roles was not asked.

7   Another aspect of the rational model would hold that people's perceptions of reality, that is, in this case how things work, should be independent of their preferences. Is there a relationship between how people answer the preference and perception questions (1 and 4 in table 4.5) pertaining to the party–individualistic dilemma? The answer is that there seems to have been a slight relationship between preference and perception in this regard in 1968 ($r = +.22$), but by 1985 this relationship was reduced to nonsignificance. Thus, in this context, preference and perception are relatively independent of one another, and this may be due to the (apparently increasing) lack of ambiguity in the stimulus referred to in the perception question. Given the way the Swedish Parliament works, it may be said that the minority of Swedish citizens who prefer the individualistic role over the party role, and who perceive that Members of Parliament usually resolve a conflict between their personal views and their party's position by voting individualistically, are indulging in a bit of "wishful thinking."

5 Parties, leaders, and candidates

1   This transformation, done so that the results for Sweden and the United States could be more directly compared, should be kept in mind. It has, of course, no substantial effect on the coefficients reported in this chapter.

2   It may seem too obvious that this would be so. After all, don't people in the U.S. vote for individuals running for the presidency while people in Sweden vote for one of the parties? Technically, this is not true, since strictly speaking people in the United States vote for electors pledged to vote for particular presidential and vice-presidential candidates, while in Sweden, people vote for a list of candidates

nominated by a party to serve in the Parliament. More importantly, the party, leader, and candidate voting decisions are inextricably linked in both of the two countries. That is, there is no way that people in the U.S. could vote for Ronald Reagan for President without simultaneously voting in favor of having the executive branch of the government being administered by Republicans. Similarly, in Sweden one could not vote for the Social Democratic Party without simultaneously indicating a preference that the party's leader serve as the Prime Minister. In both countries, it may be said that the voters "can't have one without the other."

It is also possible to make comparisons of the averages for Sweden in table 5.1 with the averages for the U.S. in table 5.2. If these results were to be taken at face value, they would indicate that people in Sweden rate their preferred party ($+3.5$) and their preferred party leader ($+3.3$) higher than people in the U.S. rate their preferred party ($+2.5$) and their preferred nominee ($+2.7$). Here, however, it is important to remember that the U.S. scale was transformed from 0–100 to -5 to $+5$, thus making the comparisons highly tenuous. That is, the observed differences could be due to methodological differences. Our view is that these differences should be viewed as no more than suggestive, but they may warrant a further look in future research. If the difference here is reliable, it could be related to the greater number and range of alternatives available to Swedish voters. That is, if people have a broader range and larger variety of alternatives from which to choose, it is not unreasonable that they might have a more positive attitude toward the alternative they select.

3 This number would be even larger if we were to also consider people who said "don't know" or who gave some other answer outside the -5 to $+5$ range on one or more of the questions.

4 This could be changing. There is the strong possibility that the role of party leader has gradually become a more prominent role within the Swedish political system (Esaiasson, 1985a). However, no one has argued seriously that party leaders play a more prominent role than parties in the Swedish system. Rather, it is thought that party leaders now have a more important role than they used to have, especially since the advent of television.

5 It is quite possible in the U.S. for people to bypass or make "an end run" around the party to get the nomination, and it has become more possible to do that with the increased use of primary elections to select delegates to the nominating convention. Jimmy Carter's successful campaign to get the nomination of the Democratic Party in 1976, in spite of very limited support within the party for his candidacy, exemplifies the point being made here.

6 This could be the result of some people thinking of both Democrats and Republicans as politicians or political groups and rating them similarly – which could balance the negative correlation that would otherwise result from some people liking one and disliking the other group. It may also be noted that attitudes toward the opposing parties are correlated more strongly than attitudes toward the vice-presidential candidates in each of three comparisons. In fact in 1980, there was even a slight positive correlation ($+.06$) between attitudes toward the opposing vice-presidential candidates, Walter Mondale and George Bush, a rather strange result. Beyond the fact that they were both in the political

mainstream and had worked hard for their respective parties, it is not easy to see what they held in common politically. It is also of interest that attitudes toward Democrats and Republicans were positively correlated in three instances and the average correlation was .00 in the four available instances.

6 Ideology and proximity voting

Portions of this chapter were published previously in *Research in Political Sociology*, 1986, 2, 107–143.

1 These authors sought to minimize "rationalization" ("the tendency to see a preferred candidate as close to, and a disliked candidate as far from, oneself on issues, regardless of the actual issue position," in other words what has been called in preceding chapters and elsewhere assimilation and contrast effects). This was done by separating the attitude and attribution questions into different parts of the questionnaire. The implication is that the order of questions, in which for instance respondents in the CPS surveys are typically asked to place themselves first and then immediately thereafter to place the candidates and the parties on the same scale, might be important. The only way, however, to demonstrate this conclusively would be to manipulate the order of the attitude and attribution questions within the same study, and that has not been done in any studies of political perception.

2 That is, holding as Thomas and Merton did that what is real in people's minds is real in its consequences is not to argue necessarily that this subjective component is all that is real or consequential.

3 This is roughly analogous to looking for the simultaneous effects of objective social class and subjective social class (Campbell *et al.*, 1960), or more generally, the presumption that both membership group and reference group may have an effect on attitude, perception, and behavior (Granberg *et al.*, 1981; Siegel & Siegel, 1957).

4 We are speaking here of direct relationships (i.e., assuming that insofar as there is a relationship it will be a positive one). The possibility that there could even be an inverse relationship between perceived and actual similarity has occurred to us but seems rather unlikely and somewhat perverse. Wilcox and Udry (1986) reported a very large "autistic" component in adolescents' perceptions of peer group attitudes regarding sexuality. The implication is that in that context, the link between objective reality and subjective perceptions of it was very tenuous.

5 See chapter 5 for a close examination of these attraction measures.

6 If one wanted to be technically correct about this, there are a variety of ways it could be done. For instance, given the stability of the placement of the parties in Sweden across elections, one would not be far off the mark if the scale values were derived from the previous election. In the United States where the candidates are usually not the same in succeeding elections, such a procedure might be more hazardous. Alternatively one could divide the sample in half, using half to derive the scale values and the other half in the final analyses. It is easy to see that such procedures would not alter our findings or conclusions in any significant way.

7 For candidates who have served in the U.S. Congress, one could use ratings by

liberal or conservative organizations (based on roll call votes) to estimate the candidates' positions. By this measure, for instance, among people who have seriously contested for the presidency in recent years, Robert Kennedy would be the farthest to the left (followed closely by Hubert Humphrey and Walter Mondale), Barry Goldwater the farthest to the right and Lyndon Johnson nearest the center. George McGovern, Gary Hart, and Eugene McCarthy would form a cluster close to Robert Kennedy, Humphrey, and Mondale, though not quite so close to the liberal extreme. There are, however, several problems in the use of such ratings for this purpose, not the least of which is that some key figures such as Ronald Reagan, Jimmy Carter, and Dwight Eisenhower never served in the Congress and thus would have received no ratings comparable to those available for others. One could also use content analysis of campaign speeches and party platforms to infer the ideological positions of candidates and parties. Page (1978) did this sort of analysis but more with the purpose of inferring the candidates' positions on specific issues. To do so with the purpose of inferring the more general ideological position would not only be complex and tedious, but also highly problematical. There would certainly be no guarantee that the results would be regarded as definitive.

8 The within-voting groups analysis was also done for the other parties. Results for the Center and Liberal voting groups were weak, but this may be due to a much constricted range and relatively small numbers at the various values of the independent variables. Among Communist Party voters, attraction to the party varied significantly both as a function of self-placement and perceived similarity on ideology.

9 It might be supposed that 5 being the modal self-placement in Sweden could be an artifact of using an 11-point 0–10 left–right scale. However, other studies of left–right self-placement in Sweden have used a 1–7 scale and found the midpoint (4) to also be the mode (Granberg, 1987).

7 The preference–expectation link

This chapter draws upon articles published previously in the *Journal of Personality and Social Psychology*, 1983, **45**, 477–491; *Social Psychology Quarterly*, 1983, **46**, 363–368; and *Social Science Quarterly*, 1986, **67**, 379–392.

1 We also considered the possibility that the causal flow might move in different directions as a function of involvement. It could be, for instance, that among the highly involved, preference leads to expectation, while among those low in involvement, expectation leads to preference. In this view, a bandwagon effect would occur but only among those low in involvement. Thus, we repeated our regression analyses using concern about the outcome of the election as the indicator of involvement, analyzing the categories of low and high involvement separately. In none of the nine years was there evidence of a direct effect of expectation on behavior when intention was controlled, that is, a bandwagon effect, among those low in involvement. In fact, analysis of the only year in which there was a significant bandwagon effect overall (1960) revealed that this effect occurred to a significant degree among the highly involved but not among those low in involvement.

2 We also isolated their symmetrical counterparts, i.e., those who had a preference but lacked an expectation. Among these people, preference predicted the vote significantly in each election (Granberg and Brent, 1983). It appears that preference is more consequential than expectation.

3 These six correlations were all based on an N of 473. The same study (Granberg & Brent, 1983) demonstrated that the preference–expectation link extends beyond the presidential level to races for the U.S. Senate (+.44), a Governorship (+.62), and a seat in the House of Representatives (+.43).

4 In experimental game studies, people predict others will choose in a manner similar to the way they chose (Dawes, McTavish, & Shaklee, 1977; Kelley & Stahelski, 1970). There appears to be some underlying tendency to assume similarity to self when making attributions (Granberg, 1972; Miller & Marks, 1982; Ross, Greene & House, 1977).

5 The preference–expectation link is even found among those who are sufficiently uninvolved to not vote. Across years, the link was only slightly lower among people who did not intend to vote than among those who did intend to vote. Among those who reported not voting for one of the two major candidates, the preference–expectation link involving those two candidates averaged .61 across years, which was even slightly higher than the .56 for those who did vote for one of the two major candidates. In 1956, 1964, 1972, and 1984, when the actual outcome was not close, the preference–expectation link was actually slightly stronger among the nonvoters than among the voters, probably because of a higher level of information among voters.

6 One can ask, of course, whether the rational democratic model might not require perception of poll results to be constant. That is, were perceptions of poll results themselves affected by candidate preference? There was, in fact, no more than a marginal relationship in that direction. Of those who preferred Reagan, 77 percent thought he was ahead in the polls, compared to 61 percent of those preferring Carter. Moreover, the bivariate relation between perception of the poll results and voting was not significant. Of those who thought Reagan to be ahead in the polls, 62 percent later voted for Reagan, compared to 55 percent of those who thought Carter was ahead in the polls. There were fluctuations in the many polls reported in the mass media during the eight-week period of interviewing for the 1980 survey, and until the final weekend the 1980 election was anticipated to be very close. So it is not unreasonable in that context that people would vary in perceptions of poll results.

7 This was the actual outcome of the 1982 election and gave the Communists an implicit power that they would not have had if the Social Democrats had won an absolute majority. The result of the 1982 election was that the Social Democratic party received more votes than the three bourgeois parties combined but less than an overall majority. Thus, to form the government and to get their bills passed, the Social Democrats had to count on the Communists *not* voting against them in the Parliament. The majority of Social Democratic supporters in this study, being somewhat overly optimistic, had anticipated that their party would win an absolute majority.

8 Comparing the two largest party preference groups, the Social Democrats preferred that the Social Democratic Party get 55 percent of the vote, on the

average, to 13 percent for the Conservative Party. Conservatives preferred that the Social Democratic Party get 31 percent to 37 percent for the Conservative Party. These differences are obviously significant, but their absolute level may be of some interest. Respondents generally did not want their preferred party to get all or most of the vote. This condition can be thought of as supportive, in some sense, for democracy (Lipset, 1981). These two party preference groups did not differ significantly in the percentage they wanted to be obtained by the Center and Liberal Parties. However, Social Democrats wanted the Communists to get 7 percent of the vote, on average, while the Conservatives wanted the Communists to get only 2 percent, less than the 4 percent minimum required to win seats in the Swedish Parliament.

9 Of course, we have not proven that a bandwagon effect did not occur in 1968. It is generally difficult to prove the absence of something, and in scientific affairs, the absence of proof is not proof of absence. We can say with confidence that we tried to conduct fair tests for the presence of a bandwagon effect but did not find it.

10 If there were such skepticism, would it have a basis in recent Swedish history? The most recent prior referendum held in Sweden in 1957 dealt with pension plans, and this was an instance in which the proposal which got the most votes, though not a majority, was later implemented into public policy. That alternative, supported by the unions and the Social Democrats and which called for a mandatory pension plan funded by employers, received 46 percent of the vote. Of course, it is also true that the other two alternatives, which rejected the notion that the pension fund should be mandatory and administered by the government, received together a majority of the vote (54%). A parliamentary election was held between that referendum and when the policy decision was made on the pension fund. The final vote in the parliament was as close as possible (115–114) and included a famous and consequential abstention (Hadenius, 1985). In the only other post-World War II national referendum in Sweden, 83 percent of the voters in 1955 indicated a preference to keep left-side driving. Twelve years later, with no subsequent referendum on the same topic, Sweden made the transition to right-side traffic.

11 In fact, interpreting the relationship between E_1 and E_2 is a complex matter. Granberg and Holmberg (1983) reported an intensive analysis of this question and concluded that 47 percent anticipated that the referendum would have an impact, 28 percent that it would have no impact, and 25 percent that it would have a doubtful impact on policy. Also, although difficult to prove, the nuclear power question, particularly as posed to the voters in the Swedish referendum, may be more complex than the subject of other referenda. For instance, a nation either does or does not join the Common Market, the subject of referenda in Norway and England (Pierce, Valen & Listhaug, 1983). Similarly, as in an earlier referendum in Sweden, a nation either does or does not change from left-side to right-side driving.

12 The questions asked people their attitude toward nuclear power in general as an energy source, to choose among five policy alternatives including two more extreme than those included in the referendum, and to rate their own attitude toward nuclear power on a −5 to +5 scale. Results indicated that pronuclear

people outnumbered antinuclear people, but the latter held more intense attitudes. Only a small minority (10%) chose an alternative more antinuclear than Line 3 or the alternative more pronuclear than Line 1 (2%). There was about 75 percent shared variance between scores on this attitude index and how people voted in the referendum (Hill, 1981).

13 The coding for voting behavior (V) presented a problem. It was well known that Lines 1 and 2 were much more similar than Lines 2 and 3 (i.e., that the intervals were not equal). In fact, one could have, with some justification, grouped supporters of Lines 1 and 2 together. That, however, loses some meaningful variance. Supporters of Line 1 rated themselves as significantly more pronuclear than did supporters of Line 2, and when asked to place the three alternatives on an 11-point scale, Line 1 was placed significantly more toward the positive extreme than Line 2. Comparing the voting groups, as to their scores on the preference index, and comparing perceptions of the three lines pointed toward the same solution. The interval between Lines 2 and 3 was four times as large as the interval between Lines 1 and 2. Therefore, in the regression analyses, voting for Line 1 was coded 1, Line 2 as 2, and Line 3 as 6.

14 Overall, in this referendum study, 94 percent of the people with an intention to vote for one of the three lines later reported having voted for their intended line (N = 1125, r = .92). This percentage was 91, 93, and 96 for Line 1, 2, and 3 intenders, respectively (cf. chapter 8).

8 From intention to behavior

1 Admittedly, the whole question of volatility in voting is much larger than this (Holmberg, 1981, 1984; van der Eijk & Niemöller, 1983), but here we limit ourselves, for the most part, to the intention–behavior relationship.

2 Pollsters also have the difficult tasks of deciding who are the likely voters and allocating the likely vote of people who are undecided, i.e., those who lack an intention (Traugott & Tucker, 1984). While important, these problems have been defined as beyond the scope of our analysis.

3 The values for Sweden are based on validated vote, in which the person's report as to whether they voted is checked against official records by the Central Statistical Bureau. This procedure has been followed in each of the Swedish election studies considered here. For the U.S., the values in figure 8.1 and throughout the chapter are based on unvalidated vote. In those years for which validated vote measures are available for the U.S. studies (1964, 1972, 1976, 1980, and 1984), each analysis was done twice, first for the entire sample and then for validated voters only. No differences of any consequence were observed. In figure 8.1, for example, the data points would be the same for validated voters for 1964 (5%), 1976 (7%), 1980 (12%), and 1984 (4%). The estimate of intention–behavior changers would decrease by 1 percent for 1972 (from 7 to 6%) if validated voters had been used. However, the vote for 1972 was not validated until four years after the fact as part of the 1972–1976 panel study. The reason the unvalidated vote is used for the U.S. is to preserve the comparability across elections within the U.S. It appears in figure 8.1 that the percentages of people in Sweden and the U.S. for whom intention and behavior

are different are roughly the same – with the exception of the U.S. elections of 1968 and 1980. However, one should also keep in mind that the chance level agreement is much higher in the two-candidate U.S. elections than in the five-party Swedish elections.

4 A better way to determine across-election volatility is to compare how people report having voted just after election A with how they report having voted just after election B. Such data, however, are available for the U.S. for only two across-election panels, 1956–1960 and 1972–1976. The results for these two methods can be compared to see what correction factor might be appropriate for the across-election volatility values in figure 8.2. The value for 1960 is 19 in figure 8.2 and increases to 22 in the panel. The corresponding values for 1976 are 22 and 26. This suggests that the values in figure 8.2 probably underestimate the amount of across-election volatility in the U.S. by about 3 or 4 percent. If one uses the 1979–1982 and 1982–1985 panels to derive a correction factor, the Swedish values in figure 8.2 may underestimate the amount of across–election volatility by about 2 percent.

5 This can be expressed in correlation terms as well. For the U.S. the correlations, averaged across elections, were .87 for intention–behavior, .67 for party preference–behavior, and .62 for prior behavior–subsequent behavior. The comparable correlations for Sweden, scaling the five parties on their positions on the left–right scale as in chapter 2, averaged .96, .93, and .88. While intention predicts behavior better than party preference, there is less attrition with preference. That is, there are more people who express a party preference but lack an intention than who have an intention but lack a preference. A more thorough treatment of the topic of volatility would use a combination of intention when available and preference when intention is lacking (Holmberg, 1974; Holmberg & Gilljam, 1987). When this is done, it appears that across-election and within-campaign volatility has increased somewhat in recent years in Sweden, indicating that the party's "grip" on the voters may have loosened ever so slightly. It may also be noted that the ordering of the correlations with behavior is not affected if one equalizes the N by using a list-wise deletion of cases. For instance, averaging across years but with a constant N within each election, the correlations for the U.S. averaged .88 for intention–behavior, .70 for party preference–behavior, and .66 for prior behavior–subsequent behavior.

6 However, it is not easy to visualize what the shape of that function might be, and it is doubtful that any one function would fit many, let alone all, intention–behavior situations.

7 This, of course, is not to say the campaign had no effect as events progressed toward election day. Several things could have happened which would not be reflected in the intention–behavior relationship we have reported, such as being mobilized to vote, changing from undecided to having a preference, becoming alienated to the point of not planning to vote, switching from a party outside the five-party structure to one within it, or vice versa, etc. (Holmberg, 1981).

8 The 1984 U.S. election study omitted the question asking how people had voted in the prior election. The data point for across-election volatility in the U.S. in figure 8.2 was estimated from the *CBS/New York Times* exit poll. In the present analysis the data are from the 1952–1980 U.S. election studies.

9 Given our impression that prior behavior and self-identity have rather strong intervening effects on the intention–behavior relation, we also wanted to see what effect these factors might have on the behavior of people who *lack* an intention. That is, among people who say they do not know for whom or which party they intend to vote, can we predict their behavior accurately on the basis of their prior behavior and party preference when that information is available? Among the no intention people in Sweden, combining across six elections, 84 percent (N = 508) voted for a party if prior behavior and party preference both pointed them in the direction of voting for that party. The corresponding figure for the U.S., summing across eight election studies, is 72 percent (N = 522). When the two cues, prior behavior and party preference, were in conflict and the no intention people voted for one of them, they tended to vote in line with party preference in Sweden by a ratio of 64:36 and also in the U.S. but there by the slim margin of 52:48.

10 They have nonetheless been included in the calculations in this chapter as having intentions. For example, in figure 8.1, the percentage of intention–behavior changers is based on the people who either directly said which party or candidate they intended to vote for or who answered the follow-up question about which party or candidate they would vote for, and later reported voting for one of the alternatives. Including the latter people has little effect on the results in that they are only a small percentage within any of the studies as could be inferred from the numbers in table 8.3.

11 The Swedish question on interest in politics provides four alternatives and the U.S. question on interest in the political campaign three alternatives. Given the marginal distributions, there did not seem to be any fair way of collapsing categories so they would be comparable for the two countries. Therefore, as shown in figure 8.3, they were scaled to take into account the distribution of answers to the interest questions. For instance, a much larger percentage of people in the U.S. chose the highest (of three) interest alternatives than people in Sweden (choosing among four alternatives). Therefore, it seemed reasonable to scale the highest interest group in Sweden closer to the maximal end of the interest continuum.

12 It should be noted that the interest question in the U.S. studies pertains to interest in the campaign, while the interest item in the Swedish surveys deals with a more general interest in politics. That *could* be the source of the difference between the U.S. and Sweden in figure 8.3, but we do not think so.

13 When this was done after both the pre- and postelection interviews in 1968, the two ratings correlated at +.75 (N = 1319). As one would expect, that correlation was somewhat higher if the ratings were made by the same interviewer (r = +.77) than if by different interviewers (r = +.61).

14 We also did a comparable analysis of across-election volatility. Within Sweden, the interested nonpartisans are the most likely (34%) to change across elections, followed by uninterested nonpartisans (30%). The uninterested partisans in Sweden are, once again, the least likely to change (8%), although their results are virtually the same as for the interested partisans (also 8%). Partisanship clearly has a strong effect on across-election volatility in Sweden, while the effect of interest is quite weak. If anything, in Sweden those who are interested may be

slightly more likely to change across elections than those who are uninterested in politics. In the U.S., interested partisans are less likely (14%) to show across-election volatility than uninterested partisans (20%). Among nonpartisans, both those lacking an interest (27%) and those interested (27%) are more likely to change.

15 We must also consider the possibility that this difference, as well as some of the differences in table 8.2, *could* be due in part to a methodological artifact resulting from measurement error in panel studies (Maccoby, 1956; van der Eijk & Niemöller, 1983, pp. 102–105). However, we tend not to favor that interpretation.

16 "Comrade 4%" is the expression used in Sweden to refer to such tactical voting. (To gain seats in the Swedish Parliament, a party must gain 4 percent of the vote nationally or 12 percent within a given district.)

17 In fact, their evidence in support of this proposition was not very strong. For instance, they cited a study by Lipset (1953) which supposedly found that in a controversy at the University of California that (a) Jews were more likely than non-Jews to indicate an intention to refuse to sign a loyalty oath and (b) among those who intended to refuse, Jews were more likely than non-Jews to behave in line with this intention (i.e., to actually refuse to sign the loyalty oath). If true, it would have been a neat finding that nicely supported the proposition Berelson *et al.* (1954) were seeking to advance. In fact, however, the study done by Lipset, the one cited by Berelson *et al.*, dealt with student attitudes toward the loyalty oath and had no information in it whatsoever about the intention–behavior relationship among faculty members. Nonetheless, the proposition offered by Berelson *et al.* is worth considering and may still be generally correct.

18 Scores on the 0–100 degree feeling thermometer are transformed here, as in Chapter 5, to a −5 to +5 scale. In 1968, the candidates were rated on the feeling thermometer only on the post-election survey.

19 The analogous comparison for Reagan intenders is not possible because in the 1980 panel there are too few Reagan intenders who switched and later voted for Carter.

9 Prior, recalled, and subsequent voting behavior

An earlier version of this chapter was published in *Human Relations*, 1986, **39**, 135–148.

1 Lewin's concept of life space is closely akin to the frame of reference concept (Sherif & Sherif, 1969b). The individual's frame of reference consists of external and internal factors operating at a given time, which jointly determine psychological structuring from which behavior follows (cf. Newcomb, Converse & Turner, 1965, figure 3.6).

2 On the other hand, if one were one of nine Supreme Court Justices, with many decisions made on a 5–4 vote, it would be hard to imagine feeling that one's vote did not matter.

3 It should be emphasized that it is not only those who are low in political involvement who, on occasion, have a difficult time recalling how they voted. Members of the U.S. Congress, for instance, cast so many votes on such a wide

variety of topics that they ordinarily have a clear memory only of their votes on especially salient and controversial issues. In fact, it is common for members of Congress to review their own voting record prior to meeting with constituents, so as to avoid mistakes and to be better prepared to state why they voted as they did – rather than simply rely on their fallible memories.

4 Due to refusals, not voting, and attrition as the panel study proceeds, the samples in our analyses are not precisely random or representative, but they do encompass a wide variety of people within these two nations (Granberg & Holmberg, 1986d).

5 Also, the same methodological problem mentioned in the panel analyses of the intention–behavior problem in chapter 8 could be relevant here. That is, when the percentage with accurate recall is noticeably higher for the Social Democratic voters than for the other four parties this could be due, in part, to the fact that the Social Democratic Party is much larger than any of the other parties. Assuming there is some measurement error in both waves of the panel, the percentage answering Social Democratic both times could be inflated somewhat as a consequence of being the larger group. Nonetheless, we feel that the high percentage of accurate recall for Social Democratic voters reflects the stability, high identification, and loyalty these people have for their party.

6 In this section we must rely on self-reported vote since the attempts at validating the vote are not comparable for the Swedish and U.S. panels. There was no attempt at validating the vote for the 1956–1960 U.S. panel. In 1976, an attempt to validate the 1972 vote was made, but this was four years after the fact and there was much missing data. In Sweden, whether people actually voted is determined by checking the records. When self-reported behavior was compared against the validated voting measure for the seven most recent parliamentary elections in Sweden, it was found that about 98 percent of the Swedes had told the truth when asked whether they voted. Among those who voted, less than 1 percent say they did not vote. Among those who did not vote, about 28 percent incorrectly claim they did vote. Across these seven elections with a combined N of 19 550, about 93.2 percent were true positives (voters who said they voted), 1.7 percent false positives (nonvoters who said they voted), 0.5 percent false negatives (voters who said they did not vote), and 4.6 percent true negatives (nonvoters who said they did not vote). The percentage of people successfully interviewed who voted is somewhat higher than the turnout for the population. This may be due to a slight "stimulus" effect in which people interviewed before the election are more likely to vote (Clausen, 1968; Adams & Smith, 1980), and more substantially to the higher percentage of nonvoters who, for one reason or another, are not successfully interviewed.

7 The Ns for these percentages are 122 and 332 for Sweden and the U.S., respectively.

8 In the correlations and the regression analyses in figure 9.2, we were faced with the problem of how to code the five political parties of Sweden. These parties can be ordered on a *vänster–höger* (left–right) scale with considerable consistency and accuracy (Holmberg, 1974, 1981). But it is also known that the intervals among the parties are by no means equal. In 1979, 1982, and 1985, a representative sample of Swedish voters placed the five parties on the left–right scale (see

chapter 2). The average placement judgments, on a scale from 0–10 are quite stable and, thus, these values could be used in our analyses as the codes for the five parties.

10 Political systems and voting behavior

1 Sidanius *et al.* (1987) have recently reported similar results on this matter, based on their comparison of students in Sweden and in the U.S.

References

Abramowitz, A. (1978). The impact of a presidential debate on voter rationality. *American Journal of Political Science*, **22**, 680–690.

Adams, W. & Smith, D. (1980). Effects of telephone canvassing on turnout and preferences: A field experiment. *Public Opinion Quarterly*, **44**, 389–395.

Ajzen, I. & Fishbein, M. (1980). *Understanding attitudes and predicting social behavior.* Englewood Cliffs, NJ: Prentice-Hall.

Almond, G. & Verba, S. (1963). *The civic culture: Political attitudes and democracy in five nations.* Princeton, NJ: Princeton University Press.

Åsard, E. (1986). Industrial and economic democracy in Sweden: From consensus to confrontation. *European Journal of Political Research*, **14**, 207–219.

Asch, S. (1956). Studies of independence and conformity: A minority of one against a unanimous majority. *Psychological Monographs*, **70** (9, Whole No. 416).

Bartels, L. (1985). Expectations and preferences in presidential nominating campaigns. *American Political Science Review*, **79**, 804–815.

Barton, A. (1955). The concept of property space in social research. In P. Lazarsfeld & M. Rosenberg (eds.), *The language of social research* (pp. 40–53). New York, NY: Free Press.

Bentler, P. & Speckart, G. (1979). Models of attitude–behavior relations. *Psychological Review*, **86**, 452–464.

Berelson, B., Lazarsfeld, P. & McPhee, W. (1954). *Voting: A study of opinion formation in a presidential campaign.* Chicago, IL: University of Chicago Press.

Biddle, B. J. (1979). *Role theory: Expectations, identities, and behaviors.* New York, NY: Academic Press.

Biddle, B., Bank, B., Anderson, D., Hauge, R., Keats, D., Keats, J. & Marlin, M. (1985). Social influence, self-referent identity labels, and behavior. *Sociological Quarterly*, **26**, 159–185.

Bishop, G., Oldendick, R., Tuchfarber, A. & Bennett, S. (1978). The changing structures of mass belief systems: Fact or artifact? *Journal of Politics*, **40**, 781–787.

Bohrnstedt, G. (1969). Observations on the measurement of change. In E. Borgatta (ed.), *Sociological methodology*. San Francisco, CA: Jossey-Bass.

Boulding, K. (1970). Ecology and environment. *Trans-Action*, **7**, 38–44.

Brent, E. & Granberg, D. (1982). Subjective agreement with the presidential candidates of 1976 and 1980. *Journal of Personality and Social Psychology*, **42**, 393–403.

Brown, C. (1982). A false consensus bias in 1980 presidential preferences. *Journal of Social Psychology*, **118**, 137–138.

References   239

Burnham, W. (1986). Foreword. In M. Wattenberg, *The decline of American political parties 1952–1984* (pp. ix-xiv). Cambridge, MA: Harvard University Press.

Butler, D. & Stokes, D. (1974). *Political change in England.* London: Macmillan.

Byrne, D. (1971). *The attraction paradigm.* New York, NY: Academic Press.

Byrne, D., Bond, M. & Diamond, M. (1969). Response to political candidates as a function of attitude similarity–dissimilarity. *Human Relations*, 22, 251–262.

Byrne, D., Ervin, C. R. & Lamberth, J. (1970). Continuity between the experimental study of attraction and "real life" computer dating. *Journal of Personality and Social Psychology*, 16, 157–165.

Campbell, A., Converse, P., Miller, W. & Stokes, D. (1960). *The American voter.* New York, NY: Wiley.

(1966). *Elections and the political order.* New York, NY: Wiley.

Campbell, A., Gurin, G. & Miller, W. (1954). *The voter decides.* Evanston, IL: Row, Peterson.

Campbell, D. (1963). From description to experimentation: Interpreting trends as quasi-experiments. In C. Harris (ed.), *Problems in measuring change.* Madison, WI: University of Wisconsin Press.

Carlson, E. & Habel, D. (1969). The perception of policy positions of presidential candidates. *Journal of Social Psychology*, 79, 69–77.

Carroll, J. (1978). The effect of imagining an event on expectations for the event: An interpretation in terms of the availability heuristic. *Journal of Experimental Social Psychology*, 14, 88–96.

Ceci, S. & Kain, E. (1982). Jumping on the bandwagon with the underdog: The impact of attitude polls on polling behavior. *Public Opinion Quarterly*, 46, 228–242.

Clausen, A. (1968). Response validity: Vote report. *Public Opinion Quarterly*, 32, 588–606.

(1977). The accuracy of leader perceptions of constituency views. *Legislative Studies Quarterly*, 2, 361–384.

Clausen, A., Holmberg, S. & deHaven-Smith, L. (1983). Contextual factors in the accuracy of leader perceptions of constituents' views. *Journal of Politics*, 45, 449–472.

Conover, P. (1981). Political cues and perception of candidates. *American Politics Quarterly*, 9, 427–448.

Conover, P. & Feldman, S. (1982). Projection and the perception of candidates' issue positions. *Western Political Quarterly*, 35, 228–244.

(1984). How people organize the political world: A schematic model. *American Journal of Political Science*, 28, 95–126.

(1986). The role of inference in the perception of political candidates. In R. Lau and D. Sears (eds.), *Political cognition* (pp. 127–158). Hillsdale, NJ: Lawrence Erlbaum.

Converse, P. (1964). The nature of belief systems in mass publics. In D. Apter (ed.), *Ideology and discontent* (pp. 206–261). New York, NY: Free Press.

(1975). Public opinion and voting behavior. In F. Greenstein & N. Polsby (eds.), *Handbook of political science, Vol. 4* (pp. 75–169). Reading, MA: Addison-Wesley.

Converse, P. & Markus, G. (1979). Plus ça change... The new CPS election study panel. *American Political Science Review*, 73, 32–49.

Converse, P. & Pierce, R. (1979). Representative roles and legislative behavior in France. *Legislative Studies Quarterly*, **4**, 525–562.

(1986). *Political representation in France*. Cambridge, MA: Harvard University Press.

Crandall, V., Solomon, D. & Kellaway, R. (1955). Expectancy statements and decision times as functions of objective probabilities and reinforcement values. *Journal of Personality*, **24**, 192–203.

Dawes, R., McTavish, J. & Shaklee, H. (1977). Behavior, communication, and assumptions about other people's behavior in a common dilemma situation. *Journal of Personality and Social Psychology*, **35**, 1–11.

Deming, W. (1943). *The statistical adjustment of data*. New York, NY: Wiley.

Downs, A. (1957). *An economic theory of democracy*. New York, NY: Harper.

Eiser, J. (1984). *Attitudinal judgment*. New York, NY: Springer-Verlag.

(1986). *Social psychology: Attitudes, cognition and social behaviour*. Cambridge: Cambridge University Press.

Eiser, J. & Stroebe, W. (1972). *Categorization and social judgment*. London: Academic Press.

Esaiasson, P. (1985a). *Partiledarna inför väljarna: Partiledarnas popularitet och betydelse för valresultatet*. Forskningsrapport 1985:4, Statsvetenskapliga institutionen. Göteborgs universitet.

(1985b). Partiledareffekter även i Sverige? – Partiledarpopularitetens betydelse för valresultatet i Sverige ur ett jämförande perspektiv. *Statsvetenskaplig Tidskrift*, **2**, 105–121.

Festinger, L. (1957). *A theory of cognitive dissonance*. Evanston, IL: Row, Peterson.

Fiorina, M. (1981). *Retrospective voting in American national elections*. New Haven, CT: Yale University Press.

Fishbein, M. (1963). An investigation of the relationship between beliefs about an object and attitude toward that object. *Human Relations*, **16**, 233–240.

(1980). A theory of reasoned action: Some applications and implications. *Nebraska Symposium on Motivation*, **27**, 65–116.

Fishbein, M. & Ajzen, I. (1975). *Belief, attitude, intention and behavior: An introduction to theory and research*. Reading, MA: Addison-Wesley.

Fishbein, M., Ajzen, I. & Hinkle, R. (1980). Predicting and understanding voting in American elections. In I. Ajzen & M. Fishbein (eds.), *Understanding and predicting social behavior* (pp. 173–195). Englewood Cliffs, NJ: Prentice-Hall.

Fleishman, J. (1986). Types of political attitude structure: Results of a cluster analysis. *Public Opinion Quarterly*, **50**, 371–386.

Frenkel, O. & Doob, A. (1976). Post-decision dissonance at the polling booth. *Canadian Journal of Behavioural Science*, **8**, 348–350.

Gant, M. & Sigelman, L. (1985). Anti-candidate voting in presidential elections. *Polity*, **18**, 329–339.

Gilljam, M. (1988). *Svenska folket och löntagarfonderna*. Lund: Studentlitteratur.

Ginsburg, H. (1983). *Full employment and public policy: The United States and Sweden*. Lexington, MA: Lexington Books.

Granberg, D. (1972). Authoritarianism and the assumption of similarity to self. *Journal of Experimental Research in Personality*, **6**, 1–4.

(1980). An analysis of the House Judiciary Committee's recommendation to impeach Richard Nixon. *Political Psychology*, **2**, 50–65.

References 241

(1982). Social judgment theory. In M. Burgoon (ed.), *Communications Yearbook*, *Vol. 6* (pp. 304–329). Beverly Hills, CA: Sage.

(1983). Preference, expectations, and placement judgments: Some evidence from Sweden. *Social Psychology Quarterly*, **46**, 363–368.

(1984). Off the bandwagon. *Psychology Today*, **18**, 12–13.

(1985a). An assimilation effect in perceptions of Sweden's political parties on the left–right dimension. *Scandinavian Journal of Psychology*, **26**, 88–91.

(1985b). An anomaly in political perception. *Public Opinion Quarterly*, **49**, 504–516.

(1987). A contextual effect in political perception and self-placement on an ideology scale: Comparative analyses of Sweden and the U.S. *Scandinavian Political Studies*, **10**, 39–60.

Granberg, D. & Brent, E. (1974). Dove-hawk placements in the 1968 election: Applications of social judgment and balance theories. *Journal of Personality and Social Psychology*, **29**, 687–695.

(1980). Perceptions of issue positions of presidential candidates. *American Scientist*, **68**, 617–625.

(1983). When prophecy bends: The preference-expectation link in the U.S. presidential elections, 1952–1980. *Journal of Personality and Social Psychology*, **45**, 477–491.

Granberg, D. & Burlison, J. (1983). The abortion issue in the 1980 elections. *Family Planning Perspectives*, **15**, 231–238.

Granberg, D. & Holmberg, S. (1983). Modeling the relationships among preference, expectations and voting behavior. Göteborgs Universitet, Statsvetenskapliga Institutionen.

(1986a). Subjective ideology in Sweden and the United States. In R. Braungart & M. Braungart (eds.), *Research in Political Sociology*, **2** (pp. 107–143). Greenwich, CT: JAI Press.

(1986b). Political perception in Sweden and the U.S.: Analyses of issues with explicit alternatives. *Western Political Quarterly*, **39**, 7–28.

(1986c). Preference, expectations, and voting behavior in Sweden's referendum on nuclear power. *Social Science Quarterly*, **66**, 379–392.

(1986d). Prior behavior, recalled behavior, and the prediction of subsequent voting behavior in Sweden and the U.S. *Human Relations*, **39**, 135–148.

Granberg, D., Jefferson, N., Brent, E. & King, M. (1981). Membership group, reference group, and the attribution of attitudes to groups. *Journal of Personality and Social Psychology*, **40**, 833–842.

Granberg, D. & Jenks, R. (1977). Assimilation and contrast in the 1972 election. *Human Relations*, **30**, 623–640.

Granberg, D. & King, M. (1980). Cross-lagged panel analysis of the relation between attraction and perceived similarity. *Journal of Experimental Social Psychology*, **16**, 573–581.

Granberg, D., Nanneman, T. & Kasmer, J. (1988). An empirical examination of two theories of political perception. *Western Political Quarterly*, **41**, 29–46.

Granberg, D. & Seidel, J. (1976). Social judgments of the urban and Vietnam issues in 1968 and 1972. *Social Forces*, **55**, 1–15.

Hadenius, S. (1985). *Swedish politics during the 20th century*. Borås: Central-tryckeriet.

Hayes, S. (1936). The predictive ability of voters. *Journal of Social Psychology*, **7**, 183–191.

Heclo, H. & Madsen, H. (1986). *Policy and politics in Sweden: Principled pragmatism.* Philadelphia, PA: Temple University Press.

Heider, F. (1958). *The psychology of interpersonal relations.* New York, NY: Wiley.

Hennessy, B. (1975). *Public opinion.* Belmont, CA: Wadsworth.

Henshel, R. (1980). The purposes of laboratory experimentation and the virtues of deliberate artificiality. *Journal of Experimental Social Psychology*, **16**, 466–478.

Hill, R. (1981). Attitudes and behavior. In M. Rosenberg & R. Turner (eds.), *Social Psychology: Sociological Perspectives* (pp. 347–377). New York, NY: Basic Books.

Himmelweit, H., Biberian, M. & Stockdale, J. (1978). Memory for past vote: Implications of a study of bias in recall. *British Journal of Political Science*, **8**, 365–375.

Himmelweit, H., Humphreys, H., Jaeger, M. & Katz, M. (1981). *How voters decide: A longitudinal study of political attitudes and voting extending over fifteen years.* London: Academic Press.

Hochschild, J. (1981). *What's fair? American beliefs about distributive justice.* Cambridge, MA: Harvard University Press.

Holmberg, S. (1974). *'Riksdagen representerar Svenska folket' Empiriska studier i representativ demokrati.* Lund: Studentlitteratur.

(1981). *Svenska väljare.* Stockholm: Liber.

(1982). Väljarna och löntagarfonderna. In K. Asp *et al. Väljare partier massmedia. Empiriska studier i Svensk demokrati.* Stockholm: Liber.

(1984). *Väljare i förändring.* Stockholm: Liber.

Holmberg, S. & Asp, K. (1984). *Kampen om kärnkraften. En bok om väljare, massmedier och folkomröstningen 1980.* Stockholm: Liber.

Holmberg, S. & Gilljam, M. (1987). *Väljare och Val i Sverige.* Stockholm: Bonniers.

Holmberg, S. & Petersson, O. (1980). *Inom felmarginalen. En bok om politiska opinionsundersökningar.* Stockholm: Liber.

Hovland, C. & Pritzker, H. (1957). Extent of opinion change as a function of the amount of change advocated. *Journal of Abnormal and Social Psychology*, **54**, 257–261.

Hovland, C. & Sherif, M. (1952). Judgmental phenomena and scales of attitude measurement: Item displacement in Thurstone scales. *Journal of Abnormal and Social Psychology*, **47**, 822–832.

Inglehart, R. (1985). Aggregate stability and individual-level flux in mass belief systems: The level of analysis paradox. *American Political Science Review*, **79**, 97–116.

Inglehart, R. & Klingemann, H. (1976). Party identification, ideological preference and the left–right dimension among western mass publics. In I. Budge, I. Crewe & D. Fairlie (eds.), *Party identification and beyond: Representation of voting and party competition* (pp. 243–273). New York, NY: Wiley.

Irwin, F. (1953). Stated expectations as functions of probability and desirability of outcomes. *Journal of Personality*, **21**, 329–335.

Judd, C., Kenny, D. & Krosnick, J. (1983). Judging the positions of political candidates: Models of assimilation and contrast. *Journal of Personality and Social Psychology*, **44**, 952–963.

References 243

Judd, C. & Milburn, M. (1980). The structure of attitude systems in the general public: Comparisons of a structural equation model. *American Sociological Review*, **45**, 627–643.

Kahle, L. & Berman, J. (1979). Attitudes cause behaviors: A cross-lagged panel analysis. *Journal of Personality and Social Psychology*, **37**, 315–321.

Katz, R., Niemi, R. & Newman, D. (1980). Reconstructing past partisanship in Britain. *British Journal of Political Science*, **10**, 505–515.

Kelley, H. & Stahelski, A. (1970). Social interaction basis of cooperators' and competitors' beliefs about others. *Journal of Personality and Social Psychology*, **16**, 66–91.

Kelley, S. & Mirer, T. (1974). The simple act of voting. *American Political Science Review*, **68**, 572–591.

Kelman, S. (1981). *Regulating America, regulating Sweden: A comparative study of occupational safety and health policy*. Cambridge, MA: MIT Press.

Kenny, D. (1975). Cross-lagged panel correlation: A test for spuriousness. *Psychological Bulletin*, **82**, 887–903.

Key, V. O. (1949). *Southern politics in state and nation*. New York, NY: Knopf.
(1961). *Public opinion and American democracy*. New York, NY: Knopf.
(1966). *The responsible electorate*. Cambridge, MA: Harvard University Press.

Kiesler, C. (1971). *The psychology of commitment*. New York, NY: Academic Press.

Kinder, D. (1978). Political person perception: The asymmetrical influence of sentiment and choice on perceptions of presidential candidates. *Journal of Personality and Social Psychology*, **36**, 859–871.

Kinder, D. & Sears, D. (1985). Public opinion and political action. In G. Lindzey and E. Aronson (eds.), *Handbook of social psychology*, Vol. 2 (3rd ed., pp. 659–741). New York, NY: Random House.

King, M. (1978). Assimilation and contrast of presidential candidates' issue positions. *Public Opinion Quarterly*, **41**, 515–522.

Knight, K. (1984). The dimensionality of partisan and ideological affect: The influence of positivity. *American Politics Quarterly*, **12**, 305–334.

Korpi, W. (1981). *Den demokratiska klasskampen: Svensk politik i jämförande perspektiv*. Stockholm: Tiden.

Lane, R. (1962). *Political ideology*. New York, NY: Free Press.
(1973). Patterns of political belief. In J. Knutson (ed.), *Handbook of political psychology*. San Francisco, CA: Jossey-Bass.

LaPiere, R. (1934). Attitudes vs. actions. *Social Forces*, **13**, 230–237.

Lau, R., Sears, D. & Centers, R. (1979). The "positivity bias" in evaluation of public figures: Evidence against instrument artifacts. *Public Opinion Quarterly*, **43**, 347–358.

Lazarsfeld, P. (1946). Mutual effects of statistical variables. In P. Lazarsfeld, A. Pasanella & M. Rosenberg (eds.), *Continuities in the language of social research*. New York, NY: Free Press.

Lazarsfeld, P., Berelson, B. & Gaudet, H. (1944). *The people's choice: How the voter makes up his mind in a presidential campaign*. New York, NY: Columbia University Press.

Lee, A. & Lee, E. (1939). *The fine art of propaganda*. New York, NY: Harcourt, Brace.

244 *References*

Legge, J. (1983). The determinants of attitudes toward abortion in the American electorate. *Western Political Quarterly*, **36**, 479–490.

Lemert, J. (1986). Picking the winners: Politician vs. voter predictions of two controversial ballot measures. *Public Opinion Quarterly*, **50**, 208–221.

Levitin, T. & Miller, W. (1979). Ideological interpretations of presidential elections. *American Political Science Review*, **73**, 751–771.

Lewin, K. (1943). Defining "the field at a given time." *Psychological Review*, **50**, 292–310.

Lipset, S. (1953). Opinion formation in a crisis situation. *Public Opinion Quarterly*, **17**, 20–46.

(1981). *Political man*. Baltimore, MD: Johns Hopkins University Press.

(1984). George Gallup: 1901 to 1984. *Public Opinion*, **7** (No. 4), 2–4.

Liska, A. (1984). A critical examination of the causal structure of the Fishbein/Ajzen attitude–behavior model. *Social Psychology Quarterly*, **47**, 61–74.

Lundqvist, L. (1980). *The hare and the tortoise: Clean air policies in Sweden and the United States*. Ann Arbor, MI: University of Michigan Press.

Luttbeg, N. & Gant, M. (1985). The failure of liberal-conservative ideology as a cognitive structure. *Public Opinion Quarterly*, **49**, 80–93.

Maccoby, E. (1956). Pitfalls in the analysis of panel data: A research note on some technical aspects of voting. *American Journal of Sociology*, **61**, 359–362.

Mair, P. (1986). Locating Irish political parties on a left–right dimension: An empirical enquiry. *Political Studies*, **34**, 456–465.

Marks, R. (1951). The effect of probability, desirability, and privilege on the stated expectations of children. *Journal of Personality*, **19**, 332–351.

Markus, G. (1982). Political attitudes during an election year: A report on the 1980 NES panel study. *American Political Science Review*, **76**, 538–560.

Markus, G. & Converse, P. (1979). A dynamic simultaneous equation model of electoral choice. *American Political Science Review*, **73**, 1055–1070.

McGuire, W. (1980). In R. Evans (ed.), *The making of social psychology: Discussions with creative contributors*. New York, NY: Gardner.

(1981). The probabilogical model of cognitive structure and attitude change. In R. Petty, T. Ostrom & T. Brock (eds.), *Cognitive responses in persuasion*. Hillsdale, NJ: Erlbaum.

(1983). A contextualist theory of knowledge: Its implications for innovations and reform in psychology research. In L. Berkowitz (ed.), *Advances in experimental social psychology*, Vol. 16 (pp. 1–47). New York, NY: Academic Press.

McLean, I. (1981). *Dealing in votes*. Oxford: Martin Robertson.

Merton, R. (1948). The self-fulfilling prophecy. *Antioch Review*, **8**, 193–210.

Miller, N. & Marks, G. (1982). Assumed similarity between self and other: Effect of expectation of future interaction with that other. *Social Psychology Quarterly*, **45**, 100–105.

Miller, W. & Stokes, D. (1963). Constituency influence in Congress. *American Political Science Review*, **57**, 45–56.

Mosteller, F. (1968). Association and estimation in contingency tables. *Journal of the American Statistical Association*, **63**, 1–28.

Mueller, J. (1973). *War, presidents and public opinion*. New York, NY: Wiley.

Myers, D. (1987). *Social psychology*. New York, NY: McGraw-Hill.

Myles, J. (1979). Differences in the Canadian and American class vote. *American Journal of Sociology*, **84**, 1232–1237.

Natchez, P. (1985). *Images of voting/Visions of democracy*. New York, NY: Basic Books.

Navazio, R. (1977). An experimental approach to bandwagon research. *Public Opinion Quarterly*, **41**, 217–225.

Neuman, W. (1986). *The paradox of mass politics: Knowledge and opinion in the American electorate*. Cambridge, MA: Harvard University Press.

Newcomb, T., Converse, P. & Turner, R. (1965). *Social psychology*. New York, NY: Holt, Rinehart & Winston.

Nie, N., Verba, S. & Petrocik, J. (1976). *The changing American voter*. Cambridge, MA: Harvard University Press.

Niemi, R., Katz, R. & Newman, D. (1980). Reconstructing past partisanship: The failure of the party identification recall questions. *American Journal of Political Science*, **24**, 633–651.

Niemi, R. & Weisberg, H. (1976). *Controversies in American voting behavior*. San Francisco, CA: W. H. Freeman.

Niemi, R. & Westholm, A. (1984). Issues, parties, and attitudinal stability: a comparative study of Sweden and the United States. *Electoral Studies*, **3**, 65–83.

Nilsson, I. & Ekehammar, B. (1985). The positivity bias: A general effect in social perception (Tech. Rep. No. 642). Stockholm: University of Stockholm, Department of Psychology.

(1987). Person positivity bias in political perception. *European Journal of Social Psychology*, **17**, 247–252.

Nimmo, D. & Savage, R. (1976). *Candidates and their images: Concepts, methods, and findings*. Pacific Palisades, CA: Goodyear.

Noelle-Neumann, E. (1974). The spiral of silence: A theory of public opinion. *Journal of Communication*, **24**, 43–51.

(1984). *The spiral of silence: Public opinion – our social skin*. Chicago, IL: University of Chicago Press.

Page, B. (1978). *Choices and echoes in presidential elections: Rational man and electoral democracy*. Chicago, IL: University of Chicago Press.

Page, B. & Brody, R. (1972). Policy voting and the electoral process: The Vietnam War issue. *American Political Science Review*, **66**, 979–995.

Page, B. & Jones, C. (1979). Reciprocal effects of policy preferences, party loyalties and the vote. *American Political Science Review*, **73**, 1071–1089.

Petersson, O. (1977). *Väljarna och valet 1976: Valundersökningar-rapport 2*. Stockholm: SCB och Liber.

Pierce, R., Valen, H. & Listhaug, O. (1983). Referendum voting behavior: The Norwegian and British referenda on memberships in the European community. *American Journal of Political Science*, **27**, 43–63.

Popper, K. (1959). *The logic of scientific discovery*. London: Hutchinson.

Pruitt, D. & Hoge, R. (1965). Strength of the relationship between the value of an event and its subjective probability as a function of method of measurement. *Journal of Experimental Psychology*, **69**, 483–489.

Przeworski, A. & Teune, H. (1970). *The logic of comparative social inquiry*. New York, NY: John Wiley.

Rabinowitz, G., Prothro, J. & Jacoby, W. (1982). Salience as a factor in the impact of issues on candidate evaluation. *Journal of Politics*, 44, 41–63.

Reimer, B. & Rosengren, K. (1986). Maps of culture: Macro and micro. Paper presented at the World Congress of Sociology, New Delhi, India.

Robinson, J. (1984). The ups and downs and ins and outs of ideology. *Public Opinion*, 7 (No. 1), 12–15.

Robinson, J. & Fleishman, J. (1984). Ideological trends in American public opinion. *Annals of the American Academy of Political and Social Science*, 472, 50–60.

Rogosa, D. (1980). A critique of cross-lagged correlation. *Psychological Bulletin*, 88, 245–258.

Rokeach, M. (1973). *The nature of human values*. New York, NY: Free Press.

Rook, K., Sears, D., Kinder, D. & Lau, R. (1978). The "positivity bias" in evaluation of public figures: Evidence against interpersonal artifacts. *Political Methodology*, 5, 469–499.

Ross, L. (1977). The intuitive psychologist and his shortcomings: Distortions in the attribution process. In L. Berkowitz (ed.), *Advances in experimental social psychology* (Vol. 5). New York, NY: Academic Press.

Ross, L., Greene, D. & House, P. (1977). The "false consensus effect": An egocentric bias in social perception and attribution process. *Journal of Experimental Social Psychology*, 13, 279–301.

Samuelson, P. (1970). *Economics*. New York, NY: McGraw-Hill.

Sani, G. & Sartori, G. (1983). Polarization, fragmentation and competition in western democracies. In H. Daalder & P. Mair (eds.), *Western European party systems: Continuity and change* (pp. 307–340). Beverly Hills, CA: Sage.

Särlvik, B. (1969). Representationsundersökningens forskningsprogram. Göteborgs Universitet: Statsvetenskapliga Institutionen.

Särlvik, B. & Crewe, I. (1983). *Decade of dealignment: The conservative victory of 1979 and electoral trends in the 1970s*. Cambridge: Cambridge University Press.

Sartori, G. (1976). *Parties and party systems: A framework for analysis*. Cambridge: Cambridge University Press.

Schuman, H. & Johnson, M (1976). Attitudes and behavior. In A. Inkeles (ed.), *Annual review of sociology* (pp. 151–207). Palo Alto, CA: Annual Reviews.

Sears, D. (1969). Political behavior. In G. Lindzey & E. Aronson (eds.), *The handbook of social psychology* (2nd ed., Vol. 5). Reading, MA: Addison-Wesley.

(1983). The person-positivity bias. *Journal of Personality and Social Psychology*, 44, 233–250.

Sears, D., Freedman, J. & Peplau, A. (1985). *Social psychology*. Englewood Cliffs, NJ: Prentice-Hall.

Segall, M., Campbell, D. & Herskovits, M. (1966). *The influence of culture on visual perception*. Indianapolis, IN: Bobbs-Merrill.

Shaffer, S. (1981). Balance theory and political cognitions. *American Politics Quarterly*, 9, 291–320.

Sherif, C., Sherif, M. & Nebergall, R. (1965). *Attitude and attitude change: The social judgment-involvement approach*. Philadelphia, PA: Saunders.

Sherif, M. & Hovland, C. (1961). *Social judgment: Assimilation and contrast effects in communication and attitude change*. New Haven, CT: Yale University Press.

Sherif, M. & Sherif, C. (1964). *Reference groups: Explorations in conformity and deviation of adolescents*. New York, NY: Harper & Row.

(1969a). *Interdisciplinary relationships in the social sciences.* Chicago, IL: Aldine.

(1969b). *Social psychology.* New York, NY: Harper & Row.

Sherrod, D. (1972). Selective perception of political candidates. *Public Opinion Quarterly*, **28**, 483–496.

Sheth, J. & Newman, B. (1981). Determinants of intention-behavior discrepancy in the 1980 national election. Paper presented at the annual meetings of the American Psychological Association.

Sidanius, J., Brewer, R., Banks, E. & Ekehammar, B. (1987). Ideological constraint, political interest and gender: A Swedish–American comparison. *European Journal of Political Research*, **15**, 471–492.

Siegel, A. & Siegel, S. (1957). Reference groups, membership groups, and attitude change. *Journal of Abnormal and Social Psychology*, **55**, 360–364.

Sigel, R. (1964). Effect of partisanship on the perception of political candidates. *Public Opinion Quarterly*, **35**, 554–562.

Skinner, B. (1973). *About behaviorism.* New York, NY: Knopf.

Smallwood, F. (1983). *The other candidates: Third parties in presidential elections.* Hanover, NH: University Press of New England.

Smith, T. (1984). Recalling attitudes: An analysis of retrospective questions on the 1982 GSS. *Public Opinion Quarterly*, **48**, 639–649.

Sniderman, P. & Tetlock, P. (1986). Interrelationship of political ideology and public opinion. In M. Hermann (ed.), *Political psychology* (pp. 62–96). San Francisco, CA: Jossey-Bass.

Stimson, J. (1975). Belief systems: Constraint, complexity, and the 1972 election. *American Journal of Political Science*, **19**, 393–418.

Strömberg, L. (1986). *Values among Swedish local leaders.* Statsvetenskapliga Institutionen, Göteborgs Universitet, Sweden.

Sullivan, J., Piereson, J. & Marcus, G. (1978). Ideological constraint in the mass public: A methodological critique and some new findings. *American Journal of Political Science*, **22**, 233–249.

Taylor, G. (1982). Pluralistic ignorance and the spiral of silence: A formal analysis. *Public Opinion Quarterly*, **46**, 311–335.

Thomas, W. I. & Znaniecki, F. (1919). *The Polish peasant in Europe and America.* Boston, MA: Gorham.

Thurstone, L. (1928). Attitudes can be measured. *American Journal of Sociology*, **33**, 529–554.

Törnblom, K., Jonsson, D. & Foa, U. (1985). Nationality, resource class, and preferences among three allocation rules: Sweden vs. USA. *International Journal of Intercultural Relations*, **9**, 51–77.

Traugott, M. & Katosh, J. (1979). Response validity in surveys of voting behavior. *Public Opinion Quarterly*, **43**, 359–377.

Traugott, M. & Tucker, C. (1984). Strategies for predicting whether a citizen will vote and estimation of electoral outcomes. *Public Opinion Quarterly*, **48** (Spring), 330–343.

Triandis, H. & Triandis, L. (1965). Some studies of social distance. In I. Steiner & M. Fishbein (eds.), *Current studies in social psychology.* New York, NY: Holt, Rinehart & Winston.

Upton, G. & Särlvik, B. (1981). A loyalty-distance model for voting change. *The Journal of the Royal Statistical Society*, **144**, 247–259.

van der Eijk, C. & Niemöller, B. (1979). Recall accuracy and its determinants. *Acta Politica*, **14**, 289–342.

(1983). *Electoral change in the Netherlands: Empirical results and methods of measurement.* Amsterdam: CT Press.

Verba, S. & Orren, G. (1985a). The meaning of equality in America. *Political Science Quarterly*, **100**, 369–387.

(1985b). Rendering what's due: Views on income inequality. *Public Opinion*, **8** (No. 2), 48–52.

Waldahl, R. & Aardal, B. (1982). Can we trust recall-data? *Scandinavian Political Studies*, **5**, 101–116.

Wattenberg, M. (1986). *The decline of American political parties 1952–1984.* Cambridge, MA: Harvard University Press.

(1987). The hollow realignment: Partisan change in a candidate-centered era. *Public Opinion Quarterly*, **51**, 58–74.

Weir, B. (1975). The distortion of voter recall. *American Journal of Political Science*, **19**, 53–62.

Weisberg, H. & Grofman, B. (1981). Candidate evaluations and turnout. *American Politics Quarterly*, **9**, 197–219.

Weisberg, H. & Rusk, J. (1970). Dimensions of candidate evaluation. *American Political Science Review*, **64**, 1167–1185.

Wilcox, S. & Udry, R. (1986). Autism and accuracy in adolescent perceptions of friends' sexual attitudes and behavior. *Journal of Applied Social Psychology*, **16**, 361–374.

Zajonc, R. (1980). Feeling and thinking: Preferences need no inferences. *American Psychologist*, **35**, 151–175.

Zetterberg, H. (1982). Höger-vänster. *Sifo Indikator: Sifos Politiska Nyhetsbrev*, **9**, 1–10.

Zuckerman, M. & Reis, H. (1978). Comparison of three models for predicting altruistic behavior. *Journal of Personality and Social Psychology*, **36**, 498–510.

Index of names

Index of subjects

intentions, 4, 155, 162, 166–194, 215–216. 232–235
interest, 69–70, 146–147, 181–189, 192–193, 199, 201, 234
involvement, 72, 77–78, 146–148, 158–161, 229, 235
irrational assimilative model, 28, 36, 120–121, 223
issue importance, 54–55, 62
issue voting, 40–41, 50–54, 74–82, 132, 218, 224

knowledge, 69–70, 72, 147–148, 168, 181, 183–185, 193–194, 216, 225

leaders, *see* party leaders
life space, 110, 235
liking, *see* attraction
looking glass phenomenon, 136

missing data, 21, 28–29, 36, 60, 71, 220–221, 236

negative voting, 89, 99
nonattitudes, 66–67, 82, 85–86, 223
nuclear power, 9, 41–42, 45, 49–57, 59–65, 154–162, 164, 178, 190, 224, 231–232

opinion formation process, 11, 74–75, 218
optimism, 150, 164–165

panel design, 4, 7–8, 66, 82, 121–123, 128–129, 143–145, 163–164, 169, 197–203, 221, 233–235, 237
parliament, 6, 9, 72–73, 80–81, 83–86, 118–119, 190, 196, 217, 219, 226–227, 231
parties *see* political parties
partisanship, 185–189, 199, 201 *see also* party identification
party identification, 15, 69–70, 72, 75–76, 84, 142, 147, 152, 172, 174, 176, 205–207, 211, 233
party leaders, 90–93, 97–99, 106–107, 214, 220, 227
perception, 4, 15–17, 21–22, 30–36, 38–40, 60–61, 132–135, 219, 224, 226
perceptual consensus, 19–21, 38, 41–47, 61–62, 65, 212–213, 220–221
perceptual distortion, *see* assimilation, contrast effects
person positivity bias, 88–89, 94–103, 107
polarization, 217
policy, *see* public policy
political parties, 11, 17, 31, 35, 90–93, 97–99, 106–107, 111–115, 217–218, 220, 227

political system, 1–2, 35–37, 107
polls, 136, 149, 151, 155, 168, 173, 230
positivity bias, 89–93, 106
pragmatic optimism, 150
preferences, 3–4, 83–86, 136–165, 217, 226, 230
presidency, 7, 17, 90, 92, 136, 139–149, 195, 197, 226–227
principal actor hypothesis, 103, 107, 214
prior behavior, 168, 176–178, 192–211, 215, 234
proportional representation, 6
proximity, 11, 19, 32, 34, 36, 110–115, 215
psychoanalytic theory, 223
public policy, 2, 155–159, 217, 231

rational democratic model, 27–30, 36, 109–110, 120–122, 135, 138–139, 149, 157–162, 164, 215, 226, 230
rational selection, 11–12, 41–48, 196
reasoned action, theory of, 166–168, 178–179
recalled behavior, 176–178, 196–211, 215
referendum, 9, 59–64, 150, 154–162, 164, 178, 225, 231–232
region, 191
reliability, 4, 154, 164
response rate, 8
retrospective voting, 131–132
roles of parliamentarians, 83–86, 226

self-identity, 168, 177–178, 192–193, 210–211, 216, 234 *see also* party identification
self-placement, 14–15, 17–18, 37, 42–44, 61, 130, 214, 220, 222, 229
semantic differential, 89
similarity, 55–56, 108–109, 115–116, 120–129, 214–215, 229
social class, 2, 192, 228
social distance, 109
social judgment theory, 13, 223
stability coefficients, 23, 36, 66, 82, 106, 214
subjective agreement, 11–12, 23–30, 36, 40, 48–55, 62–63, 212
subjective placement model, 13–15, 25–27, 221–222

tactical voting, 190, 235
taxes, 41, 44, 47, 49–53, 64, 224
time, 121–123, 128–129, 173–174, 193, 204–206
transitivity, 82–86
turnout, 204, 207–208, 219, 236

valence, 1
validity, 4, 69, 197, 232, 236

DISCHARGED